CHINA, VIETNAM, AND THE UNITED STATES

c

CHINA, VIETNAM, AND
THE UNITED STATES

Highlights of the Hearings of the

Senate Foreign Relations Committee

Public Affairs Press, Washington, D. C.

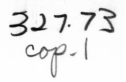

Published in 1966 by Public Affairs Press
419 New Jersey Avenue, S.E., Washington, D. C. 20003
Library of Congress Catalog Card No. 66-25442

INTRODUCTION

As is increasingly evident, the American people know far too little about China, Vietnam and the nature of U.S. policies regarding those countries.

What we have been officially told in the past decade certainly leaves much to be desired. The State Department's position concerning Communist China has often seemed like a melange of well-intentioned but negative generalities. If today there is widespread uneasiness about American involvement in Vietnam, it is at least in part because many official representations have not been sufficiently informative.

Congress shares, of course, some responsibility in this connection. Although it possesses unique powers to ask questions and evaluate policies, it has until recently played a somewhat passive role. At long last, fortunately, the Senate Committee on Foreign Relations has been holding hearings in the finest tradition of democratic government. Thanks to those hearings, much that has in the past been considered undiscussable is now being discussed both boldly and authoritatively. And thanks to the stimulus provided by the committee the policies of the United States government are today being stated somewhat more clearly than in the past.

The most significant statements made at the hearings held during February and March are published herewith in the hope they will contribute to better understanding of our problems and prospects in Southeast Asia.

In preparing this book, Public Affairs Press has benefited by the cooperation of Arthur Kuhl, an aide to Senator Fulbright, and the various experts whose testimony is included herein. Without their help prompt publication of the work would not have been possible.

M. B. SCHNAPPER

Editor, Public Affairs Press

CONTENTS

CHINA AND THE U.S.

Vietnam and the U.S.

(Biographical notes about the authors on page 214)

HISTORICAL OVERVIEW

By Senator J. William Fulbright

Speaking of China, United Nations Secretary General U Thant recently made the point that "When a country is obsessed with fear and suspicion, all sorts of tensions are likely to develop, all sorts of unreasonable reactions are likely to come forth." "Countries, like individuals," he said, "have nervous breakdowns," and it is the duty of the community to try to understand and find some remedy. The Secretary General pointed out that "China is going through a difficult stage of development and," he said, "in such a delicate stage, countries will show certain emotions, certain strong reactions, certain rigidities, and even certain arrogance."[1]

The Secretary General's words are supported by modern knowledge of human behavior. "Frightened, hostile individuals tend to behave in ways which aggravate their difficulties instead of resolving them," says the distinguished psychiatrist Dr. Jerome D. Frank, "and frightened, hostile nations seem to behave similarly."[2] A nation, like an individual, Dr. Frank suggests, is likely to respond to a feared rival by breaking off communications, by provocative behavior, or by taking measures which promise immediate relief, regardless of their ultimate consequences.

Fearful and hostile behavior is not rational but neither is it uncommon, either to individuals or to nations, including our own. In retrospect most Americans would agree that our national behavior was unduly fearful and irrational during the McCarthy period of the early fifties and the "red scare" after World War I. And just about all of us would agree that our nation suffered something worse than a "nervous breakdown" just over a hundred years ago.

Perhaps we Southerners have a sensitivity to this sort of thing that other Americans cannot fully share. We—or our forebears—experienced both the hot-headed romanticism that led to Fort Sumter and the bitter humiliation of defeat and a vindictive Reconstruction. The indignities suffered by the South during that era have burdened not just the South but the entire nation with a legacy of bitterness far more durable and, in retrospect, more damaging than the physical destruction wrought by the war itself. Even today, although the South has long since recovered its political rights and has begun at last to share in the nation's economic prosperity, the very word "Yankee" still awakens in Southern minds historical memories of defeat and humiliation, of the burning of Atlanta and Sherman's march to the sea, or of an ancestral farmhouse burned by Cantrell's raiders, or a family fortune lost and never recovered, or of arrogant carpetbaggers and the helpless rage of the people they dispossessed.

These memories are irrational but not irrelevant. They are pertinent because they persist and, by persisting, continue to work a baleful influence on our national life. They may be pertinent as well in helping us to understand the bitterness and anger and unreason in the behavior of other peoples who once were great but then were struck down and finally rose again only after a long era of degradation at the hands of foreigners.

I am thinking about China. Not being an expert in such matters, I cannot claim with anything approaching certainty that the indignities suffered by China in the nineteenth century have had human consequences comparable to those of the injustices suffered by the American South in the wake of the Civil War. It may be, however, that there is a similarity. Unless we are to believe that there is a "Chinese nature" which is entirely different from the "American nature," unless we believe that there is no such thing as a common human nature, it would seem to me logical to suppose that, national differences—great as they are—notwithstanding, the people of one nation are likely to respond to success and to humiliation, to victory and to defeat, in about the same way as the people of another nation.

Relations With the West. China has experienced very little except humiliation and defeat in its relations with the West, including Russia and, to some degree, America. One of our leading Chinese scholars, Professor John K. Fairbank, who is the Director of the East Asian Research Center of Harvard University, believes that the rapacious behavior of Europeans in China in past centuries has a great deal to do with the irrationality and hostile behavior of China's current leaders.

"The sources of China's revolutionary militancy," writes Professor

Fairbank, "are plain enough in Chinese history. The Chinese Communist regime is only the latest phase in a process of decline and fall followed by rebirth and reassertion of national power. China's humiliation under the unequal treaties of the nineteenth century lasted for a hundred years. An empire that had traditionally been superior to all others in its world was not only humbled but threatened with extinction. Inevitably, China's great tradition of unity, as the world's greatest state in size and continuity, was reasserted." [2]

Words like "extraterritoriality" and "unequal treaties" are far too antiseptic, too bland, to describe China's humiliation by Western imperialism. In human terms, the coming of Western civilization to China in the nineteenth century meant the plundering of China's wealth by foreigners and the reduction of most of the Chinese to an inferior status in their own country. Missionaries were immune from Chinese law and treated the Chinese as heathen, except of course for the converts who also claimed immunity from Chinese law and used the power conferred by their foreign association to intimidate their fellow citizens. Foreign goods were exempted by treaty from internal toll taxes imposed by the Manchu Dynasty to pay for the Taiping rebellion of the mid-nineteenth century, with the result that Western companies destroyed their Chinese competitors in the sale of such products as timber, oil, tobacco and, of course, opium. Each of China's disastrous nineteenth century wars with the West was followed by the levy of a huge indemnity or some further incursion on the economic life of the country.

The first of these wars, the opium war of 1839 to 1842, came about when the Chinese government tried to end the traffic in opium. The destructive narcotic was destroying the health and the lives of alarming numbers of Chinese addicts but it was also a source of great profit to foreign and Chinese opium merchants. British businessmen were the major foreign dealers in opium but Americans, French, and others also participated; opium became an important factor in the trade balance between some Western countries and China. When the Chinese government tried to ban the import of opium in 1839, the British refused to pledge their compliance, whereupon a number of incidents occurred culminating in war between China and England. The British won easily and under the Treaty of Nanking of 1842 China was forced to cede Hong Kong to Britain, open five treaty ports for British trade, accept tariffs that could not be changed without

Britain's consent, and, in addition, pay an indemnity to compensate the British for lost opium and for expenses incurred in the war.

Following the British example, other powers exacted concessions from China through persuasion and the threat of force. The United States, for example, signed a treaty with China in 1844 under which the United States acquired trading privileges and extraterritoriality for both civil and criminal cases.

The opium war and the Treaty of Nanking exposed China's vulnerability and opened the way to extensive exploitation by foreign powers. In the eighteen-fifties the British Prime Minister Lord Palmerston judged that "The time is fast approaching when we shall be obliged to strike another blow in China." In Palmerston's words, "these half-civilized governments such as those of China, Portugal, Spanish America . . . require a dressing down every eight or ten years to keep them in order."

The Chinese got many a "dressing down" in the years that followed. The British and French fought another war with China in 1856. Under the treaties of Tientsin new concessions were granted and old ones enlarged. The European powers acquired new trading ports and additional authority over Chinese tariffs as well as other privileges. The Chinese were required to pay indemnities, and there was also an article guaranteeing the protection of missionaries since, in the words of the treaty, "the Christian religion, as professed by the Protestants and Roman Catholics, inculcates the practice of virtue, and teaches man to do as he would be done by."

The Chinese refused to ratify these treaties. Hostilities were renewed and the British burned the emperor's summer palace in Peking. Under the Peking Convention of 1860 more ports were opened, more indemnities were paid and the Chinese were compelled to cede Kowloon to England.

The treaties of 1842 and 1844 and of 1858 and 1860, known for fairly obvious reasons as the "unequal treaties," formed the basis of China's relations with the West until the Second World War.

The Chinese also had their difficulties with the Russians. In 1858, while the Chinese were beset with British and French attacks from the sea and the Taiping rebellion in the interior, the Russians presented the Chinese with certain territorial demands. The Chinese were forced thereupon to cede to Russia all of the hitherto Chinese territories north of the Amur River. In 1860 the Russians demanded and received additional territory on the Pacific coast, including the area at which the port of Vladivostok was subsequently established. Under these two treaties Russia deprived China of a territory larger than Texas.

In the last decade of the nineteenth century Japan joined the Western powers in their depradations against China. Japan attacked China in 1894 and under the treaty of Shimonoseki, which ended that war, Japan exacted large cessions of territory as well as extensive commercial privileges. Pressure by the European powers forced the Japanese to withdraw some of their demands, notably for Port Arthur on the Liaotung peninsula, but Japan acquired the island of Taiwan and extensive trade privileges, and of course China was compelled to pay an indemnity.

Having joined with the powers in forcing Japan to return the Liaotung peninsula to China, Germany now demanded a "reward." The Chinese failed to see the equity of this claim but were brought around when the Germans landed troops. China was thereupon forced to lease the port and bay of Kiaochow to Germany for ninety-nine years and was also forced to yield commercial privileges on the Shantung peninsula.

The other powers also sought "rewards." Russia demanded and received the lease of Port Arthur and Dairen and the right to build a railroad across Manchuria. France, which had forced China to recognize French authority in Indochina in the eighteen-eighties, demanded and received in 1898 an extensive sphere of influence in South China, including the lease of Kwangchow Bay for ninety-nine years. The British, not to be outdone, now demanded and acquired control of the Chinese maritime customs, lease of a naval station at Weihaiwei, and the extension of the lease of Kowloon to ninety-nine years.

China had become a virtual colony with many masters. "Yet," said Sun Yat-sen, then a rising revolutionary, "none of the masters feels responsible for its welfare."

The Society of the Righteous and Harmonious Fists, better known as the Boxers, was a secret organization composed largely of poverty stricken peasants. Their grievances might well have been directed against the Manchu rulers of China, but government officials had no great difficulty in persuading the Boxers that the foreigners were the cause of the misery of the people. With great savagery, the Boxers fell upon foreigners and their Chinese cohorts in 1900; they were especially merciless toward missionaries and their Chinese converts.

The Boxers went on a rampage against the foreigners in Peking, besieging the foreign legations.

An international rescue force made up of Japanese, Russians, British, Germans, French, and Americans was sent to relieve the legations. The commander of the allied force, Field Marshal Count Von Waldersee, was under instructions from the Kaiser "to give no quarter and to take no prisoners," so that "no Chinese will ever again dare to look askance at a German."

The allies proved the equal of the Boxers in their ferocity. The defeated Chinese were now compelled to sign a new treaty under which the foreign powers received the right to station troops in their legation sites, a new Chinese tariff system was imposed, an indemnity of $333 million was to be paid, and the Chinese were obliged to punish "war criminals."

The United States returned a large part of the $25 million which was its share of the Boxer indemnity with the provision that the fund be used to educate Chinese students in the United States. Many Americans have regarded this as an act of extraordinary philanthropy.

America's Open Door Policy. The United States thereafter announced its Open Door policy toward China. The Open Door policy purported to preserve the territorial integrity of China and to safeguard for all nations equal commercial access to China. Limited and ineffective as it was, the Open Door policy induced the Chinese to think of the United States as the only major foreign power which might be thought of as their friend and possible protector. The Open Door remained the basis of American policy toward China until the Communists came to power in 1949 and closed China's door.

Political history hardly begins to convey the human effects of Western imperialism on the Chinese people. Something of the meaning of life in China under the impact of Western imperialism is conveyed by a Chinese engineer's account of his return to China in 1913 with his Belgian wife and son. He wrote as follows:

"In Shanghai it was agony, for there it was only too plain that in my own country I was nothing but an inferior, despised being. There were parks and restaurants and hotels I could not enter, although she could. I had no rights on the soil of a Chinese city which did not belong to the Chinese; she had rights by reason of something called skin.

"We boarded the English steamer from Shanghai to Hankow; the first class was for Europeans only, and there was no other steamer.

Marguerite leaned her arms on the railings and stared at the river. She was in first class, with our son. I went second class. I had insisted it should be so. 'It is too hot for you here below.' "

Some years earlier as a student in Shanghai the young man had written to his brother about his inability to understand the Europeans: "They always bewilder me," he wrote. "At once most ruthless in the pursuit of their interests, caring nothing for the wholesale misery they bring, at the same time their papers are full of verbiage of their nobility, rightness and the good they do. They become indignant at our public executions, and our cruelty to dogs. Yet the record of their lootings and killings in our country shows no such correct compassion."

The humiliations to which the Chinese were subjected would be difficult for any people to endure. Consider how shocking they must have been to a nation with a far longer and in many ways more illustrious history than that of any nation in the West, to a people who have always—and not without some justification—regarded their civilization as superior to any other. Before the time of Christ the Chinese had developed the principles and methods which were to hold together their empire until the twentieth century. In science and technology as well as government, China was well ahead of Europe by the time Marco Polo visited China in the thirteenth century. China became the center of civilization in eastern Asia and it became the model for smaller states, such as Korea and Vietnam, whose rulers accepted the obligation of tribute to the Chinese Emperor as their suzerain.

When European merchants and missionaries and buccaneers first came to China, they did not come to a land of primitives and pagans. They came upon a rich and ancient civilization, but one which had fallen behind in its technology, especially its military technology, with the result that it was thrown open to exploitation by foreigners whose power vastly exceeded their wisdom. "It is a regrettable fact," writes C. P. Fitzgerald, Professor of Far Eastern History in the Australian National University, "that the value of a nation's contribution to civilization, her place in the world, tends to be judged, from age to age, by the strength or weakness of her military power. When China under K'ang Hsi or Ch'ien Lung was manifestly too strong for any European encroachment to succeed, the real and serious weaknesses of the government and economy were not regarded; the achievements in art and literature were much respected. When China fell behind

Europe, her military power becoming negligible, encroachment was continual, and the value of Chinese civilization fell sharply in Western eyes." '

The Chinese revolutions of the twentieth century were in part spawned by the ravages of the West. Finding themselves militarily inferior to the West, but unshaken in their faith in the superiority of their own civilization, the Chinese undertook, first through the unsuccessful democratic revolution of Sun Yat-sen, then through the successful Communist revolution of Mao Tse-tung, to acquire those Western techniques of science and technology, of political organization and military power, which would make it possible to expel the West from China. It is ironic and significant that the Western political doctrine that China finally adopted was the one which the West itself had repudiated.

Basic Questions. It is of great importance that we try to learn something more about the strange and fascinating Chinese nation, about its past and its present, about the aims of its leaders and the aspirations of its people. Before we can make wise political—and perhaps military—decisions pertaining to China, there are many questions to be asked and, hopefully, answered: what kind of people are the Chinese? to what extent are they motivated by national feeling? to what extent by ideology? why are the Chinese Communist leaders so hostile to the United States and why do they advocate violent revolution against most of the world's governments? to what extent is their view of the world distorted by isolation and the memory of ancient grievances? and to what extent, and with what effect on their government, do the Chinese people share with us and with all other peoples what Aldous Huxley has called the "simple human preference for life and peace?"

We need to ask these questions because China and America may be heading toward war with each other and it is essential that we do all that can be done to prevent that calamity, starting with a concerted effort to understand the Chinese people and their leaders.

The danger of war is real. It is real because China is ruled by ideological dogmatists who will soon have nuclear weapons at their disposal and who, though far more ferocious in words than in actions, nonetheless are intensely hostile to the United States. In the short run the danger of war between China and America is real because an "open-ended" war in Vietnam can bring the two great powers into conflict with each other, by accident or by design, at almost any time. Some of our military experts are confident that China will not enter the war in Vietnam; their confidence would be more reassuring if it did not bring to mind the predictions of military experts in 1950 that China would not enter the Korean War, as well as more recent predictions about an early victory in Vietnam. In fact, it is the view of certain China experts in our government that the Chinese leaders themselves *expect* to be at war with the United States within a year, and it is clear that some of our own officials also expect a war with China.

The *expectation* of war, even though it is not desired, makes war more likely. "The crux of the matter," writes social psychologist Gordon Allport, "lies in the fact that while most people deplore war, they nonetheless *expect* it to continue. *And what people expect determines their behavior. . . .* the indispensable condition of war," says Professor Allport, "is that people must *expect* war and must prepare for war, before under war-minded leadership, they make war. It is in this sense that 'wars begin in the minds of men.' "[5]

The first vital step toward altering the fatal expectancy of war is the acquisition of some understanding of our prospective adversary. Most of us know very little about Communist China, partly for lack of qualified observers in China and partly because there are so few China experts in our own government and universities. At present, I am told, there are only about six full-time analysts of Chinese affairs in the Department of State. Some of the most knowledgeable "Old China hands" were driven out of the State Department by the McCarthy investigations and there are now few if any well-known and influential "sinologists" at the highest level of government comparable to such Soviet experts as George Kennan and Llewellyn Thompson. There are some highly competent China specialists below the top levels of government but they are not exerting a major influence on policy. Some of these experts, according to James Reston, do not subscribe to the view that the war in Vietnam can be enlarged without drawing China into the conflict.[6]

We must acquire knowledge not only of China but of the Chinese. To most of us China is a strange, distant, and dangerous nation, not a society made up of 700 million individual human beings but a kind of menacing abstraction. When Chinese soldiers are described, for example, as "hordes of Chinese coolies," it is clear that they are being thought of not as people but as something terrifying and abstract, or as something inanimate like the flow of lava from a volcano.

Abstractions and Judgments. Both China and America seem to think of each other as abstractions: to the Chinese we are not a society of individual people but the embodiment of an evil idea, the idea of "imperialist capitalism"; and to most of us China represents not people but an evil and frightening idea, the idea of "aggressive communism." Man's capacity for decent behavior seems to vary directly with his perception of others as individual humans with human motives and feelings, whereas his capacity for barbarous behavior seems to increase with his perception of an adversary in abstract terms. This is the only explanation I can think of for the fact that the very same good and decent citizens who would never fail to feed a hungry child or comfort a sick friend or drop a coin in the church collection basket celebrated the dropping of the atomic bomb on Hiroshima and can now contemplate with equanimity, or indeed even advocate, the use of nuclear weapons against the "hordes of Chinese coolies." I feel sure that this apparent insensitivity to the incineration of thousands of millions of our fellow human beings is not the result of feelings of savage inhumanity toward foreigners; it is the result of not thinking of them as humans at all but rather as the embodiment of doctrines that we consider evil such as fascism and communism. "If you want war," wrote William Graham Sumner, "nourish a doctrine. Doctrines are the most frightful tyrants to which men ever are subject, because doctrines get inside of a man's reason and betray him against himself. Civilized men have done their fiercest fighting for doctrines." [7]

For these reasons it is important that Americans and Chinese come to know each other in human terms. There is no easy way for us to make ourselves known to the Chinese as the decent and honorable people we really are, and it is not likely that the dogmatic men who rule in Peking will soon remove the blinders of ideology and look at the world in realistic and human terms. This makes it all the more important for Americans to be open-minded and inquisitive, to set aside ideological preconceptions and try to learn all that we can about the Chinese and their behavior and attitudes, and especially to try to find out why exactly the Chinese are so hostile to the West and what if anything can be done to eliminate that hostility.

In the hope of making some contribution to a better understanding of China the Committee on Foreign Relations began on March 8th a series of public hearings on China and on American attitudes toward China. The immediate purpose of the inquiry was educational rather than political. It seems to me that at this stage the best contribution the Committee can make is to provide a forum through which recognized experts and scholars can help increase Congressional and public knowledge of China. Whether and in what way the inquiry will influence American foreign policy will depend upon the value of the information provided and the attentiveness and open-mindedness with which it is received.

Major Goals. Our ultimate objective must of course be political: the prevention of war between China and America. At present there appears to be a growing *expectation* of war in both countries and, as Professor Allport points out, "what people expect determines their behavior." Perhaps a concerted effort to increase our understanding of China and the Chinese would alter that fatal expectancy, and perhaps if our expectations were altered theirs too would change. It is anything but a sure thing but, considering the stakes and considering the alternative, it seems worth a try.

The Chinese today, like Americans a hundred years ago, are in an agitated and abnormal state of mind. It is not only within our means but, as a great and mature nation, it is our responsibility, as U Thant so wisely pointed out, to try to understand the causes of China's agitation and to try to find some remedy.

On November 14, 1860, Alexander Hamilton Stephens, who subsequently became Vice-President of the Southern Confederacy, delivered an address to the Georgia Legislature in which he appealed to his colleagues to delay the secession of Georgia from the Union. "It may be," he said, "that out of it we may become greater and more prosperous, but I am candid and sincere in telling you that I fear if we yield to passion and without sufficient cause shall take that step, that instead of becoming greater or more peaceful, prosperous and happy—instead of becoming Gods, we will become demons, and at no distant day commence cutting one another's throats. This is my apprehension. Let us, therefore, whatever we do, meet these difficulties, great as they are, like wise and sensible men, and consider them in the light of all the consequences which may attend our action." [8]

What a tragedy it is that the South did not accept Stephens' advice in 1860. What a blessing it would be if, faced with the danger of a war with China, we did accept it today.

1. *The Washington Post,* January 21, 1966.

2. Letter from Dr. Frank to Senator Fulbright, September 13, 1960.

3. John K. Fairbank, "How to Deal with the Chinese Revolution," *The New York Review of Books,* February 17, 1966.

4. C. P. Fitzgerald, *The Chinese View of their Place in the World* (London: Oxford University Press, 1964), pp. 34-35.

5. Gordon W. Allport, "The Role of Expectancy," Hadley Cantril, Ed., *Tensions That Cause Wars* (Urbana: University of Illinois Press, 1950), pp. 43, 48.

6. "The New China Experts," *New York Times,* February 16, 1966.

7. "War" (1903).

8. Alexander Hamilton Stephens, "Secession," in *Modern Eloquence* (New York: P. F. Collier & Sons, 1928), Vol. II, p. 203.

2

AMERICAN POLICY ALTERNATIVES

By A. Doak Barnett

The question of how to deal with China is now—and certainly will continue to be during the decade ahead—one of the most crucial foreign policy issues facing us. It will demand not only firmness, determination, and commitment, but also flexibility, understanding, and patience. Rigid dogmatism cannot point the way toward sound policies. We need creative and imaginative thinking about a wide range of questions—not only about how to contain and check China's pressures on its neighbors and how to achieve a more stable military balance in Asia, basic as these questions are, but also about how to avoid war, minimize conflict, and reduce tension, how to meet the multiple nonmilitary challenges which China poses, how to evolve policies which can exert a moderating influence on Peking's leaders, how to accommodate to Communist China's legitimate interests as a major power, how to reestablish a reasonable basis for contact and discourse between the United States and mainland China, how to create a broader consensus among non-Communist nations on reasonable approaches to dealing with the Chinese, and how over time to involve Communist China increasingly in more responsible roles in the general international community.

It has been suggested to me by Senator Fulbright that in initiating the hearings of the Senate Foreign Relations Committee on China I attempt to outline briefly some of the broad areas of inquiry that the committee, the American Government, and the American people might well consider in any systematic effort to reexamine the problems of U.S. relations with China, and I will try to do this.

It is my understanding that while the committee does intend, during the course of these hearings, to probe the interconnections between our policy toward China and the pressing problems that we now face in Vietnam, the intention is to examine China policy also in a broader

15

and longer term perspective, and that is the kind of perspective which I have adopted in formulating my remarks.

I would like, right at the start, to state my own belief that there is a need for basic changes in the overall U.S. posture toward Communist China. For almost 17 years, we have pursued a policy that might best be characterized as one aimed at containment and isolation of Communist China. In my view, the element of containment—using this term in a broad sense to include both military and non-military measures to block threats posed by China to its neighbors—has been an essential part of our policy and has been, in some respects at least, fairly successful. Our power has played an important and necessary role in creating a counterbalance to Communist China's power in Asia, and we have contributed significantly to the task of gradually building stable non-Communist societies in areas that lie in China's shadow. But the U.S. attempt to isolate Communist China has been, in my opinion, unwise and, in a fundamental sense, unsuccessful, and it cannot, I believe, provide a basis for a sound long-term policy that aims not only at containing and restraining Chinese power but also at reducing tensions, exerting a moderating influence on Peking, broadening the areas of non-Communist agreement on issues relating to China, and slowly involving Communist China in more normal patterns of international intercourse.

Containment But Not Isolation. I strongly believe, therefore, that the time has come—even though the United States is now engaged in a bitter struggle in Vietnam—for our Government to alter its posture toward Communist China and adopt a policy of containment but not isolation, a policy that would aim on the one hand at checking military or subversive threats and pressures emanating from Peking but at the same time would aim at maximum contacts with and maximum involvement of the Chinese Communists in the international community. Such a policy would involve continued commitments to help non-Communist regimes combat Communist subversion and insurrection, as in Vietnam, and continued pledges to defend areas on China's periphery, including Taiwan. But it would involve changes in many other aspects of our policies. While continuing to fulfill our pledge to defend Taiwan against attack, we should clearly and explicitly acknowledge the Chinese Communist regime as the de facto government of the China mainland and state our desire to extend de jure recognition and exchange diplomatic representatives with Peking if and when it indicates that it would be prepared to reciprocate.

We should press in every way we can to encourage nonofficial contacts. We should, instead of embargoing all trade with the China mainland, restrict only trade in strategic items and encourage American businessmen to explore other opportunities for trade contacts. And within the United Nations we should work for the acceptance of some formula which would provide seats for both Communist China and Nationalist China. In taking these steps, we will have to do so in full recognition of the fact that Peking's initial reaction is almost certain to be negative and hostile and that any changes in our posture will create some new problems. But we should take them nevertheless, because initiatives on our part are clearly required if we are to work, however slowly, toward the long-term goal of a more stable, less explosive situation in Asia and to explore the possibilities of trying to moderate Peking's policies.

Some people believe that a policy combining the differing elements I have suggested—that is, containment but also increased attempts to deal directly with Peking—would involve contradictory and inconsistent elements. I would argue that, on the contrary, in terms of our long term aims the seemingly contradictory elements would in fact be complementary and mutually reinforcing. Others argue that a change of posture such as the one I have suggested might be interpreted as a sign of weakness and irresolution on our part, and therefore be dangerous, particularly if taken while we are engaged in a major struggle against Communist insurrection in Vietnam. I would argue that our commitments and actions in Vietnam make it wholly clear, to both friend and foe, that we are not acting out of weakness and that while we search for areas of possible agreement and accommodation we will also continue in our determination to protect the interests of ourselves and our friends, to oppose violence as a means of political change, and to assist in the growth of viable, progressive, non-Communist regimes, in Asia as elsewhere.

I hope that later in our discussion we will have an opportunity to examine in more concrete terms some of the detailed aspects of our China policy. But before proceeding further perhaps I should try to outline briefly, in response to your suggestion, Mr. Chairman, some of the broad areas of inquiry that it would be desirable to cover in any examination of U.S. relations with China that attempts to probe background factors as well as immediate issues. Briefly stated I think it is necessary to examine: the historical background to the Chinese revolution, including both the general characteristics of the historic confrontation between China and the West and the causes of the rise of Communism in China; the internal situation in Communist China since 1949, including the domestic political situation, recent trends, and possible changes in the future, and the state of the Chinese economy; and Communist China's general international position and foreign policy, with special attention to the Sino-Soviet split and China's military strength and potential. I can do no more than make a few comments on each of these complicated subjects, but if time permits I would like to do that much.

Historical Perspective. It is important, I think, to view recent developments in China and the present state of American-Chinese relations in some kind of historical perspective. The perspective of the policymaker must, of necessity, be very different from that of the historian, and analysis of the past does not necessarily provide answers to the urgent policy issues of the present. But unless one has some understanding of the broad forces that have been at work over time, it is difficult to evolve a rational or coherent framework even for policies designed to meet immediate problems.

For roughly 2,000 years prior to the mid-19th century, China was the center of one of the great world civilizations. It was relatively isolated from comparable centers in Europe and elsewhere; it considered itself superior to all of its neighbors, and it played a role of unchallenged primacy in the world as Chinese leaders knew it. Then, in the mid-19th century, its isolation was shattered by the restless, expanding, technologically superior nations of the West, and it became an arena for, and pawn of, competing imperial and colonial powers. The "Chinese revolution," if one uses this term in a broad sense, started at that time, in response to the traumatic impact of the West as well as to mounting domestic problems. It has been underway, therefore, for over a hundred years. In this revolution the Chinese people have been groping, painfully and slowly, to find effective means to modernize and develop their country, to build a strong modern nation-state, and to reassert China's role in the world.

It is worth noting that to date there has been no extended period of peaceful relations between China and the Western world on the basis of reasonable equality. Before the mid-19th century, the Chinese held a superior position and attempted, unsuccessfully, to fit the Western powers into its traditional imperial system of relations with subordinate states. During the next hundred years, the Western powers held a superior position and attempted, also without great success, to fit China into the modern international system of relations. The still unresolved problem for the future is whether both China and the West can, in time, reach an acceptable peaceful accommodation within the modern nation-state system, on the basis of reasonable relationships in which the rights and obligations of both will be recognized.

Part of the legacy of the past hundred years is the intense nationalism and self-assertiveness that all Chinese—whatever their ideology— now feel. All Chinese, non-Communist as well as Communist, are now determined to end China's recent position of inferiority and see their country achieve recognized major power status. There seems little doubt that in due time it will. The question is whether both China and the West can discover and accept roles for the Chinese in the international community as a whole—or whether China and the West must face an indefinite period of dangerous confrontation and high risk of major military conflict.

Recent Successes. One obviously cannot look at the Chinese historical background simply in the terms I have suggested, however. China has been, and still is, undergoing not just a revolution, but more specifically a Communist revolution, led by men dedicated to promoting their own pattern of revolutionary struggle and change abroad as well as at home. It is important for us to understand the reasons for Communist success in China and the impact of their success elsewhere.

The explanations for Chinese Communist successes in the 1930's and 1940's are numerous, but I would say that the most important ones were the following: One was the Sino-Japanese war, which had a shattering effect on China and helped to create a revolutionary situation. Another was the failure of the non-Communist leaders in China to achieve unity in their own ranks, to define and pursue effective programs designed to cope with such basic problems as landlordism, inflation, and corruption, or to build a firm grassroots base of support—a failure which in effect created a vacuum into which the Communists moved. Still another was the Communists' success in building an unprecedently disciplined and strong revolutionary organization, in appealing to nationalism and reformism especially during the war, in developing a shrewd revolutionary strategy, and in implementing their programs with determination and, whenever necessary, ruthlessness.

Peking's leaders now maintain that their experience provides a primary model for revolutions throughout the underdeveloped world. It is a model calling for the creation of Communist-led peasant armies, the establishment of so-called "liberated areas" as bases for revolutionary struggle, the creation of broad anti-imperialist united fronts, and the overthrow of existing non-Communist regimes by violence. There is little doubt that the Chinese model has had, and will continue to have, an impact far beyond China's borders; revolutionary leaders in many parts of the world look to it for inspiration. We need, therefore, to understand it, and to grasp not only how it helps to explain Communist success in China, but also how it may influence events elsewhere.

We should not, however, magnify its significance. Careful analysis indicates, I think, that the particular constellation of factors and forces which make it possible for Mao Tse-tung's strategy to succeed in China are not widely duplicated, and there are many reasons to believe that the Chinese model cannot be exported as easily as Mao and some of his colleagues have hoped. The available evidence also suggests that while the Chinese leaders would like to see their model widely emulated, their capacity to promote, and willingness and ability to support, Chinese-style revolutions elsewhere is definitely limited.

The historical background is important, but obviously the primary focus of any inquiry into current problems must be on developments in China in the 17 years since Communist takeover. Communist China in 1966 is a very different country in many respects from China in 1949.

Perhaps the first thing that should be noted about the political situation in China is that the Communists have created a very strong totalitarian apparatus that has unified and exercises effective control over the entire China mainland, and they have used their power to promote uninterrupted revolution aimed at restructuring the nation's economy, social structure, and system of values. While the impact of the regime has been harsh and painful for millions of Chinese, the Communists have built a strong base of organized support, partly on the basis of appeals to nationalism as well as promises of future accomplishments. They have also demonstrated a remarkable capacity to make and implement decisions and an impressive ability to mobilize people and resources. Not surprisingly, however, there are many tensions in the society and, in my opinion, fairly widespread—even though largely unarticulated—dissatisfaction with numerous Communist policies and methods of rule. But there is no significant organized opposition and no foreseeable prospect of its developing. In short, the regime is not a passing phenomenon. In time it may change its character, but it will continue to exist, as we will continue to have to deal with it, for the predictable future.

There are some important questions one can raise, however, about the future. I believe that among the leaders in China there are significant differences on policies, under the surface—especially differences regarding domestic policies but some of them are relevant to foreign-policy issues as well—and that one can differentiate between groups that might be labeled the technical-bureaucrats and the specialists in power, politics, and ideology. I further believe that these differences are reflected, even today, in the complex mixture of policies in China, and that in the future they are likely to become increasingly important, especially after the death of Mao.

Period of Transition. The biggest question about the future arises from the fact that Communist China is on the verge of an historic transition period in which virtually the entire top leadership will pass from the scene in a relatively brief period of time. To date the unity as well as the longevity of the Chinese Communist leaders has been remarkable, but what has been an asset to the regime in the past is now becoming a liability, as the leaders steadily age and resist bringing younger men into the top inner circle. When Mao and other top leaders die, therefore, I would expect China to enter a period in which there could be a great deal more fluidity and uncertainty about both leaders and policies than in recent years. It would be reasonable to expect, I think, that the outcome of the competition between leaders and policies that is likely to occur, and the resulting balance between "radicals" and "moderates" will be definitely influenced by perceptions that the new leaders have of the international environment as it affects China. While it may not be possible for outsiders to exert very much influence on the outcome, our hope, certainly, should be that the balance will in time shift in favor of technical-bureaucrats promoting relatively moderate policies.

The economic performance of the Chinese Communist regime to date has been a very mixed one, characterized by some notable successes, some serious failures, and some basic unanswered questions.

When the Chinese Communists first came to power they were impressively successful in bringing order out of economic chaos, and in initiating an ambitious development program. During their first 5-year plan, under a Stalinist-type program, China's annual increase in gross national product—about 6 or 7 percent—was as rapid or more rapid than that of any other important underdeveloped nation at the time. But the momentum of growth started to decline by 1957, the last year of the first plan—as a result of the lag in agricultural output, the steady increase in population, and the ending of Soviet credits. And in 1958 Peking's leaders embarked on their radical and reckless "great leap forward" and commune program, hoping to achieve the impossible by unprecedented political and ideological mobilization.

The failures of the "leap" produced an economic crisis of major proportions in China, which lasted from 1959 through 1961. The result, in effect, was a Communist version of a great depression. It compelled the regime to abandon many of its most extreme policies and ambitious goals, and Peking redefined its economic policies to include some sensible elements, showing realism and pragmatism. Emphasis was placed on the need to promote agriculture, various sorts of incentives were restored, needed food was imported from the West, major industrial projects were postponed, and in general more modest goals were adopted.

Since 1962 there has been a slow but steady recovery of both agricultural and industrial production in China, and today overall Chinese output is comparable to what it was just before the "leap"—although it is still not that high in per capita terms. The primary stress on developing agriculture continues, and its results, plus continuing grain imports, have greatly eased the food situation. This year a new 5-year plan, the third, has begun, and even though no details on the plan have yet been published, undoubtedly there is renewed growth in industry— although at a more gradual pace than in earlier years.

In any overall assessment of the Chinese economy since 1949, several things would have to be noted. The Communists have not yet converted China into a major industrial power, but they have begun to build a significant industrial base. At one point, in 1960, steel output was claimed to be 18 million tons; production now is below peak capacity but is probably between 8 and 10 million tons. Moreover, since the regime decides how output will be used, current production fully supports the nation's military power and further industrialization. There has been no appreciable overall increase in living standards in

China since 1949, but, except during the worst post-leap years, the regime has met the population's minimum requirements, distributed available goods fairly equitably, and kept the economy running—a not insignificant accomplishment in China. However, the Communists have not found panaceas capable of rapidly solving the nation's most basic economic problems. Agriculture continues to lag, and it will take time for present improvement programs to change the situation. And the population steadily rises; a birth control program has been initiated, but quick results cannot be expected.

As a consequence of the Sino-Soviet split, and the ending of Soviet technical assistance as well as credits, the Chinese Communists have decided to glorify the virtues of economic "self-reliance." On a more practical level, however, they have pragmatically adapted to the changed situation and have done all they could to expand trade with Japan and a variety of Western nations. As a result, Communist China's international economic orientation has fundamentally changed, and now a majority of its trade is with the non-Communist world. Even though to date this fact has not greatly affected Peking's over-all foreign policy, the shift has slowly created new and diversified patterns of relations which could be of some significance over time.

Foreign Policy Ambitions. In examining Peking's general foreign policy, the first thing to note is that China's leaders obviously have very ambitious long-term goals. Moved by intense nationalism, they aim to build a strong base of power at home and to strengthen China's security; they also hope to recover what they consider to be "lost territories" (including Taiwan); and they are determined to play the role of a major power on the world stage. At the present time, they view the United States as the major obstacle and threat to many of their aims and interests—and call, therefore, for the removal of American power from Asia—but they also regard the Soviet Union at present as a serious obstacle to Chinese aspirations and therefore compete with it too, whenever and wherever feasible.

As first generation revolutionary leaders, and true believers in the Maoist version of Marxism-Leninism, Peking's leaders are also dedicated to the promotion of revolutionary struggles, especially in the underdeveloped world. Their public pronouncements now tend to concentrate on this aim and in at least some areas, such as Vietnam, they are prepared to give significant support to revolutionary forces, even though they have avoided direct Chinese military intervention.

While it is important to recognize Peking's ambitious goals, it is equally important to note that, on the basis of available evidence and Communist China's performance to date, the Chinese Communists do not appear to think primarily in terms of spreading their influence through direct military and territorial expansion; they appear to recognize the limits to their capabilities for military action outside of China's borders; they have usually been quite realistic in assessing the power balance in concrete situations; they have generally been calculating and even cautious in avoiding military "adventurism" and limiting their risks; they have tended to think in long-range terms about their most ambitious goals; and they have repeatedly been flexible and pragmatic (at least until recently) in adapting their strategy and tactics to fit changing situations in pursuit of their shortrun goals.

If one analyzes the Chinese Communists' overall foreign policy strategy since 1949, one can identify at least three major periods in which their approach to the outside world has been distinctive. In the period immediately after 1949, Peking — like Moscow at the time — adopted a militant posture of struggle against the entire non-Communist world and called for revolutions wherever possible in the underdeveloped countries. By contrast, in the mid-1950's, during the so-called Bandung period, it adopted a much more moderate and flexible strategy and promoted friendly relations with a wide variety of non-Communist countries, especially in the underdeveloped world. Then, in the late 1950's, it shifted back to a militant posture and renewed its calls for worldwide revolutionary struggle. Further shifts of this sort are certainly possible, in the future as in the past.

Even in the recent period of militancy, moreover, Peking's doctrinaire and rigid ideological statements have not fully represented Chinese Communist policies, which in practice have included a variety of elements. In fact, even its major ideological statements on strategy have not been wholly consistent. For example, while Peking's leaders have sounded the trumpet for "people's wars" wherever feasible and for the mobilization of the rural areas of the world (the underdeveloped nations) against the cities of the world (North America and Western Europe), at the same time they have called for closer links with many countries in the so-called "intermediate zone"—including Japan and many Western countries—since their practical requirements, dictated by economic considerations, make it seem desirable to promote trade and other contacts with these nations.

Revolutionary Militancy. On balance, nevertheless, Peking's primary stress in the most recent period has been a revolutionary militancy. But developments of recent months must have raised questions in the minds of at least some of the policy planners in Peking as to whether they should continue present policies or consider a new shift in overall foreign policy strategy. Where the Chinese Communists have been dogmatically and rigidly militant in the recent period, they have suffered a series of major setbacks and policy defeats—in relations with the Soviet Union, at the Algiers Conference last fall, and in such widely scattered countries as Indonesia, Cuba, and Ghana. It seems probable, also, that Peking's leaders misestimated the probable extent of American involvement and commitment in Vietnam.

Recent events demonstrate, in short, that Peking's ability to manipulate or control even those situations where receptivity to Chinese influence has been greatest is severely limited. It remains to be seen whether Peking's leaders will grasp this fact and modify their policies as a result. Mao and some other top leaders may well resist doing so. But changes in Chinese policies are certainly within the realm of possibility—after Mao's death if not before.

What is required, it seems to me, to maximize the possibility of a desirable sort of shift in Peking's posture and policies, is a combination of two elements: developments in Vietnam as well as elsewhere that will help to convince Chinese Communist leaders that excessive militancy is counterproductive, but at the same time indications in the general international environment, as they see it, that there are other reasonable and promising policy options—that they can see some possibility of expanding China's role in international affairs and achieving at least some of China's legitimate aspirations by moderate rather than militant means.

The Sino-Soviet Dispute. In any careful examination of Communist China's international role, two subjects certainly deserve special attention: the Sino-Soviet dispute and its implications for the rest of the world, and China's military position and potential.

The Sino-Soviet dispute as it has evolved in recent years is clearly one of the most important developments in the international politics of the 1960's—just as the formation of the Sino-Soviet alliance was in the 1950's. There can be no doubt that the conflicts between Peking and Moscow now are very real, very bitter, and very deep. The dispute has involved basic clashes of national interests as well as major ideological differences, and it has resulted in worldwide competition between the two countries.

In a fundamental sense the Sino-Soviet dispute has weakened Peking's international position, which has been to our advantage in many respects, since it imposes increased restraints on the Chinese Communist regime. But not all of the results of the dispute have been good from our point of view. It appears, for example, to have been a significant factor reinforcing Peking's tendency in recent years to maintain a highly militant posture. We cannot, moreover, rely on the dispute to solve our own basic problems in relations with the Chinese. In certain situations, Soviet interests and policies may run parallel to ours, as appears to be the case even in Vietnam today, to a very limited degree. But we cannot expect such parallelism to be dependable or believe that it will result—as some suggest—in a kind of Soviet-American anti-Chinese axis. Even when a degree of parallelism does exist, it cannot be expected to resolve all the difficult problems of dealing with the Chinese. Furthermore, although it is difficult to see in the predictable future any full restoration of the type of Sino-Soviet relationship that existed in the early 1950's, it is certainly possible that Communist China, particularly under new leaders, might decide to try to repair at least some of the damage that has been done to the alliance in recent years. In any case, the United States will itself have to work toward a solution of at least some of our problems with Communist China; the Sino-Soviet dispute will not solve them for us.

Turning to the question of Communist China's military position, several things should be noted. First of all, the Peking regime has developed China into a significant military power, with large, modernized, conventional land forces and a sizeable air force. However, these forces appear to be designed mainly for defense, and Peking lacks many of the prerequisites for successful operation outside of China against the forces of a major power such as the United States. The strength of Communist China's military establishment far exceeds that of its Asian neighbors, though, and its mere existence argues for the maintenance of adequate counterbalancing forces in Asia, which at the present time must be provided largely by the United States.

Despite Peking's formal entrance into the "nuclear club," and despite the fact that Communist China will probably acquire some sort of missile delivery system in the not distant future, the Chinese Communists are not close to achieving superpower status. For the predictable future, therefore, Peking's leaders are likely to use China's limited nuclear arsenal primarily for political purposes—although they doubtless also hope that they will be able to deter and cancel out the significance of American nuclear power in Asia.

Peking's leaders will probably continue to be sensitive to the actual balance of military strength, and reluctant to take excessive risks; for a while, in fact, the vulnerability of their embryonic nuclear establishment may actually impose additional restraints on them.

The Risk of War. However, it would be a dangerous error to conclude that Communist China would not risk major war if it genuinely felt that its vital interests were threatened. In regard to Vietnam particularly, there is considerable evidence, I believe, that while Peking hopes to avoid any major conflict with the United States, it fears that American escalation will create situations demanding escalation on the Chinese side, which could lead to major conflict. In recent months, in fact, Peking has repeatedly warned its own people of the dangers of American attacks and major war, and there appears to be a genuine apprehension that this may take place. No one can say with certainty what actions might provoke an increased Chinese response. Since Peking appears to view North Vietnam, like North Korea, as a vital buffer area, it is likely that if the Chinese concluded there was a major threat to the existence of the North Vietnamese regime, the result could be large-scale, direct Chinese intervention. There is no guarantee, however, that even less drastic forms of American escalation—such as bombing of North Vietnam's major cities— might not impel the Chinese to escalate their involvement in smaller ways which might lead to much higher risks of direct American-Chinese clashes that are not desired by either side. In view of this uncertainty, it is essential that the United States exercise great restraint in the use of its power, especially in North Vietnam, and demonstrate by deeds as well as words that we are determined to avoid provoking any direct American-Chinese conflict.

Let me at this point return again to questions relating to U.S. policy.

On February 23rd, President Johnson clearly stated that our desire is to avoid major conflict with China. "Some ask," he said, "about the risks of wider war, perhaps against the vast land armies of Red China. And again, the answer is no. Never by any act of ours—and not if there's any reason left behind the wild words from Peking. We have threatened no one, and we will not. We seek the end of no regime, and we will not." He declared that we will employ a "measured use of force," with "prudent firmness," and that "there will not be a mindless escalation."

This is a wise posture for us to adopt—although to insure against major war resulting from miscalculation we must firmly hold the line against further escalation in practice as well as theory. This stand is excellent, as far as it goes. But in my opinion we should go still further, especially in regard to policy toward China, and, as I suggested earlier, we should alter our basic posture toward the Chinese Communist regime from one of containment plus isolation to one of containment without isolation.

I indicated earlier that such a change of posture would call for re-examination of many specific aspects of our current policy toward China, and I would like now to make a few comments on some of these.

The United Nations Issue. The China issue in the United Nations is in many respects an urgent question, since unless we can soon evolve a new and sounder position on this issue, we are likely to be defeated in the General Assembly, and then our entire policy of isolation of Peking will begin to unravel as a result of a major political defeat, even before we can, on our own initiative, attempt to redefine our posture.

Last fall, we were barely able to get enough votes to sustain our position. Conceivably we might do so once or twice again; but it is equally conceivable that next fall the General Assembly might, despite our opposition, vote to seat Peking in the present China seat occupied by the Chinese Nationalist regime. If this takes place there is little likelihood that the Nationalists could later be brought back into the United Nations, since this would then be a question of admitting a new member, which is subject to the veto.

It would be to our interest, therefore, to take the initiative in the General Assembly in promoting a solution in which the Assembly would declare that there are now two "successor states" ruling the territory of the original China which joined the United Nations when it was formed in 1945, and that both should have seats in the Assembly. Neither the Chinese Communists nor the Chinese Nationalists is presently willing to accept such a solution, and conceivably both might boycott the United Nations for a period of time, if such a solution were adopted. Nevertheless, it is a realistic and reasonable position for the international community as a whole to adopt, and I believe that, if it were adopted, there would be numerous pressures operating overtime to induce Peking and Taipei eventually to reexamine their positions and consider accepting seats even under these conditions.

If and when Communist China does assume a seat in the United Nations, its initial impact is likely to be disruptive, but I firmly believe that over the long run it is nonetheless desirable to involve Peking in this complicated political arena, where it will have to deal on a day-to-day basis with such a wide variety of countries and issues. It will soon learn, I think, that dogmatic arrogance will result only in self-isolation and that even a major nation must make compromises to operate with any success in the present world community.

A shift of American policy on the United Nations issue—and, in fact, any significant change in our posture toward Peking—will inevitably require some modification of our policy toward the Nationalist regime on Taiwan. For many reasons—political, strategic, and moral—we should continue defending Taiwan against attack and should firmly support the principal of self-determination in regard to the 13 million inhabitants of the island. But we will not be able to continue sustaining the fiction that the Nationalist regime is the government of mainland China. Our view of the Nationalist regime should be one in which we recognize it as the legal government of the territories it now occupies, essentially Taiwan and the Pescadores, rather than as the government of all China; this, one might note, is the position which the Japanese Government already maintains in regard to the Nationalists. We should do all we can to obtain representation for the Taipei regime in the United Nations and to urge the international community to accept and support it as the government of its present population and territory. But we cannot indefinitely sustain the fiction that it is the government of all China.

Unofficial Contacts. The desirability of increased unofficial contacts with Communist China has already been accepted, at least to a limited degree, by the U.S. Government, and there is now a sizable number of American newsmen, and some doctors and medical scientists, who would be permitted to visit mainland China if the Chinese Communists would grant them visas. The present obstacles to limited contacts, in short, are created by Peking, not by us. But despite Peking's general intransigence, we should continue searching for every possible opportunity for contact, in the hope that Peking will eventually modify its present stand, and should encourage scholars, businessmen, and others, as well as newsmen and doctors, to try to visit mainland China.

As a part of our effort to increase unofficial contacts with Communist China we should end our embargo on all trade and permit trade in nonstrategic items. The present significance of our embargo, it should be stressed, is wholly symbolic, since no other major trading nation maintains such an embargo, and Peking is able, therefore, to purchase in Japan, Germany, England, or elsewhere any goods that are denied to it by us. The ending of our embargo might well be largely symbolic, too, since the Chinese Communists are likely to prefer trading with countries other than the United States. Nevertheless, it is conceivable that over time some limited trade contacts might develop, and be desirable from our point of view.

The question of de jure recognition of Communist China—which in some discussions of China policy is given more attention than it deserves—is really a question for the future rather than the present. Until Peking indicates a willingness to exchange diplomatic representatives with us, there are no strong arguments for our unilaterally extending official recognition that would not be reciprocated. Our aim, certainly, should be to work toward eventual establishment of normal diplomatic relations, but it is likely to be some time—even if we alter our own overall position—before that is possible. We can and should, however, clearly indicate now—in much more explicit fashion than we have to date—that we do recognize the Peking regime in a de facto sense. One might argue that our frequent ambassadorial meetings with the Chinese Communists in Warsaw already constitute a form of de facto recognition, but officially we have refused to acknowledge any sort of recognition—de jure or de facto—and we should now do so.

American Public Opinion. No discussion of China policy would be complete without at least a word on American public opinion. Although there are many persons in the United States—in the Government, in universities, and elsewhere—who are relatively well informed about Communist China, there is no doubt that the American people, as a whole, know far too little about China, or about the problems of evolving effective policies to deal with it. At the same time, issues relating to China policy have been among the most emotional in

American public life ever since the late 1940's. It is probably fair to say that there has been less responsible public discussion of China policy than of any other foreign policy issue of comparable importance. I believe, therefore, that the holding of these hearings is of very great importance, and I hope that they will stimulate nationwide interest and will encourage widespread discussion of U.S. policy toward China.

It is sometimes assumed that, because issues relating to China policy have tended to be viewed emotionally, it has not been politically wise to discuss them. I do not know to what extent this has been true in the past, or to what extent it has inhibited responsible public debate. I do believe, however, that public opinion has been slowly changing and is increasingly receptive to a reexamination of China policy. In support of this view, I would like to call your attention to a book just published, called "The American People and China." It is written by A. T. Steele, formerly of the New York Herald Tribune, and published by the Council on Foreign Relations as part of its broad study, which will result in almost a dozen books, on the United States and China in world affairs. Steele concludes that "American public opinion would, on the whole, welcome a public reappraisal in Congress and among the people, of our China policy," and that public opinion would respond to both congressional and presidential leadership on this issue. I believe he is right, and I hope, therefore, that these hearings will mark the start of the most important public reexamination of China policy since the Communist takeover of China in 1949.

3

PERSPECTIVE ON CONTAINMENT

By John K. Fairbank

Dealing with the Peking rulers is so frustrating because they are so implacably doctrinaire. They call us all lackeys of "Wall Street capitalist imperialism," lumping together indiscriminately Democrats and Republicans, professors and public servants, even the executive and legislative branches, all of us due for extinction by the laws of Marxist history.

Peking is not only unrealistic about us. Chairman Mao even thinks of himself as the successor to Marx, Lenin, and Stalin, whereas in actual fact, as the ruler of China, he is much more the successor of the emperors who ruled at Peking until 1912 when Mao was already eighteen years of age. To hear the Peking leaders talk you would think they were an offshoot of European Socialism. Actually the problems they face and the methods they use are in large part inherited from Chinese history.

We Americans talk every day about our founding fathers of the eighteenth century. Our founding fathers lived in the period of the Emperor Ch'ien-lung, who ruled for sixty years at the height of a two-thousand-year development of imperial monarchy. Chairman Mao doesn't seem to know it, but he owes something of his style and world view to his predecessors in Peking in ages past. Since we have now given up calling Communism a great international monolith, everywhere and always the same, it is high time for us to examine the Chineseness which is now showing through the Communism in Peking.

I am a professional historian but we all know that everybody is his own historian, and history can be cited selectively on all sides of every question. I think we need more perspective on the Chinese style of political behavior. What did the world look like from Peking? How was the power held there down to 1912, within the lifetime of many of us? How did Peking handle her foreign relations, and what kind of heritage is operating today in Peking's motives and toward the outside world?

I imagine we would all agree on a first point — China's remarkable feeling of superiority. Here was a very big, ancient, isolated, unified and self-sufficient empire, stretching from the latitude of Hudson's Bay to Cuba or from the Baltic Sea to the Sahara Desert, with a great deal of domestic commerce to meet its needs, cut off from West Asia by the high mountains and deserts of Central Asia and thus isolated throughout most of its history, preserving a continuity of development in the same area over some three or four thousand years, during most of which time the Chinese state has been a unified entity. As we might expect, this biggest, most isolated and distinctive, most long-continued culture and society developed a strong tendency to look inward, an attitude of ethnocentrism or Sinocentrism, China being the center of the known world and of civilization, the non-Chinese being peripheral and inferior, China being superior to all foreign regions.

It is fascinating to note how this cultural isolation is still reinforced by the Chinese writing system. Because it uses ideographic characters, it cannot easily take in foreign words by sound but only by representing the foreign ideas in Chinese characters, yet the Chinese characters have their own meaning already. Our current research finds that foreign ideas have come into Chinese most easily when the Chinese have already had the same general idea. The writing system makes for continuity and inertia in Chinese ways. Unlike Japan, Korea, or Vietnam, who all had a phonetic writing system combined with Chinese characters, the Chinese cannot take in foreign words purely by transcribing their sound even today.

A second point is that the old Peking rulers were the custodians and propagators of a true teaching, the Confucian classical doctrines of social order, an orthodoxy which told every man how to behave in his proper place and kept the social pyramid intact with the emperor on top. The emperor was himself the high priest of a cult of social order. The three main bonds of the Confucian social order were the filial piety of children to their superior parents, the admirable devotion of wives to their superior husbands, the loyalty of scholar-officials to their superior the emperor. This system did not believe in the equality of all men, which was obviously untrue. It believed in selecting the talented, training them in the orthodoxy, and promoting them as officials to keep the populace under control and maintain the system. We need not labor the point that China today still has a ruling class selected for their abilities who propagate a true teaching under a sage ruler and strive to keep the various social classes in order.

The Myth of Rule by Virtue. If we try to generalize about the ideological sanction for holding power in China, I think we must conclude that China was ruled by a great Confucian political fiction, the myth of rule by virtue. According to this, the right conduct of a superior man, acting according to the correct principles, set an example which moved others and commanded their respect and allegiance. In particular, the emperor's right conduct, the most perfect example among mankind, was thought to exert an influence over all beholders. His virtuous conduct commanded their loyalty, providing they also understood the correct principles of conduct as laid down in the classics. Persons too uneducated to be so moved could, of course, be dealt with by rewards and punishments.

This national myth of rule-by-virtue fills the Chinese historical record. It corresponded in political life, I suppose, to the Western concept of the supremacy of law and the natural rights of the individual and his civil liberties under law, which I take to be still one of our chief articles of faith, including the idea of self-determination for nations. Ancient China never developed these concepts of supremacy of law and natural rights or civil liberties. Instead it spread the Confucian faith as to proper conduct in all relationships and so reinforced the ruler's claim that he ruled by his virtuous example.

In their foreign relations the Chinese rulers down to 1912 extended their domestic doctrines across their frontiers and applied the national myth of rule-by-virtue to their foreign relations. Foreign rulers could have contact with the Peking monarch only by sending tribute to him and having their envoys perform the three kneelings and nine prostrations of the kotow ritual. This elaborate and prolonged ceremony, kneeling and prostrating oneself at command in front of the emperor — quite a lot of exercise! — was absolutely insisted upon by the court to preserve the image of China's superiority and show the foreigner his proper place in the world hierarchy. It became well established that all foreign relations must be tributary relations, reinforcing the myth of Chinese supremacy and particularly the myth that foreign rulers were attracted by the emperor's virtue and "turned toward him" to offer their submission to the center of civilization. This grandiose concept reminds one of other ancient kings. The interesting thing is that the Chinese state was able to preserve it intact down to this century. The last tribute mission came from Nepal in 1908.

When China was weak, she could still maintain the fiction of supremacy by maintaining the rituals and the written records. For example, three thousand Mongol horsemen might come to Peking on a so-called "annual tribute mission," being royally entertained and given expensive gifts at great cost to the government, having as much fun as a Shriner's Convention and letting the Chinese court call it "tribute" just to keep its fictions intact. In short, the tribute system was sometimes maintained by giving gifts.

The long record of Chinese foreign relations shows the importance attached to the political myths of China's superiority and rule by virtue. Maintaining this ideological orthodoxy in written form helped the emperor keep power in fact, because the recorded "facts" sustained the theory. It was like the advertisement for paint — "Save the surface (or the record) and you save all."

We can conclude, I think, that the ideological component of power in China has been proportionately greater than in the West. Calling everything by its orthodox name helped keep things in order. The emperors were constantly spelling out the true doctrines, having them read in the Confucian temples and studied by all scholars. Heterodoxy and deviation could not be permitted, or if they did exist, could not be acknowledged to exist. Even when the foreigners were more powerful, the myth of China's superiority had to be solemnly recorded and preserved in ritual. This stress on orthodoxy strikes one today when Peking is continuing its nation-wide indoctrination in Chairman Mao's true teachings.

Applying all this background to the present moment, I suggest we should not get too excited over Peking's vast blueprints for the onward course of the Maoist revolution. Some American commentators who really ought to know better have over-reacted to the visionary blueprint of world revolution put out by Lin Piao last September in Peking (about the strangling of the world's advanced countries or "cities" from the underdeveloped countries or "countryside.") This was, I think, a re-assertion of faith, that the Chinese Communists' own parochial example of rural-based revolution is the model for the rest of the underdeveloped world to emulate. It was put out mainly as compensation for China's recent defeats in many parts of the globe. To compare it to Hitler's *Mein Kampf* would be quite misleading. Rule by virtue required that the rulers proclaim their true teaching, claiming that it will still win the world even if they themselves are too weak to support it in practice.

China's Modern Disaster. The disaster that hit China in the nineteenth century is one of the most comprehensive any people ever experienced. The ancient tradition of China's superiority, plus this modern disaster, has undoubtedly produced one first-class case of frustration. It cannot seem right that a civilization once at the top should have been brought so low.

The nineteenth century disaster began with a great population increase during the peaceful eighteenth century, a consequent weakening of administrative efficiency and maybe some popular demoralization, evident in the beginning of opium smoking. In the Opium War of 1840 the Chinese were fighting against the opium trade, conducted by both foreigners and Chinese, while the British were fighting in the broad sense against the tribute system, demanding that China drop her claim to superiority and join the modern international trading world, the same thing we are waiting for today more than a century later.

The Opium War and the unequal treaties in the 1840's gave our merchants and missionaries a privileged status as agents of Westernization in the Chinese treaty ports. Throughout the next century, Western influence gradually disintegrated the old Chinese civilization. As the disaster gained momentum, Western gunboats proved that China had to have scientific technology, and then had to have Western industries, for which it was necessary to have Western learning, and eventually Western institutions and even a Western type of government. The prestige of the Confucian classics evaporated. The Confucian type of a family-structure began to crack. China's superiority vanished even culturally.

The generation of Chinese that lived through this long-continued disaster, which happened in our grandfathers' time, experienced a deepening crisis. The sacred values of proper conduct and social order proved useless. The ancient faith in China's superiority as a civilization was slowly strangled. The privileged foreigners came in everywhere and gradually stirred up a Chinese nationalism.

So complete was the disaster that a new order had to be built from the ground up. Western doctrines of all kinds were tried out. The thing that proved effective was the Leninist type of party dictatorship, an elite recruited under discipline according to a new orthodoxy, organised something like an old Chinese secret society, united in the effort to seize power and recreate a strong state. This nationalistic aim overrode every other consideration. The kind of Western individualism propagated by our missionaries had no chance.

The retrospective humiliation and sense of grievance over the enormous disaster of the nineteenth century had made modern Chinese feel that their country was victimized. So it was, by fate. Circumstance made China the worst accident case in history. But Marxism-Leninism offers a devil-theory to explain it: how "capitalist imperialism" combined with "feudal reaction" to attack, betray and exploit the Chinese people and distort their otherwise normal development toward "capitalism" and "socialism". Thus a great Communist myth of "imperalist" victimization becomes the new national myth.

Maoism as a Minor Tradition. It would not be naive to agree that China's early sense of superiority had some justification, and that her modern sense of victimization also has some justification. To have been so advanced and superior and then to find herself so backward and weak was a shattering experience. Now that Maoism is in power, we see the continued desire to set a model for mankind, to be the center from which civilization is derived. We can also see the tactic of having relations with other powers only in so far as they fit into the Chinese world view. But what has happened to the old Confucian tradition of balance, harmony, and tolerance for private variations in faith and custom? The training of bureaucrats who were also humanists, artists and scholars, to carry on the established order, was the major tradition, dominant over most of the centuries, whereas the present regime seems to be in a minority rebel tradition of dynastic founders, more like a band of sworn brothers rising from the countryside as leaders of peasant rebellion, animated by an extreme fanaticism.

The Peking leaders of today remind one of the leaders of the Taiping rebellion of the 1850's who picked up Christianity as a foreign ideology, rebuilt it to suit their needs, and took over half the country. The Taipings came from the back country, not from the foreign trade centers. They began as a secret society with a cult, invoked the radical tradition in the Chinese classics, and sought a utopian collective or communal society, at one time even segregating the sexes. But the Taiping leaders were so dogmatic and doctrinaire that they alienated both the Chinese scholar class who might have helped them and the foreign merchants and missionaries who also might have helped them. Their simple fanaticism and xenophobia led them to pluck disaster from the jaws of victory.

In the course of time Peking should see a resurgence of the more humanistic and bureaucratic tradition of government by well-educated administrators who keep society in balance. While the past is gone forever, the present is not permanent either. Eventually we may expect the Chinese revolution to mellow down a bit.

American Sentiment About Our China Policy. As Americans we can only begin to imagine how the Chinese have suffered from being on the receiving end of modernization rather than the giving end. It has been hard for them to take, because under their traditional code there should be reciprocity between people, one should not accept gifts without paying them back. For China to be always receiving from the West not only hurts national pride. Being on the receiving end with no chance of repaying the favors of missionaries, for example, also hurts personal self-respect.

We Americans, being on the giving end of modernization, got a great deal more fun out of Sino-American relations. In the privileged status thrust upon them by the treaty system, most Americans enjoyed their contact with China, the chance to be an upper-class foreigner riding in a rickshaw while still remaining an egalitarian grass-roots democrat in one's own conscience. For an average American to go abroad and find himself a rich man by comparison with the local people is also quite enjoyable. The Chinese were very polite, and countless Americans made warm friends among them. The American people built up a genuine, though sometimes patronizing fondness for China.

Unfortunately, this now turns out to have been an unrealistic and rather naive attitude for two reasons. In the first place, the Americans were conscious of their own good intentions and less conscious of the humiliation that their superior circumstances often inflicted upon their Chinese friends.

In the second place, the Americans were able in the nineteenth century to share all the special privileges of foreigners in China under the unequal treaties without fighting for them. The British and others fought the colonial wars and the Americans enjoyed the fruits of such aggression without the moral responsibility. By 1900 the British, the French, and the Japanese had all fought wars with China; the Russians had seized territory; and all of them together, with the Germans, had seized special privileges in spheres of influence.

The Americans had done none of these things and came up instead with the Open Door doctrine, which soon expanded to include not only the open door for trade but also the idea of China's integrity as a nation. Thus we Americans prided ourselves on championing China's modernization and self-determination. We considered ourselves above the nasty imperialism and power politics of the Europeans. We developed a self-image of moral superiority. The Open Door and benevolence toward Chinese nationalism became the bases of our Far Eastern policy until war with Japan brought us up against the realities of power politics. Then we began to realize, for almost the first time, that the power structure of East Asian politics had been held together by the British navy in the nineteenth century, and by the British and Japanese navies under the Anglo-Japanese Alliance from 1902 to 1922.

Today we find ourselves in an onerous situation trying to maintain the power balance in East Asia. It is reminiscent in some ways of the colonial wars of the nineteenth century, a type of situation that we generally succeeded in avoiding in that era. I do not contend that we today are simply nineteenth-century imperialists come back to life, any more than Chairman Mao is actually a resurrected Son of Heaven in a blue boiler suite. But I don't believe we can escape our historical heritage entirely, any more than he can. We have been part and parcel of the long-term Western approach to East Asia and ought to see ourselves in that perspective, just as any view of our China policy has to include a perpective on our program in Vietnam.

Echoes of Colonial War in Vietnam. Our Vietnam war differs from colonial wars of the past in certain basic ways, but still the similarities are rather striking. Colonial wars in East and Southeast Asia had half a dozen common features:

First, an expansive ideological interest on the part of the modernizing colonial power — whether it was British faith in "commerce as the handmaiden of civilization," the French "civilizing mission" in support of Catholic Christianity, Russia's sacred mission to "liberate" the oppressed peoples of the Orient, Japan's "co-prosperity sphere," or merely the "white man's burden" and "manifest destiny".

Second, a rival to keep ahead of in power politics — witness the long-continued Anglo-French rivalry in Southeast Asia, Russo-Japanese rivalry in Korea and Manchuria, Anglo-Russian rivalry all across Asia, and so on.

Third, marked uncertainties of policy, much debated at the time — but which usually wound up in a refusal to back down or scuttle out. As the Tsar said of Vladivostok in 1860, "Where the flag has once been raised, it must not be lowered."

Fourth, a superior logistic capacity and fire-power — evident all the way from the British iron-hulled steam gunboats of the Opium War that could sail against wind and tide (!) to the Japanese tank-and-dive-bomber teams of the 1930's. The superior killing capacity gave colonial wars their particular brand of inhumanity.

Fifth, a local regime to work with — either inherited like Vietnam's Nguyen dynasty from 1885 to 1945, or Korea's Yi dynasty from 1905 to 1910, or else built up anew; but in either case staffed by native and foreign administrators working together.

Sixth, a period of military "pacification" after the foreign power moved in. Britain in Upper Burma after 1886 needed five years and 40,000 troops to suppress the resistance. After the French had defeated China and seized North Vietnam (Tongking) in 1885, their network of posts and punitive flying columns needed ten years to "pacify" the guerrillas. After the United States seized the Philippines in 1898, military suppression of Aguinaldo's Philippine Republic took three years. When Japan moved into Formosa in 1895 she needed seven years to suppress the resistance. In Korea Japan faced three years of nationwide rebellion even before 1910.

Finally, disruption and modernization of the colonial society — accelerated change on all levels, neither wholly "bad" nor wholly "good," and still much disputed in retrospect.

Most of these criteria seem to apply to Vietnam today. "Self-determination" and "defense against aggression" are ideals we all, I am sure, deeply believe in, yet they have expansive implications. In Vietnam we are bent on forestalling the Chinese Communist model of nation-building by subversion and regimentation, which we regard as a dangerous rival to our own trade-and-aid model. Our fire-power is superb and our killing capacity is superior. We have a local regime to work with. The American build-up in South Vietnam is so massive it comes very close to a colonial take-over, even though it is firmly intended to be only temporary. "Pacification" is naturally scheduled to ensue for several years, probably in the towns more than the back country, together with the further disrupion of Vitnamese sociey and its further modernization. The Americans bring with them their culture, its good and its ills. Refugee shanty towns and traffic jams in the Saigon metropolis are only the most superficial evidence of shattering changes in the urban part of South Vietnam that we can hope to dominate.

Of course this war is not for colonial territory nor our own aggrandizement. Asian nationalism and nuclear capacity are great new factors. Times have changed. The age of imperialism has given way to the age of nationalism, which we now champion, although we supported the French in Vietnam not so long ago. National interest is now tied in with international stability.

But Vietnam today gives us a more severe crisis of moral concience partly because during most of our history we felt morally superior to the imperialist powers of the nineteenth century. Why must our land of the free now send its boys to kill and be killed in a civil war so far away? I would not claim that the history of power politics in East Asia automatically gives us the justification, but I do believe it helps explain how we got in. The problem of power relations has to be faced. Perhaps power has to be used in smaller wars if we are to avoid bigger wars. In any case, in Vietnam we seem unlikely either to lose or to win completely. Therefore I think the most important issue is our non-military, or more-than-military, program there.

Containment and Competition in Southeast Asia. The main fact about our containment of the Chinese revolutionary influence in South Vietnam is that it is only in part military. In larger part, it is a competition in how to help in nation-building. Warfare is only the visible top of the iceberg. Most of the problem is not only political but also social, how to mobilize the people and organize their participation in politics.

The real test for us is not whether we can fight but whether we can be more constructive than destructive while we are fighting, right now and not later on. At present we seem more destructive. Whatever our level of effort, the balance of it should be weighted much, much more than it is on the side of helping civil action, recruitment and training for "pacification," and the other good things envisioned at Honolulu.

This kind of military containment-plus-social competition in helping to build up a new nation in South Vietnam, is obviously a much harder task than our original containment-plus-Marshall Plan effort in industrialized Europe. We should not expect a comparable success. Yet to burn up Vietnam and go away and leave it will not smell as good as to make the much greater effort to help build up the society whenever we can.

Some argue, feeling culturally closer to Europe, than Vietnam is beyond our proper realm of concern. I don't agree. The Western powers have played major roles in Southeast Asia for four hundred years even if we have not. The West has made its contribution while also precipitating the nationalist revolutions. American merchants and missionaries joined in making this Western contribution. We cannot now condemn and disown the old British empire, for instance, just because we let the British fight dirty colonial wars while we got the benefits. We were and are involved in East Asian power politics at least as much as in those of Europe, cultural differences notwithstanding.

Stuck in a dirty war today, we would do well to lower our self-esteem, be not so proud, acknowledge our Western inheritance of both good and evil, and see ourselves as hardly more noble and not much smarter than the British and French in their day. We must be steadfast and restrained. We cannot take East Asia *or* ourselves out of power politics. The real test, I repeat, is whether we can be more constructive than destructive in areas of Vietnam we can influence.

Preparing to Get Peking Into the World. My conclusion is that the alternative to war with Peking, over Vietnam or elsewhere, lies along two lines of effort — one is to achieve a better balance between destruction and construction in our own efforts in Vietnam, so that the non-Communist model of nation-building there can compete more effectively with the Chinese Communist model of nation-building. The other line of effort is to defuse or dampen Peking's militancy by getting China into greater contact with the outside world, more connected with the international scene and more interested in participating in it like other countries.

How to get the Peking leadership into the international order, instead of their trying to destroy it according to their revolutionary vision, is primarily a psychological problem. Therapy for Peking's present almost paranoid state of mind must follow the usual lines of therapy: it must lead the rulers of China gradually into different channels of experience until by degrees they reshape their picture of the world and their place in it. The remolding of Chairman Mao, the greatest remolder of others in history, is not something I would advocate as feasible. But I think it is high time we got ourselves ready to deal with his successors and with *their* successors in years ahead.

In practice this means getting Peking into a multitude of activities abroad. China should be included in all international conferences, as on disarmament, and in international associations, both professional and functional, in international sports, not just ping-pong, and in trade with everyone, including ourselves, except for strategic goods. One thinks naturally of the U.N. agencies and participation in the Security Council as well as the Assembly. Yet all this can come only step by step, with altercation all along the way — Not an easy process but a lot more constructive than warfare.

American policy should work toward a gradual shift from trying to isolate Peking, which only worsens our problem, to a less exposed position where we can acquiesce in the growth of contact between Peking and other countries and let *them* suffer the impact of Peking's abrasiveness.

In gradually manipulating Peking into an acceptance of the international world, as an alternative to trying to subvert it, we must motivate Chinese behavior according to China's needs: 1) One of these is the craving for greater prestige in the world to redress the balance of the last century's humiliations. For China to be in the center of the world's councils would seem to a Chinese patriot only right and proper.

(2) We can also use the Peking government's need for prestige to maintain itself domestically. It is still true that the virtue of the rulers, as advertised in their acknowledged achievements, is a vital element sustaining any regime in China.

(3) In addition, the Chinese people positively need certain kinds of aid through exchanges of technology or of goods, like all developing countries.

(4) Peking may also be motivated by the opportunitiy to manipulate foreigners against one another. This traditional way of dealing with outsiders can be attempted in any conclave like the United Nations. But any number can play this game, and, in fact, it is the essence of diplomacy.

As these types of motives come into play, we may expect the Peking regime to be involved in bilateral relationships and be influenced by others whose desire is for peace rather than violence. In the end all this may make coexistence more attractive and feasible.

Opening the door for China's participation in the world scene is only one part of an American policy. The other part is to hold the line. The Chinese are no more amenable to pure sweetness and light than other revolutionaries. Encouraging them to participate in the U.N. and other parts of the international scene has to be combined with a cognate attitude of firmness backed by force. Military containment on the Korean border, in the Taiwan Straits, and somehow in Vietnam cannot soon be abandoned and may have to be maintained for some time. But containment alone is a blind alley unless we add policies of constructive competition and of international contact.

In short, my reading of history is that Peking's rulers shout aggressively out of manifold frustrations, that isolation intensifies their ailment and makes it self perpetuating, and that we need to encourage international contact with China on many fronts.

4

THE RISE OF CHINESE COMMUNISM

By Benjamin I. Schwartz

I have been asked to comment briefly on the history of the rise of the Chinese Communists to power in 1949 and on the fall of the Nationalist government. I think that it is most appropriate that the two be linked since the success of the one side was to a considerable extent the result of the failure of the other. Were it not for certain fundamental and very specific failures on the Nationalist side, the Maoist revolutionary strategy might not have succeeded.

Since much attention has been focused recently on Mao Tse-tung's formula for revolutionary success I would like to dwell for a moment on the failure of the Nationalists.

In 1911, China witnessed the collapse of one of the most imposing political systems the world has ever known. What collapsed was not merely a government but the whole cosmology on which that government was based. In the ensuing vacuum, political power gravitated into the hands of local militarists. We then have the immense anarchy and chaos of the so-called warlord period. It is, I believe, a warranted assumption that during this period of chaos and political decay, the social and economic situation of the vast masses of China — in the aggregate — continued to deteriorate.

In 1927, the Kuomintang government ostensibly carried out the political and military unification of China. This speedy unification was, however, based on a network of flimsy agreements with many of the local militarists themselves — agreements which proved highly evanescent. In fact, the government in Nanking controlled directly only certain provinces of central China. This situation had, of course, not been created by the Nationalist government and the tendency of this government to direct much of its energy during the next few years to the task of achieving the genuine military unification of China may seem entirely justifiable. Unfortunately, the resources available to this government were limited and the concentration of major energies in this task meant that other vital tasks were neglected. Furthermore, the Kuomintang itself, which was the supreme political body of the society, was not a highly integrated movement. It was riven by cliques among which there was little lateral cohesion. The reasons for this failure of the Kuomintang to achieve inner unity still remain to be studied but the fact that the Party rested on what has been called a "balance of weakness" can hardly be denied. One aggravating factor was undoubtedly the fact that these political cliques were often able to establish links with the independent military groupings mentioned above. On the whole, the ideology of the Kuomintang did not prove to be an overwhelming galvanizing force, either within or outside of the Party. One of its ingredients was, of course, nationalism, and nationalism is, as we know, one of the most potent engines in the world. The Nationalist government was, however, unable — particularly after the Japanese onslaught — to feed its engine with the fuel of success.

Positive Programs. During its early years, the Kuomintang did carry out positive programs in the realm of communications, education, foreign affairs etc., but these programs were also limited in conception. They were largely urban in orientation and paid little attention to the vast rural hinterland which was hardly affected by the Nationalist rise to power. Local power in these areas, by default, remained in the hands of the incumbent holders of power. No doubt, the rural situation in the vast territory of China was not uniform. It was obviously better in some areas than others. It was not, however, substantially improved anywhere by government action. The governments conception of the priority of tasks involved the assumption that the task of military and political unification, the tasks of industrialization and various forms of urban modernization must come first. Since the government was unable, during the whole period of its tenure on the mainland, to solve the problem of military unification or to launch a substantial industrialization program, it never did turn its attention seriously to the problem of the rural areas. There are those who contend that it could probably not have carried out substantial programs of reforms in the countryside even if it had desired to do so because it had become indissolubly linked to the local holders of power and privilege. Whether this is so or not, the fact remains that even in terms of policy, rural reform was not high on the list of priorities.

It should also be pointed out that in spite of its orientation to military tasks, the Nationalist government did not carry out substantial reforms in the military area itself. Taking the period of Nationalist control as a whole, one must say that too little was done to improve the condition of the average soldier, to improve the practices of recruitment or the relations between the military and the civilian population. Many of the deplorable practices of the warlord period had carried on into the post-1927 period. The failure in this area may have been due in part to the military crises in which the government was constantly involved. There was the seemingly common sense argument that one does not proceed to carry out sweeping reforms within a military force currently involved in combat. Even more important was the notion that one does not scrutinize the behavior of military officers who have manifested their unquestioned loyalty.

The Kuomintang government was not a totalitarian government in the Communist sense. The intellectually articulate classes were not completely repressed. There was, however, sporadic and arbitrary repression. There was not sufficient repression to prevent intellectuals and students from communicating with each other and exchanging views but there was sufficient suppression (including occasional executions) to embitter and alienate many of them.

It should also be noted that during the period from 1931-1937 the Nationalist government was unable to take full advantage of the patriotic anti-Japanese sentiment of the intellectuals and students. It was the considered view of the leadership that it was futile for China to attempt to confront Japanese power before carrying out military unification at home. While this policy may again on the surface appear eminently sensible, the campaigns against the Communist areas and against local militarists provided the unfortunate spectacle of Chinese fighting Chinese rather than the common Japanese enemy.

Maoist Strategy of Revolution. It is within the context of this situation that the Maoist strategy of revolution gradually emerged. The development of this strategy on the part of Mao and others was a gradual and groping process. There was no pre-existent blue-print. Neither Communist theory nor Russian practice provided any clear "operational code." The Chinese Communist Party in 1927 was by no means committed to an exclusive concentration on rural areas. The emergence of rural bases, the emergence of a concentration on peasant support, on the creation of peasant military forces and on guerilla warfare was precisely a response to some of the Nationalist weaknesses mentioned above. The Kuomintang was weakest in the countryside and in an environment of military disunity, the Communists in a sense took on the coloration of their environment. The Nationalists, indeed, often referred to them as a peculiar breed of warlords. Yet they were neither warlords nor "agrarian reformers." From their Communism they derived a profound faith that history was on their side and they on its side. They also derived the concept of the Communist Party as the instrument of history, as a monolithic group united by an iron discipline and a fixed purpose. Their image of the future was also profoundly influenced by Soviet Communism. By the forties, Mao Tse-tung and others had succeeded in creating a Communist Party which corresponded in the main to this ideal type. Land reform played a considerable role in their program but this does not mean that their policies were uniformly popular with the peasantry or that their dreams for the future were in any way determined by the perspectives of the peasants. Whether popular or unpopular, they succeeded during the course of the thirties and forties in involving the peasantry in their organizational network and in tapping their energies. Above all, I would stress some of the policies which they developed in the military area. They paid enormous attention to the political indoctrination and morale of the average soldier and, within the limits of the situation, to his physical well-being. They also laid constant stress on proper relations between the military and civilian population. In accounting for their victory after 1945, I would be inclined to place more weight on this factor than on the efficacy of land reform as such.

Having pointed out some of the weaknesses of the Kuomintang and some of the strengths of the Maoist strategy of revolution, as I see them, I should immediately add that had there been no Japanese assault on China, it is not inconceivable that the Kuomintang might have survived and that the Maoist strategy might have failed. In the course of time, the Nanking government might have achieved a decisive preponderance of military power in China. Whether this would then have led it to cope successfully with all its other manifold problems we shall never know, but we do know that governments often survive without solving all their problems. The Communist strategy of revolution — at least as it had developed before 1935 — did not prove invulnerable, For all its weaknesses, the Nationalist government was able to muster sufficient military power to squeeze the Communists out of the areas occupied by them in southeastern China. Mao

Tse-tung has claimed that this happened because he was not at the
time in control of the Party and because his own policy views were
not being followed. Be that as it may, the Red Army was forced to
save itself by retreating to the northwest where it arrived with its
number greatly reduced. Most impartial observers might well have
maintained during the 1935-36 period that the Communist strategy
had arrived at a dead end.

The Japanese war against China after 1937 proved, however, to be
like a disease which attacks a frail body at its weakest points. The
net effect of the war was to aggravate the weaknesses of the Nationalist government. All thought of achieving the military control of
North China had to be abandoned. The dependence on holders of
military power increased and the government became more dependent
than in the past on the rural power structure. As the was progressed
the government became convinced that the major battles against
Japan would be won elsewhere. This led to a passive posture in the
war and to policies more concerned with postwar problems of unification than with wartime tasks. Farsighted as such policies may have
been, they did nothing to improve morale or to encourage reform
within the military establishment.

Nationalistic Sentiment. The Communists, on the other hand, were
able to apply their considerable experience in organizing rural areas
to the situation in North China. Once again they were able to spread
their power through the countryside while the enemy — now the
Japanese — controlled cities and lines of communication. The fact
tha tthe enemy was now the foreign aggressor made it possible for
the Communists to add an important string to their bow. They were
now able to make a strong appeal to nationalistic sentiment (which
they undoubtedly shared) and to call for support among many elements — particularly intellectuals . . . who were deeply impressed
by their anti-Japanese activities. One may, of course, raise the question whether Chinese Communist military activities against the Japanese would have made much difference if Japanese power had not
been destroyed elsewhere. From the point of view of many nationalistic Chinese, however, there was the fact that they were actively
engaged with the enemy while the Nationalist government continued
in its passive posture. It is not easy to know how much this Communist patriotic approach affected the attitude of the masses but there
can be no doubt that it actually attracted many intellectuals and

students to the Communist areas and created an attitude of at least favorable neutrality in wide circles outside of these areas. By the end of the war the Communists had managed to establish their political authority in some depth over wide areas of the North China plain. This, of course, gave them ready access to Manchuria which had in actuality never been under firm Nationalist control.

The Nationalist government carried into the postwar period its overwhelming concern with the immediate achievement of military, political and even economic unification. Yet the factors which had made for low morale in both its political and military establishment had not been overcome during the course of the war. They had, in fact, been aggravated.

One is tempted to speculate in retrospect on what might have happened if the Nationalist government had concentrated during the years between 1927 and the later '40s on reform in depth within the areas under its firm control rather than on the will-o-wisp pursuit of the military unification of the whole of China. If it had been able to establish its power in depth in given areas, these areas might have then proven a solid base for a much more effective unification effort. This would have involved at a bare minimum a sweeping reform of the military establishment and some sort of beneficent impact on the life of the peasant village. The notion that national unification was the task of first priority is one which has a certain commonsensical plausibility. Unfortunately, ordinary "common sense" and true statesmanship do not always coincide. Whether the Nationalist government could have carried out such a policy is a question which cannot be answered here.

General Implications. In considering some of the general implications of this story, I think it must be emphasized that the success of the Maoist strategy in China must be explained in terms of the specific history of modern China and not in terms of vague generalities about underdeveloped countries in general. The political and military fragmentation of modern China, the whole phenomenon of "warlordism," the failure to carry out military reform even in those armies under firm government control played an enormous role in the ultimate success of Chinese Communist strategy. Furthermore, as a result of the Japanese aggression, the Chinese Communists were able to wed their rural strategy to a genuine national appeal. In the eyes of many Chinese, they were able to make themselves the spokesmen of a genuine Chinese nationalism even while remaining Communists.

It is by no means true that all the circumstances here described can be found in all underdeveloped countries. Warlordism and military fragmentation is by no means a universal phenomenon in the third world. Many of these states, in spite of their many debilities, do succeed in creating a fairly unified, cohesive and disciplined army. Furthermore, few of these new nations now confront a foreign enemy on their own soil. Peking has been attempting to create in the third world an attitude toward the United States which would be the equivalent of Chinese attitudes toward Japan during the '40s. This effort is not likely to succeed unless we actually choose to perform the role which Peking has assigned to us. The notion that the Chinese model of revolution is a kind of magic formula which will work everywhere in the "underdeveloped world," once certain buttons are pressed in Peking, is a notion based on the same fear of the diabolical cleverness of Communists which we used to direct to Moscow. Not only does the strategy require the existence of a local political situation favorable to its success, it requires the existence of a self-reliant, capable, indigenous leadership willing to adopt and adapt it to local conditions.

Peking may now believe that it can create such revolutionary elites through embassy staffs and manuals. Its own experience should have taught it otherwise. In Vietnam, which provides the only case until now of the successful adaptation of the Chinese strategy, one has had not only specific favorable circumstances but a leadership in Hanoi which has essentially made itself. The fact that neither the United States nor the U.S.S.R. have been quite successful in imposing their models on the third world is in itself no proof that the Chinese will succeed in doing so.

5

RECENT POLITICAL DEVELOPMENTS

By John M. H. Lindbeck

From listening to public discussions and reading newspaper articles about China, one might gain the impression that China's Communist leaders spend much, if not most, of their time thinking about promoting revolutions around the world and plotting to extend their control over China's neighbors. In actual fact, China's leaders are preoccupied with Chinese domestic issues and the country's internal problems and development.

It is true that within the framework of their doctrinal perspectives, these men believe there is a close relationship between external and domestic affairs. They believe, for example, that the main forces shaping history — economic and social changes, proletarian revolutions, opposition to imperialism, the expansion of socialism — transcend national boundaries. They see developments in China as part of a larger transnational historic movement. But the "fundamental task" which they set for themselves in the Party Constitution of 1956 during the period of transition to Communism is the "socialist transformation" of the society and economy and "the industrialization of the country." It is their own interests and those of China, as they interpret these, that are foremost in their minds.

China's Communist leaders are specialists in Chinese domestic politics, but amateurs in the field of international politics. However harsh the methods or technically and professionally primitive some of the major programs and policies they have adopted, these men have applied themselves with energy to developing and using military force for achieving power within China, to consolidating their control over the country, to modernizing the use of China's human and natural resources, and to overhauling radically China's economic, social and political systems. If power, organizational skill, and the introduction of radical programs of economic development and social modernization are criteria for success, then they have considerable achievements to their credit.

By contrast, for a regime that is professedly internationalist in orientation, relatively modest amounts of attention and resources are allocated to activities relating to external relationships. Apart from the attention and resources devoted to the country's military forces — and these were brought into being for domestic purposes and still have domestic as well as external functions, the number of people working on foreign political, economic and cultural relations, budgetary allocations for foreign affairs, and the amount of time devoted to international affairs by governmental bodies and in annual official reports represent a small proportion of the total. Instead of the firm grasp the country's leaders seem to have of Chinese realities, if not of modern science and technology, these men seem to me to reveal oversensitivity to prestige and ideological considerations, ignorance and misconceptions, lack of experience and sophistication, and narrowmindedness in their handling of China's relations with its external environment.

Instead of successfully finding ways to extend Chinese power and influence in their international affairs, as they have in domestic affairs, they now are pitted simultaneously against the United States and the Soviet Union; they are estranged from a majority of nations in the world; they are unpopular and feared by most of their neighbors in East Asia. I believe that this, in part at least, is the result of their parochial Chinese background and experience and the doctrinaire inflexibility of their perspectives on the world.

Consolidation and Maintenance of Power. The regime is solidly entrenched in China. By the regime I mean above all the Communist Party, but also the large administrative and economic institutions and mass organizations created by the party and staffed by officials who are party appointees. There is no good evidence, so far as I can see, that the continuity and basic stability of the regime is likely to be jeopardized in the foreseeable future. Even should there be a succession crisis when the present top leaders die, with a sharp struggle for power between competing groups in the party, it is unlikely, I believe, that the authority and control of the regime over the country will be seriously impaired. Contests for power are likely to be confined to groups within the party. The contestants, as influential party officials, will have a vital stake in the survival of the system and of the party as an organization. None of them is likely to seek the support of forces opposed to the regime to win power.

The strength and stability of the regime are a result of several factors. Above all it depends on the unity and efficiency of the Communist Party and the armed forces over which the party exercises particular control. We also must take account of the thoroughness and speed with which the party consolidated its power after achieving military victory. First, this victory enabled the party to destroy all rival military forces on the China mainland and enabled the Red Army, or the Peoples' Liberation Army, to acquire a monopoly of military power in the country.

Secondly, political power was consolidated by destroying the party's political opponents and empowering new political groups throughout the country. This meant the liquidation of millions of people, such as village and town leaders, members of landlord families, officials and members of the Nationalist Party and government, groups connected with industrial and commercial enterprises, warlord families and troops, leaders in secret societies, members of criminal gangs, and others. In villages and hamlets, as well as in various enterprises, new men and women selected or endorsed by the party took control. In general, they were drawn from local groups that were dissatisfied with previous conditions and hostile toward established local leaders; thus they were willing to work for the party. In this process of transferring power to new hands the number of people killed is unknown. During the land reforms of 1950-52 at least a few individuals from each village were singled out as leading "enemies of the people." In terms of long-range consequences, the way in which class conflicts were engineered to discredit, to reduce the status and to penalize those who had economic or social interests which might lead them to oppose the regime was probably more important. This process of identifying and isolating opponents or potential opponents of the party's policies is on-going.

A third measure adopted by the party was to create new governmental and administrative institutions staffed by party-approved appointees. Local assemblies were created and governmental councils established, both operating under party supervision. The party linked the operations of these institutions to the mass organizations that it also controlled.

In the fourth place, through its programs of social modernization the regime destroyed the old and created new institutions of property, production and social relationships. Collective and state farms, nationalized factories, mass organizations and small discussion groups brought the behavior attitudes and activities of the bulk of the population under the surveillance and direction of the government and party.

As the party introduced its new and sweeping programs of collectivization and social mobilization, the relationship between the regime and the people underwent a change. Tensions between the regime and major sectors of Chinese society were inevitable. The regime needed control if it was to introduce radical programs of modernization and speed up the economic development of China. Its authority could not rest on broad political support, but only upon effective organization and the use of instruments of persuasion and coercion.

Tensions Between Regime and Society. The basic source of political tensions in China is in the relationship between the regime, or party, and the people. The regime is authoritarian in character, depending principally upon an authoritarian political party to implement its policies. The primary cause of dissatisfaction and resistance to the regime is not, it seems to me, the high concentration of power in the hands of the ruling elite — for despotic power is not unknown to China. Rather it is the nature of some of the policies and programs of the regime, the disruptive pace at which they are introduced, and the intensity with which people are mobilized to implement these programs that generates stress and produces protests.

The range and degree of resistance varies. The party leaders are skilled in trying to limit popular dissatisfactions and keeping them down to manageable proportions. Occasionally, protests have broken through the bounds of control, as they did during the brief Hundred Flowers Period in 1957 when a policy of liberalization of thought and speech to win greater support from intellectuals led instead to a burst of attacks on the party and its policies; or among farmers during collectivization and communalization when slaughtering of livestock, passivity and other types of resistance appeared and forced readjustments in the regime's policies and patterns of incentives. During the worst of the post-Leap depression, sporadic armed protests occurred. Among the non-Chinese minority groups antagonism to the regime periodically has taken a militant form.

Without going into further details, we seem to see in China a fairly constant process of adjustment taking place between the party and different sectors of the population. The party politicians are responsive to a degree to popular attitudes. They are well aware of the dangers of being alienated from the masses, as the people are called. Where resistance is localized and limited to a small sector of the population, coercive means can be used. But in other, more politically significant cases, the party seeks to use persuasion — which is socially, politically and financially less expensive — rather than physical force to gain compliance or public support. In extreme cases of resistance it has retreated, as from the communes, and reintroduced economic incentives, such as the private plots and free markets, and reinstated the family as a social, housekeeping and child-care unit.

This broad dimension of Chinese politics, the polarization of power between the people and their rulers, finds reflection in the main arena of political activity in China, that is, in the party.

Intra-Party Politics. We get occasional glimpses of the kinds of political activities that go on within the party. The party is made up of individuals with varying backgrounds, experiences, skills, jobs, local connections, and different personal and institutional, as well as class, interests. In a party as large as the Chinese Communist Party, differences between groups and between supporters for different policy alternatives are unavoidable.

Broadly speaking, some groups in the party favor policies and procedures which are at least somewhat responsive to popular desires and needs; others are more inclined to push the pace of social change and economic development and to ignore public opinion. We have seen intra-party struggles between provincial and regional party groups and the top leadership in Peking. Some contests have probably been the result of personal rivalries; others have stemmed from policy differences.

In addition to pulls between central and regional or local interests, there have been differences between functional or institutional components of the party, such as between those members of the party who run the party's own organizations and those who run government and economic ministries. There is some evidence that in the past party members and leaders within the army have tried to obtain a larger slice of China's limited resources in order to promote programs for professionalizing and further modernizing the army, only to be rebuffed by others in the party. This points to the existence of bureaucratic politics within the regime.

Clearly we do not have in Communist China the kind of political activity which occurs in a pluralistic political system in which various groups openly organize to protect and advance their interests. In China, despite the formal existence of non-Communist parties and organizations, it is not possible for these groups to form coalitions and to establish parties able to enter into active competition with the Communists by mobilizing political support.

But this situation does not lead to the disappearance of politics — the struggle for power and influence and a competition between groups advocating different policy alternatives and program priorities. Politics takes a different form and, above all, is confined, so far as the party can make this possible, to the party itself.

Some of these political developments, or intra-party conflicts, are the result of the changing character of the party and its role and functions in China as a ruling party rather than as a party seeking power.

The Communist Party. By 1961 the party had 17 million members. Eighty percent of these had joined the party after 1949. When it came to power, the hard core of the party was in the army whose officers tended for a time to run the government "as the warlord would." After 1949 new recruits to party membership were not warriors but individuals and groups selected by the party leadership through its party-building programs for their usefulness in administration, social and economic management, and programs of modernization. In the first seven years of rule, the party took in over six million new members. In the three years between 1957 and 1961, over four million more were recruited. The proportion of army members in the party dropped from about 20 percent to 6 percent; the number of intellectuals increased from about 5 percent to 15 percent, or to two and a half million in number; industrial workers, once virtually non-existent in the party, made up about 15 percent of the membership by 1962. The proportion of peasant members fell from about 80 percent in 1949 to 66 percent in 1961.

After the assumption of power an important change took place in the role of the party and the activities of its members. Instead of being soldiers and administrators of rural base areas providing support for the army, party members became economic planners and factory managers; they were called upon to run railways, banks, courts, educational systems, scientific institutes, in short, to take on the whole gamut of key jobs which needed to be performed in a large and complex society.

Strains developed between the politically reliable old warriors and the newer, better educated members whose abilities promoted them to administrative jobs both in the party and outside. Top party leaders also have shown signs of uneasiness about the lack of revolutionary spirit and commitment of its new professionally and functionally oriented members. Some of them are said to have tried to use the party to advance the interests of non-party organizations in which they work. Others have shown signs of "revisionism" and "rightism," that is, they have been accused of seeking the good will and support of the people with whom they work by attempting to moderate the pace and direction of the party's policies for transforming China.

The party leaders have made intensive efforts to implant their commitments and values on party members through indoctrination, manual labor, intensified study of Mao's works and other means. At the same time, the leaders cannot achieve their goals without accepting and using groups with the skills needed for governing the country.

Political Change. While the men who came to the top in China have stayed on top, vast changes are taking place within the country. I have stressed the changes which have taken place in the party itself, the institution which is the key to their power and control. It is being transferred from an elite corps composed of politically reliable party henchmen and political activists into a complex organization with administrators, well trained military officers, young intellectuals, scientists, engineers and other professional specialists. Changes in the party reflect broader changes in the country. These changes are the results in part of programs instituted by the country's rulers. Vast educational programs are bringing new outlooks and skills to millions of people. About 10 percent of the national budget is devoted to this purpose and varying percentages of local budgets. Technological innovations and new attitudes toward science are being actively diffused throughout the country. Industry is growing, albeit slowly in the past few years.

The expectations and needs of new groups and institutions which it has brought into being shape the options and policies of the regime. In addition, the urgency and inescapability of some of the problems it faces determines in certain respects the directions in which the regime must move and the priorities it must adopt. For example, excessive population growth and pressures undoubtedly lay behind Peking's reappraisal in 1961 of once repudiated birth control programs. Again, the low productivity of agriculture compelled the party to readjust its economic development priorities at the Tenth Puenum of the Central Committee in 1962, at which time it adopted the line of "developing the national economy with agriculture as the foundation and industry as the leading factor."

Will the new economic, political and social institutions imposed by the Communist leaders of China increasingly be accepted and become domesticated? If the country's leaders maintain the relatively moderate and gradualist economic and social policies they have pursued during the past few years, this is likely to be the case. Over 300 million Chinese are children of the post-1949 era. Those 25 years and under have little or no memory of a non-Communist past. On the other hand, the experiences of the period from 1958 to 1962, when China underwent the mad pressures of the Great Leap, the disorientations of the communes, and economic recession, were undoubtedly traumatic for most Chinese, young and old, but some of the uncertainties and fears of that period are being forgotten with the passage of time. If routinization and continuity of life patterns and social work schedules are encouraged, this too will change the political atmosphere and context in which the regime operates, producing an increased sense of stability and confidence.

I believe that the political situation in China is not static. As in the past, so in the future, there will be important changes. But at present the aging leaders in Peking seem to be uncertain of the directions in which they should move. They want to preserve the fruits of their efforts, but they also seem to realize that the world cannot be remade in a day. They too apparently have learned, or perhaps have been stunned, by the failures of their excessive ambitions.

In 1957 Peking was ending on an upcurve, speedy industrialization led to the claim that China would catch up with and surpass Great Britain within 12 years in major sectors of industrial production; the Great Leap looked feasible; new forms of social organization, the communes, were on the verge of being introduced to speed China into an advanced form of socialism; increased assistance, including aid in developing nuclear facilities and weapons, seemed to be forthcoming from the Soviet Union; China was ready to challenge the United States in the Taiwan Straits.

The mood today is very different. The population pinch is growing; agricultural production has not advanced beyond the point it reached in 1957; Russia is no longer China's mainstay of help and support, but a competitor; slogans of self-reliance and frugality depress the atmosphere; the pace of industrialization has been set back; economic priorities of a less dramatic and less congenial kind have been accepted by Peking; there is reluctant acknowledgement that China's modernization will be accomplished not in a short period, but over the course of many decades.

In this statement I have dwelt only on a few aspects of the political situation in China. First I noted the central place of domestic programs and problems. These I believe will continue to have first claim on the time and energies of China's rulers and on the resources of the country. At present China's policies are more isolationist than internationalist in orientation. Self-reliance is the current watch-word. Second, the present Communist regime has successfully entrenched itself in China and its power and policies will have to be taken into account by all of China's neighbors. Third, continuing changes are taking place in China to which the country's rulers must and do respond in some fashion. Undoubtedly, the regime's reactions to domestic pressures and problems will be more immediate and direct than its response to developments outside China's borders. But China also does react to a changing world environment. Once 70 percent of its trade was with the Communist world; in 1965 about 70 percent of China's trade was with industrialized non-Communist countries. Japan has, I believe, replaced Russia as her leading trade partner. Not one of China's leading trade partners can be classed as a strong ally, and ten of these are allies or close to the United States. The rigid "lean-to-one-side" posture of 1949 seems to have crumpled.

Finally, it seems to me that the main changes which have taken place in the Chinese political scene during the past 17 years have been the result of domestic developments and problems. The country which has had the greatest influence on Chinese domestic developments and policies has been the Soviet Union, which in the past did have intimate connections with China, but even Russia's impact on Chinese politics was circumscribed. In the last few years the Chinese leaders have sought to extirpate any lingering influences the Russians might retain within the country.

6

MILITARY POSTURE AND DOCTRINES

By General Samuel B. Griffith II

I doubt if any other similar problem with which our government deals is as obscure as Communist China's military power. This is primarily due to the fact that the Peking regime has published practically no "hard" data whatever since 1960, and statistics made public prior to that time were usually inaccurate and misleading.

Western visitors to China have had no opportunity to observe military activities there, nor have we seen any significant Chinese force in action since the Korean War. The Indian "border war" of 1962 was short-lived and conducted in a special environment. The press and other media are stringently controlled and little of value is to be derived from these sources.

Thus, it is difficult to estimate the proportion of resources currently allocated to the military sector, to discern trends, or to make accurate forecasts of probable future developments. Our appreciations of the military situation there are speculative.

In 1962 a number of copies of a secret document designed for distribution to regimental levels and above were acquired by the United States, and were subsequently released by the State Department. These documents, entitled "The Bulletin of Activities," were published by the General Political Department (GPD) of the Peoples' Liberation Army (PLA) and were quite revealing. One clear inference was that as of mid-1962 the PLA was moving very slowly toward attaining the announced goal of being a powerful, fully modernized military establishment.

However, despite the paucity of factual data, one may with some confidence make a few generalizations. First, the force structure of the PLA is now, and will for some time necessarily remain, in a condition of serious imbalance. The party hopes to correct this, of course, because this imbalance restricts the strategic options open to the Chinese, and imposes severe operational constraints.

But, even given this situation, the PLA is a potent regional military instrument. True, the Chinese cannot yet project conventional power beyond immediately peripheral areas. And it will be some time, certainly ten years at least, until they will be able to do so. For them, the vista is defined by resource limitations. There simply is not enough cake to go around.

It is not yet clear in what directions they are going to move these scarce resources. But I would suspect that modernization of conventional ground forces will receive a low priority. Some selective modernization, yes, in terms of armor and motor transport. Air defense is being emphasized. A limited amphibious capability will receive attention, and as Chinese capacity to produce modern aircraft improves, some increases in airborne capabilities must be anticipated.

Her nuclear outlook, to which Professor Halperin devotes his remarks, is as yet embryonic. But it is receiving major attention.

It is in the light of these several constraints, these various limiting factors, that we might later examine the doctrine of National Liberation Wars enunciated last September by Minister of Defense Lin Piao.

As in classical China the army was a ruler's "talons and teeth," so today the People's Liberation Army is the party's "gun." This gun has been the party's indispensable tool; the party's power, as Mao wrote in 1938, grew "out of the barrel of a gun":

"Our principle is that the party commands the gun, and the gun will never be allowed to command the party. But it is also true that with guns at our disposal we can really build up the party organizations. Anything can grow out of the barrel of a gun. According to the Marxist theory of the state, the army is the chief component of the political power of a state. Whoever wants to seize the political power of the state and to maintain it must have a strong army."

As yet, the PLA is by no means as powerful a "gun" as the party could wish. But we must not for a moment underrate the party's determination to make China a great military power. Progress toward this goal was symbolized by the mushroom clouds that in October 1964 and May 1965 rose above the Takla Makan desert in remote Sinkiang province.

Locus of Power. In communist states, substantive power does not inhere to the bureaucracies established by their constitutions, and thus there was for some time considerable uncertainty as to just where the locus of power in matters military was to be found in the People's

Republic. *The Bulletin of Activities* resolved this problem. Substantive power resides in the Military Affairs Commission (MAC), the organ of the party's Central Committee (CC) and its Politburo (the "Central Authorities"), which deals with military policy. The MAC, routinely chaired by Marshal Lin Piao, generates policy directives affecting the armed forces on all but most sensitive and important matters, which are handled by the Politburo and its Standing Committee. Mao Tse-tung, party chairman, is also chairman of the MAC. Mao is kept currently informed of MAC deliberations and reads and occasionally comments on its papers.

This offspring of the Revolutionary Military Council of guerrilla and civil war days is undoubtedly the smallest and most exclusive military club in the world. Only top members of the party's hierarchy assemble at the call of "Chief" Lin. No precise information is available either as to MAC membership, the membership of its Standing Committee, or to its defined functions. *Bulletins* show that its interests in the armed forces are indeed catholic, and not confined (as one might hastily conclude) strictly to ideological problems. These are, to be sure, some of the major concerns. But the entire spectrum of military affairs falls within the MAC's purview.

For example, *Bulletins* reveal the commission's lively interest in morale; training; equipment; officer procurement; professional and technical education; rations; dispersal of military installations; rectification, emulation, and other types of campaigns; health; the militia; the state of all-weather flying proficiency in the air force; relations of the army with the people; anti-aircraft defense; marksmanship; night marching; current standards attained by the PLA in its campaigns to raise cereals, hogs, chickens and ducks; treatment of soldiers' families; literacy in the army; the unfortunate prevalence of superstition (soldiers afraid to lay communication wire near graveyards at night); the problem (which exists in all armies) of prevailing upon trained technicians to continue their military careers; the arrogant behavior of officers' wives; frugality; licentious liaisons of junior officers with women of questionable character; and the deplorable laxity in routine handling of classified material. Literally no aspect of life in the armed forces is immune from the searching attention of this vigilant and powerful party commission.

National Defense Ministry. When Marshal Lin Piao leaves a MAC meeting, he puts on another hat, that of minister of national defense.

In this capacity, he is the direct, day-to-day overseer of the PLA and, under the Chairman of the People's Republic, commands its field forces. Nine deputy ministers assist him and four department chiefs report to him. These are the chiefs of the general staff department (Lo Jui-Ch'ing), the general political department (Hsaio Hua), the general rear services department (Ch'iu Hui-tso), and the general administrative department (Hsiao Hsing-jung). The commanders of the air force, navy, air defense command, armored force, artillery, military academy, engineers, signal, technical services and railway troops have access to the minister.

Marshal Lin, his deputies, and the chiefs of staff departments command and administer the PLA through 13 regional headquarters. Of these, four strategically critical border areas — Sinkiang, Tibet, Foochow and Inner Mongolia — are designated "direct control military regions." The other nine, which are further subdivided into 22 provincial districts and subdistricts, presumably enjoy a greater degree of autonomy than do the "direct control regions." Elements of the PLA appear to be assigned to the various regions on a semi-permanent basis. This system, compatible with the army's important production and construction missions, likewise tends to nurture that close relationship between the army and the people which is one of the party's principal objectives.

Regional headquarters are organized along the same pattern as is the ministry in Peking and close liaison is maintained between corresponding departments and sections of the staff. Similarly, commanders of the arms and services deal directly with their subordinates at regional levels in matters of administrative and technical nature. Operational control, however, is centralized in the MND. It may be imagined that this system would inevitably produce conflicts of interest, as for example between the regional representatives of the GPD and the GSD in questions relating to allocation of time for political and military training. Apparently this frequently did happen in the past, but such matters are now settled at MND level.

Generally, regional commanders command all PLA ground, naval, air, and public security units (which include border guards) assigned to their regions, and are responsible for recruiting, organizing, arming and training the People's Militia. The PLA is custodian of arms and ammunition allocated the militia. Commanders render administrative support to specialized elements such as air defense, railway, airborne and amphibious troops training or operating in their geographical areas. They operate local military schools and training centers and handle induction and separation from the service. They are responsible for the maintenance of law and order, and for apprehending enemy agents. On the whole, they appear to enjoy a considerable degree of local autonomy in routine matters.

But in the sphere of policy they are kept on a very tight rein, and there is no doubt they are carefully watched for incipient tendencies which might develop into dangerous regionalism. Members of the Politburo are not likely to forget Kao Kang's attempt to create a semi-independent strategy in Manchuria between 1946 and 1953. Nor are either regional military or political commanders likely to forget his fate: in 1954 Kao Kang's "crimes" were discovered, he was arrested, deprived of all his posts, expelled from the party, and — so it was said — committed suicide.

The dual command system is designed to check such developments. At the side of every regional commander stands a political commissar of equal rank. With him, and the regional party committee, the regional commander must discuss every decision he desires to take and every order he wishes to issue. Should a deadlock be reached, the question is referred to the ministry for decision. In four strategically critical regions previously named, the posts of military commander and commisar are combined in one individual.

The armed forces of the Chinese People's Republic stand today at an overall strength of some 2.5 million. The vast majority of men wearing the uniform of the PLA serve in the ground forces, in infantry divisions. Estimates as to the number of these divisions vary from a low of 105 to a high of about 120. If a figure of 110 be presumed, there are approximately 1,800,000 now serving in the infantry arm.

The current PLA infantry division is well balanced in terms of organic weapons, but is short on service, maintenance, medical and communication personel. As yet, the divisions lack sufficient motor transport to move them or to keep lower echelons continuously supplied in fluid situations. For motive power, the PLA's infantry must still rely on the legs of its tough soldiers. As marching standards are far more rigorous than in western armies, shortage of motor transport is a matter of less concern. Still, despite their remarkable march capability, Chinese infantry formations would be at a grave disadvantage in rapidly moving situations in reasonably open terrain where cross-country mobility of tracked-vehicle task forces would greatly exceed theirs. On the other hand, in tropical jungles or mountainous country they could exploit proven cross-country capability against a road-bound enemy.

Divisional organization is triangular — *i.e.*, based on three infantry regiments — which permits ready formation of all-arms task groups appropriate to specific missions. The Chinese press has shown pictures of infantry-tank maneuvers supported by attack aircraft (and presumably artillery). There is no way to tell how frequently such maneuvers are held, or how well they are executed. However, as in more than one issue of *The Bulletin of Activities* the authorities indicated marked concern with standards of technical proficiency (particularly in respect to armor, motor transport and communication personnel), it is evident that as of 1962 performance left much to be desired.

The PLA's Armored Command is small, but its 4/5 armored divisions are formidably equipped with 80/100 Soviet Model T-34 and T-54 tanks (or Chinese copies) plus a number of JS-2 heavies. The T-54, a well-designed, high-performance medium tank, mounts a high-velocity 100 mm. gun and has excellent cross-country capability. The JS-2, a 50-ton low-silhouette, wide-track tank, carries a 122 mm. high-velocity gun, is well armored and has good cross-country performance.

Problems of replacement and maintenance of this and other modern equipment of Soviet design plagued the PLA during 1960 and 1961. Whether or not Chinese industry can yet replace obsolescing tanks, or even provide sufficient spare parts to keep what the PLA has in operable condition is questionable.

In early 1962 the MAC directed the PLA to establish and operate its own spare-parts replacement program. Obviously, this was one of the areas critically affected by the withdrawal of Soviet aid. As the Chinese have no doubt discovered, this problem cannot be solved by traditional handicraft methods and "back-yard" operations. The need to maintain aircraft, motor vehicles, armor, self-propelled artillery and other heavy and complicated equipment of Soviet origin obviously puts a very serious strain on Chinese industry, which must also simultaneously satisfy many other equally important requirements.

One may conjecture that purchase abroad of heavy equipment such as locomotives, road machinery (one list of equipment wanted named excavators, rock crushers, small, medium and heavy tractors and bulldozers) is in part designed to release personnel and plant for the manufacture of airframes, armored vehicles, artillery and military prime movers.

Air Force Strength. The personnel strength of the Air Force can be approximated only by "crewing levels." If we assume that 60/70 officers and men are required to crew one aircraft we arrive at a figure (based on 2,500 combat aircraft) of 150,000/175,000.

The latest figure for naval strength—135,000—may be somewhat low. The Navy supports a small air arm. Presumably, this component would be employed in coastal, short and medium range overwater reconnaissance and mine laying. There is also a small Landing Force.

In estimating the strength of ground force supporting arms and services we are again in the cloudy realm of uncertainty and speculation. There are, we know, a small number of lightly-equipped mountain divisions at a manning level of 8,000/10,000, and Border Guard formations. These units are well-equipped and demonstrated their combat capabilities in October and November 1962 against the Indians. In the North East Frontier Agency (NEFA) the Chinese moved rapidly and executed combat maneuvers with skill and precision.

Additionally, there are a number of Security Police units deployed throughout the country. No estimates can be made of their strength. There are several cavalry divisions, possibly two air-borne divisions and some separate brigades and regiments. It is probable that these special units are trained in guerrilla operations.

The status of the PLA's Air Force is a major enigma at the present time. What was described in 1952 by General Hoyt Vandenberg, then Chief of Staff, U.S. Air Force, as a "formidable air force" has obsolesced critically in the past fourteen years. During the Korean War MIG 15s and 17s formed the bulk of the Chinese Air Force. At present, the MIG 17 is the standard interceptor. A few—possibly as many as 100—MIG 19s were acquired from the Russians prior to 1960. There have been unconfirmed reports of PLA interceptors similar to MIG 21s sighted by Nationalist air patrols south of Shantung province. If these reports are correct—and we would be prudent to assume they are, a limited capability to produce air frames, jet engines, weapons and control systems has been developed. One must not underestimate the Chinese determination to create a modern jet air force. An important step towards this goal was taken in December

1964 when the 7th Ministry of Machine Building was established. The appointment of a very senior officer, Wang P'ing-chang, former Deputy Commander of the Air Force, as Minister, is significant. But how deeply the Chinese will commit themselves to a manned interceptor program cannot now be estimated.

To date, surface-to-air missiles (SAM) deployed in North Vietnam have not proved particularly effective. According to a good source—Mr. Khrushchev—the Russians "gave" the Chinese "some rockets" prior to 1960. It is reasonable to speculate that the "rockets" were SAM and air-to-air types, and that working model guidance systems were provided. As early as 1951 the Chinese were operating excellent Soviet-made radar-controlled anti-aircraft equipment in Korea, and heavy concentrations of AAA have been spotted for defense of critical areas in North Vietnam. It is a reasonable assumption, therefore, that the early warning and air-defense system designed to protect critical target areas in China is fairly effective, and that its continuing development is receiving a very high priority.

The Air Force is generally credited with about 400/500 IL-28 (Beagle) twin-jet bombers. This must still be considered a very good aircraft. The Chinese have also a few TU-4 (Bull) four-engined propeller bombers. (Some of these are reported to be configured for long-range reconnaissance.) This Soviet copy of the U.S. B-29 of World War II has long been obsolete in western air forces. This slow and highly vulnerable aircraft has little strategic value except as a possible launching platform for "stand-off" missiles or a fueling plane.

Despite Chinese assertions that they have attained "basic self-sufficiency" in petroleum, we may suspect that jet fuel supply will be a continuing problem for the Air Force. In 1961 and 1962 the Soviets drastically cut deliveries of petroleum products to China, and she is in the market for refineries at the present time. (The French, Italians, and Japanese are likely to be the principal beneficiaries of refinery purchases abroad). Many technical difficulties are encountered in refining, rectification, transport, storing and routine handling of volatile jet fuels, and "basic self-sufficiency" in petroleum claimed does not by any means solve the problem of adequate jet fuel for the Air Force.

Some reliable analysts have asserted that Communist pilots averaged no better than ten hours a month in 1963-1965. This figure is probably derived from observed sortie rates and may be misleadingly low. Nevertheless, Nationalist sources stated in 1964 that they believed the figure of ten hours per month representative. If so, Red pilots are getting on the average one-half the flying time considered minimum in the U.S., Japanese and Nationalist Air Forces to maintain all-weather pilot proficiency. As of 1962, training standards were poor and caused the MAC much concern.

Other than in the capacity of elite ground troops, parachute formations are not much use without the lift required to get them to the target. The PLA could conceivably muster sufficient lift to put two battalions simultaneously on related targets, but in certain areas only. Terrain, distance and transport vulnerability severely limit air lift mounted in Chinese territory against Indian targets, except in the North East Frontier Agency (NEFA).

In Tibet, the PLA is deploying the equivalent of three armies. Some sources estimate a total of six mountain (10,000-man) divisions plus a number of separate regiments and Border Guard formations. With special support units (principally transport and engineer), total commitment to this strategic region may be of the order of 200,000. Terrain, weather and communications present severe problems. Logistic constraints put a lid on the number and type of formations that can be supported north of the Western Yunnan-Himalayan arc, or that could operate south of it for sustained periods.

If there are any specially trained amphibious troops in the ground forces, they (unlike the U.S. Marines) receive no publicity. It has been reported that the Navy has a relatively small Landing Force. Possibly the function of this Force is to operate landing ships and craft, provide underwater demolition personnel, "beach-jumpers" and similar specialists. The existence of such a force has been reported but cannot be confirmed.

Shortly after the Korean War the People's Republic began to pay some attention to naval requirements, and with Soviet assistance and advice a rudimentary naval force was established. From the first, emphasis was laid on submarines and coastal defense craft.

How many long-range diesel-powered "G" and "W"-class submarines the Soviets sold the Chinese is unknown; estimates are in the range of thirty to forty, of which at least one "G"-class boat has been identified. This class boat is equipped with three launching tubes, so that it is capable of firing missiles from a submerged position. I do not agree with my friend Hanson Baldwin that one such boat affects the balance of power in the Pacific. But I would agree that 5/6 such

uipped with nuclear-armed ballistic missiles, would definitely
The type of fleet I conceive the Chinese to be constructing,
toge... r with the missiles described, would provide them with a
credible deterrent, probably by 1972, if not before.

A conventional submarine force of the size postulated would pose
a substantial threat to traffic in the far Pacific from Korea to Indonesia. A capability for some of these boats to surface launch short-
range missiles (say 300/400 miles), is probably already developed.
The submarine force described would thus constitute a respectable—
and less vulnerable—variant of the French *force de frappe.* Further—and perhaps unexpectedly rapid—growth of a sophisticated submarine fleet must be assessed as an almost certain development for
the near future.

For defense of coastal waters the Chinese relay on high-speed motor
torpedo boats and defensive mining. The U.S. Navy discovered to its
dismay in the fall of 1950 at Wonsan that Russian mines and mining
techniques were extremely good, and prudent assumption must be
that the Chinese learned from the Russians both how to manufacture mines of various types and how to sow them in effective patterns.

One aspect of an amphibious capability has been mentioned. The
Reds inherited a few landing ships and craft from the Nationalists.
Press photographs have shown Landing Ship Tank (LST), Landing
Craft Tank (LCT) and Landing Craft Vehicle and Personnel
(LCVP). Amphibious ships and craft of these types are relatively
cheap and not too difficult to produce in quantity, and could be aug-
mented by motor-junk and towed barges.

Taiwan is the obvious target for an amphibious operation but air
superiority over the Strait and the landing areas would have to be
guaranteed. Given the present state of the PLA's Air Force, such a
capability seems remote.

Strategy and Platitudes. Some concluding remarks on Chinese
Communist strategy may be appropriate.

At present, save through application of her doctrine of national
liberation wars, China cannot influence events outside peripheral
areas. This is a very frustrating situation in which an ancient, great
and proud nation finds herself. We may be sure that she will do all
that her resources allow to rectify this condition.

China wishes to regain her ancient position in Asia. She considers
this aspiration to be justified by propinquity, by history, by cul-

tural affiliation, and by economic fact. She sees us then as alien meddlers; neo-colonialists; exploiters in a word—and she wishes above all to remove our presence from Asia. Her strategy, be it ambiguous or evident, indircet or direct, will be focussed for the foreseeable future to attainment of this objective.

Chairman Mao's platitudes appear in the Chinese press with monotonous regularity, but few more frequently than his pronouncement that man is the factor of most importance in war. "Man," he said, "decides everything." To accord to weapons what Mao believes to be an undue emphasis is by implication to depreciate the place of man. Those who hold such beliefs, or make the mistake of voicing them cannot aspire to high position in the PLA. It is generally thought that P'eng Teh-huai and his hand-picked Chief of the General Staff Department, Huang K'o-ch'eng, were dismissed from office in 1959 in part because they subscribed to this "mechanistic" heresy and connived with the Soviets to implement it.

It follows that the party is expressly concerned with qualitative values in the annual selection of young men to serve in the armed forces. This is a luxury the party can well afford, for the problem of finding bodies has never been an acute one in China. But until the Communists came to power there had never been an effective conscription system. If the ingenious Chinese peasant could possibly conceive a plan to avoid serving in the armed forces without incurring a penalty, he was quick to adopt it.

General Wedemeyer remarked that the conscription system under the Nationalists was administered in a scandalous fashion. Actually the "system" he (and others) observed in operation was one of impressment rather than conscription. But, whatever the reasons may have been, the Chinese Communists did not seem to experience the difficulties the Nationalists encountered in collecting men. There is little doubt that during the anti-Japanese War and (particularly) the Civil War, they occasionally resorted to impressment. But until 1947 when wholesale integration of surrendered Nationalist formations began, the Red Army was essentially composed of volunteers, or at least of men who had not been rounded up at the point of the bayonet and roped together by press gangs.

The voluntary enlistment system did not, however, satisfy the party's requirements for a revolutionary "class-conscious" army, and in 1955 the People's Republic abandoned the voluntary system in favor of national conscription. This obviously gave the party better quality control than was possible under a voluntary program. As approximately 6,500,000 males reach the age of 18 every year, the PLA can afford to be selective, and to apply very rigid standards in respect to the mental, physical, psychological and political attributes of prospective service men. As a matter of principle, the PLA prefers to induct young men only from families with poor peasant and proletarian backgrounds. The party presumes, probably correctly, that this will preserve the ideological purity of its armed forces.

The same family background criterion is applied to aspirants to "leader" (officer) status. Young men with bourgeois or landlord parents are systematically excluded from opportunity to become "leaders." In this manner the party hopes to create a leadership corps which is "class conscious," animated with revolutionary zeal, dedicated, obedient, and of unquestioned loyalty to it.

The context of the martialized life provides the party opportunity to observe an individual's career in its children's and youth organizations and in lower and middle schools, and to spot those who tend to be too individualistic or too skeptical, or who do not otherwise enthusiastically conform to its conceptual and behavioral "norms." With equal facility the party can distinguish "progressives" at an early age. Thus the entire organizational structure may be seen as consisting of a series of built-in "filters." By the time a young man reaches his eighteenth year the party has formed a very good idea of his leadership potential. Those who have consistently displayed the characteristics wanted of "leaders" in the armed forces are encouraged to make the service a career.

As a "leader" moves up the ladder in the armed forces, he discovers again and again that intellectual "individualism" is treated as an even more grievous deviation than "bureaucratism" or "commandism." A "leader" may exercise technical initiative—indeed, is distinctly encouraged to do so—but his thoughts must be the thoughts of Mao Tse-tung. Mao's thoughts are the focus around which all life and all activity must resolve. In some effusions, these thoughts are described as "guideposts," in others, as "compasses," "arrows," or "lighthouses."

This leads us to the perplexing question implicit in the slogan "Be Red and Expert." Is there an inherent contradiction in these terms? Are they, indeed, even—or sometimes—mutually exclusive? The party obviously considers them compatible. But the party finds it difficult tc assess the degree of a person's "Redness." Is he a "beet" or a "radish," or somewhere in between? If P'eng Teh-huai and Huang K'o-ch'eng were "radishes," how many others are there? Who are they? These questions must frequently plague the PLA's General Political Department and its representatives in the armed forces. They obviously bother Senior General Lo Jui-ch'ing, who in a special message to the PLA on New Year's Day (1965) found it necessary to warn that the "overthrown exploiter class" in China had not yet been "wiped out." The PLA, he said, must be constantly vigilant, and with sober mind and open eyes continue to raise its class-consciousness, "master the skills of class struggle, resolutely support and carry out the policies of the party," and continue to develop its "hard-fighting traditions." He added that the "enemy" within the gate was secretly distributing "sugar-coated pills," and urged the PLA to be on its guard against "complacency."

Propaganda Influence. In its propaganda the party consistently emphasizes that the primary mission of the PLA is to repel "imperialist aggressors" and to foil the "nefarious plots" of the "Chiang bandits." The theme of "defense of the Motherland" is repeated in practically every speech made by a member of the military hierarchy. There is no reason to believe that the PLA would not loyally respond to any challenge directed against the Chinese Mainland.

Its behavior in a frustrating and prolonged combat situation outside China's borders would naturally depend on many factors, notably the degree of control the party can exert. A primary objective in any combat situation must be to erode the party's mechanism in the Army. Until this happens the PLA should be expected to perform in peripheral areas as creditably as it did in Korea.

The party has admitted that about five percent of the population follows its lead only with the greatest reluctance, and that another unnamed but significant percentage consists of "wavering elements." Selective induction and promotion processes will, it obviously hopes, exclude these unreliable elements from ever attaining a dangerous foothold in the PLA. But some termites are already in the woodwork, according to General Lo, who warned that they were infiltrating the PLA "trying to grab the official seats from us (the staunch party men) in certain fields."

It is statements such as this which lead some people to question the loyalty of the PLA. On Taiwan it is one of the articles of faith that the PLA is only superficially loyal. But facts do not lend any support to this view. In the great exodus during the spring of 1962, over 125,000 mainlanders came into the Crown Colony of Hong Kong (including the "New Territories"). As far as is known, not one of these was a serving officer or solider. Some few were demobilized ex-officers or non-commissioned officers, several of whom had, so their questioners discovered, been dismissed from the PLA. Surely, had dissatisfaction been as rampant in the armed forces as Taiwan sources insist it is, a great many serving soldiers would have thrown away their rifles, put on peasants' clothing, and crossed over. The brief Sino-Indian border war also refutes the claim advanced in Taiwan. There, no Chinese soldier "turned his hat around." The Indians took one prisoner. He was lost, and blundered into an Indian outpost.

Despite huge offers of money, coupled with promises of complete immunity and good treatment, the Nationalists have induced only a few Red flyers to desert to them.

Red pilots are under surveillance which would naturally be more strict than that exercised over their colleagues in the ground or naval forces. And—although there are no figures to confirm this—one may suspect that the great majority of Air Force "leaders" and senior enlisted men are party members. Nevertheless, if a trusted pilot planned to desert with his aircraft he would find means of doing so.

What I am trying to suggest here is that we should not be deluded by the hope that in a crisis the PLA leadership would necessarily issue a Latin American type *pronunciamento*. That possibility seems remote. The party did away expeditiously with Marshal P'eng Teh-huai in 1959. P'eng was one of the three army men at the top of the heap. The PLA is, in my opinion, a highly motivated, loyal, and dedicated instrument.

7

NUCLEAR STRENGTH AND STRATEGY

By Morton H. Halperin

There has been much discussion of issues of military strategy in the Chinese press and on the Chinese radio during the past six months. From these statements, previous Chinese discussions of these matters, and, more important, Chinese actions, it is possible to develop a reasonably complete understanding of Chinese views on nuclear strategy and what they call "People's War." However I would emphasize that there remains a considerable range of uncertainty, particularly in attempting to predict future Chinese behavior. In part this is true because the Chinese themselves are very likely undecided about what they would do in various possible contingencies of interest to us.

I propose to discuss the Chinese attitude toward Vietnam in the context of their commitment to People's War, to consider Chinese nuclear doctrine, and to conclude with some comments about the Chinese current strategic outlook and the implications which it may have for American policy.

The Chinese leadership recognizes that the introduction of large numbers of American troops into Vietnam has drastically changed the situation from the favorable outlook of a year or so ago. They have been forced to concede that even when on the brink of victory a revolutionary movement can be turned back by America's military power. While the Chinese talk, as they did at the time of the Korean War, of the fact that the United States may be over extended, they do not doubt that we have the military capability to suppress the revolution in Vietnam for as long as we have the will to do so. The Chinese also accept that the United States has made Vietnam into a test case of whether or not it can successfully suppress wars of national liberation which follow the Chinese pattern. Thus the Chinese believe it is important to avoid a defeat in Vietnam.

By esoteric but clearly understood signals in their public statements, the Chinese have indicated to the Viet Cong their belief that victory can come only after a protracted struggle. Drawing on their own experience, the Chinese now see the Vietnam struggle to be a stage analogous to the Japanese invasion of China. They have urged on the Viet Cong the need to adopt a strategy of survival until the American invaders tire of the war and withdraw from the country. Both by its actions and its words, Peking has told Hanoi that the Viet Cong must be almost entirely self-sufficient in generating the supplies and equipment needed for their survival and military operations. Nevertheless Peking has told the Chinese masses that they have a duty to sacrifice for the people of Vietnam, and China appears to have provided substantial amounts of economic and military assistance to the Viet Cong forces.

Thus Peking now expects a long drawn out war. The Chinese leaders would be very disappointed if Hanoi accepted a negotiated settlement which would imply an effort by the Viet Cong to come to power by other means and might increase Soviet influence in Southeast Asia. Peking, however, no longer expects a quick victory and even what may look to us like an American victory in Vietnam would look to the Chinese only as a temporary lull in revolutionary activity in preparations for the next stage of the revolution. The Chinese commitment to support for wars of national liberation is far too deep-seated to be erased by a temporary setback in a single country.

People's War Strategy. This brings me to the more general question of Chinese strategy toward what they call People's War. The Chinese doctrine as stated originally in 1949 and now reaffirmed in the Lin Piao article and in other documents, is essentially that the Chinese revolutionary model can be applied in other underdeveloped societies to bring a Communist Party to power. Mao believes that if a Communist Party is to seize control it must first establish a rural base, create a people's army and then depend on armed struggle with the support of the peasants to seize control first of the countryside and then of the cities. The Chinese feel that this process will ultimately be followed in all the countries of the third world and advise revolutionaries to adopt this pattern. They believe that other proposed routes to power are doomed to failure. China's leaders believe that they have an obligation to give what support they can to groups seeking to come to power through a People's War. They feel that revolutionaries must be primarily self-reliant but that they can give training in the techniques of guerrilla operations, provide training manuals and the writings of Chairman Mao, and, finally, give limited amounts of military equipment. The Chinese recognize that the United States is committed to helping bourgeois groups prevent Communist revolutionaries from coming to power and they believe that the struggle will be a protracted one in which a number of setbacks will be suffered.

Mao's image of what is going on in the third world seems to me to be wildly out of touch with reality. While revolutionaries inspired by China's success have tried to apply the Chinese model in some countries, these efforts have met with success only on the Indochinese peninsula. Furthermore in most countries those committed to social and economic changes have preferred to work through existing nationalistic movements and not to seek to organize guerrilla bands in the jungles and mountains of their country. Thus in the long run, the third generation of Chinese leaders may come to abandon their faith in this path to revolutionary power as it becomes clearer and clearer that it is doomed to failure.

Risks in Vietnam. Misled by the efforts of the United States to confine its opposition to guerrilla warfare to the country in which the action was taking place, the Chinese came to believe that support for such operations did not entail a risk of an attack on China. However, confronted by American bombing of North Vietnam and what from their perspective appears to be a substantial build-up of American military power in the Far East and increasing attention of American leaders to Asian problems, the Chinese have concluded that there is a substantial probability of an American attack on China growing out of the Vietnam war. The Chinese appear to believe that they may be forced to intervene to protect the political integrity of North Vietnam and that this would lead to an attack on China. In addition they fear that the United States, frustrated in Vietnam, may lash out at what it continues to describe as the source of the aggression and attack the Chinese mainland. The Chinese believe that the United States will not be deterred by concessions and that only if China shows herself to be unafraid and prepared can an attack be deterred. In Peking, no less than in Washington, the desire to avoid another Munich is a major preoccupation of political leaders. The Chinese believe that the United States may at least initially restrict its attack to conventional weapons, but they expect that nuclear weapons would ultimately be used and that the American attack may begin with a surprise nuclear strike.

Nuclear Doctrine. Because of the widespread confusion about general Chinese attitudes toward nuclear weapons, I propose to make a few assertions about Chinese nuclear doctrine. The Chinese recognize very well the destructive power of nuclear weapons. They know that these weapons could destroy all of the industry and in fact the entire modernized sector of China. Since 1946 the Chinese have been concerned about American possession of atomic weapons and have attempted to calculate the damage that the United States could do to China. When Mao in 1957 stated privately that 300,000,000 Chinese would be killed in a nuclear war, he was apparently reporting the results of a calculation and not expressing any lack of concern that such an attack would seriously damage the mainland of China.

Their perception of the damage which would be done to them in nuclear war has led the Chinese to a determination not to provoke a nuclear attack on China. While the Chinese have been prepared to risk such an attack when the survival of the Communist regime in China was at stake, they have attached a very high priority to avoiding nuclear war. In short, there is no reason to believe that the Chinese want a nuclear war or are not as determined as any political leadership to avoid a nuclear attack if possible.

Given their current military preparedness, the Chinese see no way of blunting the initial American first strike which they expect will destroy Chinese military installations, including their nuclear production facilities and industrial and urban centers. The Chinese expect the United States to follow this attack up with a ground invasion designed to conquer and control China.

There has been considerable debate between the Chinese military and the top political leadership about how to deal with such an invasion. The strategy proposed by the military and rejected by the political leaders would have relied on professional military forces to attempt to meet and destroy the invasion. Chairman Mao has preferred to rely on the same strategy of People's War which he urges on other groups of insurrectionists. If the Chinese expect an imminent nuclear attack, the political leaders of the country will retreat from the main cities and return to rural areas. The People's Liberation Army similarly will retreat from population and industrial centers and withdraw to the interior of the country. The people's militia which is now undergoing intensive military and ideological training, will be expected to bear the brunt of the invasion and to engage in People's War against the American forces. In these circumstances the Chinese believe the most important thing is to instill an ideological fervor in the Chinese people so that they will engage in guerrilla activities against the American troops. The Chinese hope that if they can make this strategy credible it will succeed in deterring an American nuclear strike by making clear that the United States will not be able to invade and control China. While they are confident that this strategy could succeed in enabling the Chinese Communist Party to survive and to begin slowly to rebuild, the Chinese place far too high a price on their ideological, political, and economic progress to be willing to take any actions that would provoke an American attack.

The intense Chinese drive for an operational nuclear capability is, I believe, related to their long standing fear of an American nuclear attack. At a fundamental level, the Chinese desire for nuclear weapons is simply a logical extension of their intention to become a great power. However, the priority given to the effort is, I believe, attributable to their belief that they need to develop a deterrent against American nuclear attack. The development of such a capability will leave the Chinese freer to press their efforts to establish their hegemony in Asia and to give such support as they can to People's Wars. In addition, the Chinese believe that they will get some increased prestige in the third world and within the Communist bloc from their development of nuclear weapons.

Recent Setbacks. Despite their nuclear detonations, the events of the last nine months have substantially reduced Chinese expectations that the world is now ripe for revolutionary advance and a major increase in Chinese influence. Partly because of the re-emergence of the Soviet Union on the world scene following the fall of Khrushchev, and partly because of the continuing growth of nationalism in the third world, the Chinese have suffered a series of setbacks in their dual effort to carve out a sphere of influence within the Communist world and to establish themselves as the leaders of a militant group of left wing, if non-Communist, regimes in Africa, Asia, and Latin America. From Indonesia to Algeria to Ghana to Cuba, and perhaps even to Albania, the Chinese have seen regimes formerly friendly to them draw away and in some cases turn to extreme hostility. Until very recently the Chinese looked to Vietnam as a hopeful area in which the balance might be redressed, but the prognosis for Vietnam now is for a long hard struggle and not for a quick victory. Thus, I believe that the Chinese are anxious to turn in and focus their efforts even more than they have in the past on the domestic concerns of the Chinese revolution. It is important to emphasize that most of the attention of the top leadership and most of the resources of China always have and will continue to be directed at creating a new revolutionary society in China and building an economically developed state. The Chinese are concerned not only with the slow growth rate of their economy, but also with the signs that the third and fourth generations are not as ideologically pure as Chairman Mao would like them to be. I believe that if the Chinese can become convinced that they do not face imminent threat of an American nuclear attack, that they are likely to withdraw even more from the world while continuing to issue revolutionary proclamations and concentrate on their internal difficulties and opportunities.

Implications for American Policy. This analysis leads me to some observations concerning American policy. From the standpoint of our relations with China, and I would emphasize that there are a great many other factors involved, it is important for the United States to remain in Vietnam and to prevent a military victory by the Viet Cong employing what the Chinese believe to be their model of revolutionary violence. This means, I think, that it is important for us to use our military forces in ways that suggest our confidence in overcoming the Viet Cong challenge and our determination not to be driven from Vietnam by the Viet Cong.

Second, China's current stance suggests the importance of American assurances to China that we are not looking for an opportunity to attack Chinese nuclear installations or to launch an even larger attack on the Chinese mainland. I believe that an American declaration that it was prepared to discuss with Peking the exchange of ambassadors would make an important contribution to this objective, as would American proposals—even though they would be deplored in Peking—to seat both China and Taiwan in the General Assembly of the United Nations.

Third, I think it is important for the United States to avoid the appearance of over-reacting to very limited Chinese capabilities. The Chinese, I believe, are correctly amused by the credit we give them for every act of violence anywhere in the world. Such statements and our overreaction to the Chinese nuclear force, which six months ago we were deprecating, only serve to increase the belief in China and elsewhere in Asia that we are overly fearful of the Chinese and are likely to respond either by preventive war or by precipitous withdrawal.

Finally, I believe that we should avoid using China as a simple justification for our policies. The policy choices that we face in Vietnam and elsewhere in Asia are exceedingly complex. We are unlikely to make the right choices if we confine ourselves to an analysis of what will best contain a China which has a desire to control its neighbors, but only a very limited capability to do so.

8

RECENT ECONOMIC DEVELOPMENTS

By Alexander Eckstein

Mainland China's economy has undergone rapid growth and considerable structural change since the advent of the Communist regime in 1949. In its early phases, this development was in part based upon rehabilitation of China's war-devastated production plant, but as a result of high rates of investment, this plant was greatly expanded. The momentum engendered by policies and measures of the new regime carried the economy continuously forward between 1949 and 1959. Development, however, did not proceed at an even pace. Althrough the economy expanded year by year, the rate of growth itself was marked by sharp fluctuations largely because of harvest changes. At the same time, expansion was confined mainly to the industrial, urban, and commercialized sector of the economy, while agriculture more or less stagnated.

In the end, agricultural stagnation and a sudden radicalization of economic policy based on a highly unrealistic assessment of the economy's capabilities produced an acute crisis. Between 1960 and 1961 this crisis led not only to a slowing down in the pace of growth but to a far-reaching decline in absolute terms as well. Thus, the economy of the Chinese mainland entered the throes of a deep depression, from which it has been recovering only quite slowly. As a result, it may take about 10 years for Chinese agriculture to recover to its 1957 level of output per capita, and the peak national product levels of 1958-60 may not be attained until the late sixties. In short, it may turn out that the Great Leap will have cost the Chinese economy roughly a decade of growth.

This set back has undoubtedly reduced China's expansionist power and forced it to pursue a relatively cautious foreign and domestic policy, at least for the time being. However, it did not undermine the basic stability of viability of the Communist regime. But with the gradual economic recovery, the regime seems to have regained its earlier sense of self-assurance and a measure of dynamism. One could even argue that since the regime survived this ordeal, its faith in its indestructibility may have been reinforced. The fact that it could weather a profound agricultural and food crisis—even if that crisis was partially of its own making—and manage to avert a mass famine without economic aid from the Soviet Union or anyone else must have been viewed by the leadership as a self-vindication. Moreover, the apparent fact that even at the depth of the crisis no organized opposition arose must have been interpreted both by the regime and by the people at large as an element of strength. Thus, there is no evidence to support the wishful, but nevertheless widely held, notion that the Chinese Communist regime was on the verge of collapse and that an inevitably "descending spiral" was about to drive it from the seat of power.

Implications for the U.S. What are the implications of this conclusion for U.S. policy? If a regime hostile to us is on the verge of collapse, there is no point in dealing with it. On the contrary, a strong case can be made for ignoring and quarantining it lest contact in any form—commercial, cultural or diplomatic—serve to strengthen it, possibly delay its demise, or even prevent its breakdown altogether. Indeed, if a hostile government is on the verge of collapse, why not apply maximum economic pressure to hasten its downfall? From this perspective, then, there is a rationale for tight trade controls and for keeping Communist China out of the United Nations.

If, on the other hand, the "collapse" theory cannot be validated by actual developments in Communist China, an entirely different range of policy implications emerges. Such a finding does not in and of itself argue for or against admission of China into the United Nations or any other specific policy. But it does suggest a different policy posture for the United States—one that accepts Communist China as a body politic, a society, and an economy that means to be here to stay for some time to come.

In the conduct of its foreign relations, Communist China can and does use military force, the threat of force, trade and aid, moral suasion, and propaganda appeals. Its ability to employ all these means, however, is in one way or another affected by the size of its national product, the structure of its economy, the state of its economic development, and the rate at which its economy is growing and being transformed from a backward and preponderantly agricultural state into a modern, industrialized one. The relationships are most direct, of course, in the field of trade and aid. Yet they are also of major importance with respect to the country's military posture. On the other hand, they carry less decisive weight as far as propaganda capabilities are concerned.

Strengths and Weaknesses. In appraising the potency of economic instruments in the conduct of Chinese Communist foreign policy, it is important to start with a brief analysis of the present state of the mainland economy, its strengths and weaknesses, its accomplishments and its unresolved problems.

Undoubtedly the most fundamental and intractable problem facing economic policy makers in China is that of population and food. On the basis of highly fragmentary and rather unreliable data, mainland China's population in 1964 is estimated to be about 730 million. This vast population is supposed to be growing at an average annual rate of 2 per cent or more. As a result the population is increased annually by about 15 million. Maintaining such a rapidly growing population just at the prevailing standards of living entails heroic efforts. It requires an annual rate of growth in food supply of 2-3 per cent; it places a heavy demand on investment resources for housing, school construction, hospitals, and other educational, health, and welfare facilities.

This population has high birth rates and fairly high death rates— i.e., it is a preponderantly young population with a high ratio of consumers to producers. These characteristics are conducive to high consumption and low saving. Furthermore, a sizable share of savings needs to be channeled into investment in social overhead rather than production facilities.

These relationships pose a series of dilemmas, which are common to all economies subject to acute population pressure. At the end of the First Five Year Plan period (1957), it seemed that China might be on the way to breaking out of this vicious circle of backwardness. Seen from the perspective of 1965, one can be much less certain of this.

There is no doubt that the Chinese Communist leadership is fully conscious of the problem and is trying to attack it from two directions simultaneously. It has in recent years accorded high priority to agricultural development. At the same time, it has embarked on a program of family planning, thus far largely confined to the urban area.

Present indications are that this two-pronged attack has produced some recovery and progress. However, unless there is a miraculous boon in the form of unusually good harvests or foreign aid on a large scale, further economic growth and advance in China may be expected to be significantly slower than in the 1950s. Correspondingly, the Chinese Communist vision of becoming a top-ranking industrial nation may have to be postponed for a long time to come.

This prospect could be altered if Communist China were to gain access to foreign credits or grants. In this respect, China is in a unique situation, for it is perhaps the only underdeveloped country today that has no long-term credits or foreign aid to draw upon. On the contrary, since 1955 it has been a net exporter of capital. These capital exports have been used to amortize the Soviet loans and to finance Chinese foreign aid programs. It would seem that in contributing to rising Sino-Soviet tensions, the Chinese Communist leadership must have chosen to buy increasing self-reliance and freedom of action in foreign affairs at the price of economic development at home.

China's development prospects could also be altered markedly by changes in domestic policy. In recent years, the Chinese Communists have pursued a prudent and more or less conservative economic policy—easing the tax and collection pressures on the peasantry, trying to foster a generally more favorable incentive system for agriculture, keeping the savings burden down, and channeling a large share of investment to agriculture and agriculture-supporting industries. However, this policy yields a pattern of resource allocation which runs strongly counter to the ideological and programmatic commitments of the leadership. It tends to produce a lower rate of investment and a lower rate of industrial growth. Therefore, the current economic policies are in many ways distasteful to the regime—so much so that they become a continuing source of tension between what the leadership desires and hopes for and what it considers possible and necessary. This tension may in turn tempt the leadership to resort once more to bold measures to break out of the vise of backwardness. Such attempts could easily lead to another economic breakdown and crisis. Consequently, one of the most serious problems for the leadership is to curb its own sense of impatience.

According to some assessments, the very intractability of the population-food dilemma might drive the Chinese Communists into adventurism, particularly in Southeast Asia. The adherents of this view maintain that Communist China's current interest in Vietnam is at least partly motivated by a desire to gain access to the rice surpluses and the rich mineral resources of Southeast Asia. However, it is difficult to see what the economic gains of conquest would be. What could China obtain through conquest of this region that she cannot now get through the normal processes of international trade?

Implicit in this view is an assumption that the Chinese Communits could move in and confiscate the rice and other commodities. Southeast Asia, however, depends on rice and mineral exports for essential imports. If Communist China conquered the region, she would have to assume responsibility for maintaining economic and political stability. This task would mean assuring a modicum of incentive to farmers to induce them at least to maintain, if not expand, production. Forced confiscation might yield some produce for a year or two but would unquestionably be counter-productive in the long run. The Chinese Communists have a great deal of difficulty with their own peasantry. It is hard to believe that they would expect to overcome these difficulties with a conquered peasantry.

For these reasons one probably has to look to historical, cultural, ideological, and strategic considerations rather than economic motivations for the primary explanation for Communist China's interest in Southeast Asia.

The Role of Imports. China's imports were crucial for the expansion of her industrial plant, the relief of her acute shortages of food after 1960, and the modernization of her defense establishment. During the period of the First Five Year Plan as a whole, about 20-40 per cent (depending at what exchange rate the dollar figures for imports are converted to yuan) of the equipment component of investment was imported. In the absence of these imports, Communist China's economic growth might possibly have fallen from an average annual rate of about 7 per cent to 3-5 per cent. Moreover, a cessation of imports would have greatly retarded technological progress and modernization of the economy, most particularly of industry. It would almost certainly have stifled the development of the iron and steel, electric power, chemicals, and other technically complex industrial branches.

Since 1960 this type of import has greatly diminished in importance, for the construction of new plants has been drastically curtailed. Because most industries are operating well below capacity, imports of equipment are confined to those branches which have continued to expand throughout the depression, i.e., chemicals and petroleum extraction and refining.

As capital goods imports diminished, food (particularly grain) imports gained greatly in importance. Although such imports have only increased China's total grain supply by 3-4 per cent, they have been of considerable importance in marginal terms. They have greatly eased the distribution burden, reduced the collection pressures in the countryside, relieved the transport system of a heavy load, and provided the cities with a guaranteed food supply. As late as 1965 indications were that Chinese Communist policy makers and planners intended to continue importing grain for at least the next two or three years. Whether such imports will become a longer-term feature of Chinese Communist trade policy is impossible to forecast at the present time. In the meantime, a total non-Communist world embargo on food exports to China would undoubtedly increase strains in the Chinese economy, particularly if the exports were cut off suddenly. Such an embargo would once more introduce difficulties of food supply, particularly in the cities, and would force the regime to step up its pressure on the peasantry.

There is no doubt that imports played a crucial role in the modernization of the Chinese Communist military establishment. While there are no data on the quantity or value of Chinese military imports, some crude guesses about the relative importance of these purchases from abroad can be made on the basis of certain assumptions. In these terms it would seem that imports of military equipment and materiel constituted at least 20-40 per cent of the total defense expenditure. In any case, the import component of defense was sizeable enough to be of considerable significance regardless of what the precise figure may have been.

Implications for U.S. Trade Policy. Since 1950 U.S. policy on trade with China has involved a virtually total embargo on all economic contacts between ourselves and the mainland and the maintenance of as stringent controls as possible on trade between our allies and the mainland. This policy was initiated as an emergency measure during the Korean War and was conceived within the context of economic warfare. It has been maintained since on the technical ground that

.orean War has never been formally terminated but ended only in ..... armistice.

To be more precise, U.S. policy and regulations concerning trade with China have remained unchanged since 1950, while those of our allies have gradually and progressively been liberalized, more or less to our displeasure and in a number of cases despite our resistance. As a result, essentially all that is left of the elaborate structure of COCOM controls constructed in the early fifties is a continuing ban on the shipment of arms, weapons, military materiel of all kinds, fissionable materials, and some other clearly strategic goods. In addition, there is an agreement to limit credits to a term of five years.

Apart from its technical and legal basis rooted in the Korean War, what is the rationale of this trade policy *vis-à-vis* Communist China? U.S. policy toward China in effect is designed to isolate it and to contain it within its present boundaries, and trade controls are intended to support both these objectives. If adhered to by all major trading countries, such controls would, of course, limit intercourse with China and therefore isolate her not only commercially but politically. At the same time, they would deprive her of modern weapons and other defense materials and thus tend to weaken her militarily. Finally, to the extent that they could deny China the wherewithal for modern industrial development, they would at least retard the country's economic growth and postpone the day when it would acquire a large enough industrial base to support a strong and more or less modern military posture. U.S. trade policy, thus, is designed to reduce Communist China's military potential in both the short and the long run.

Let us examine the logic of the rationale for this policy and then appraise the policy's practical effects.

With respect to the logic of the policy's rationale, two questions may be posed: Is it in the national interest to the United States to isolate China, and is it in the national interest of the United States to weaken China economically? In examining the question of isolation, we must remember that we are dealing with a regime which rules over a country of more than 700 million people—that is, the largest national entity in the world. On the basis of all available evidence, moreover, it seems to be a regime which is here to stay. While one can never rule out the possibility of a collapse under some hypothetical combination of circumstances, its *probability* may be rated as low.

Thus we find ourselves in the same world and on the same planet with a country which has vowed unalterable hostility to us and one

which we consider as actually or potentially a dangerous, threatening
and disequilibrating influence in the world international system. Yet
the Chinese must somehow learn to live with us, and we must learn
to live with them. Such coexistence requires increasing communication and contact between Communist China and the United States.
Continuing efforts to isolate China are bound to reinforce the regime's
implacable hostility to the United States and its determination to wage
an unrelenting campaign to isolate the United States in Asia and in
the world at large. At least to some extent, Communist China's
strategy of revolution, her propagation of national wars of liberation,
and her push for militancy in various parts of the world are related to
this effort or counter-effort to isolate the United States. Because we
have a stake in growth (national, political, and economic) under stable
conditions while the Chinese Communists have a vested interest in
disturbance, some form of coexistence is of much greater importance
to the United States.

Of course, the United States and Communist China have in one
sense been in more or less continuous contact—but within a war or
quasi-war context, such as that which prevails in Korea, in Vietnam
and Laos, and in the Taiwan Strait. Such contacts undoubtedly involve one form of communication. There have also been limited diplomatic contacts at the Warsaw talks and at occasional international
conferences such as the Geneva Conference on Laos. This kind of
contact, however, does not amount to a departure by either country
from a policy of isolating the other.

Regardless of the merits of a policy designed to isolate China, are
trade controls suitable and effective as one of the instruments for the
implementation of this policy? A cutting off of all exports to China
would undoubtedly have damaged her economy in several ways. It
would have significantly reduced the country's economic growth, would
have rendered difficult if not impossible the expansion of her heavy
industry, and in the early 1960s would have greatly complicated her
problem of food supply. The Chinese economy, however, did not
suffer these consequences because (a) no other major trading nation
followed the U.S. policy of total embargo and (b) up to 1960 China
could obtain from other Communist countries virtually any commodities which allied trade controls denied her. During the period of
intimate Sino-Soviet economic relations (1950-60), therefore, the practical consequences of the U.S. embargo and allied trade controls were
negligible. The Sino-Soviet trade relationships may possibly have

increased the cost of China's imports, but the evidence on this matter is far from conclusive. Even if some costs did result, they were probably minimal.

The situation, however, changed after 1960. Sino-Soviet economic relations deteriorated markedly. As a result, China has had difficulty in obtaining imports of armaments and military goods, and she has been unable to obtain long-term credits. For the first time, it could be argued, enforcement of the whole system of trade controls became theoretically possible. From the mid-1950s on, however, allied trade controls had gradually been eased. Therefore, Western countries were prepared and in a position to move into the breach left by the Soviets. While U.S. trade policy was formerly ineffective because China could obtain controlled and embargoed goods from the Communist countries, it is now ineffective because these same goods (except for military materiel) can be obtained from practically every country which exports them except the United States.

The only practical economic impediment to which China is still exposed under the controls lies in the field of credit. This fact raises two questions: how much damage do credit controls impose on the Chinese economy, and conversely, to what extent could credits be used to induce modifications of Chinese Communist policies?

The Chinese Communists do not seem to have any difficulties in obtaining all the short- and medium-term credits they can use or finance at present. Their international credit rating is good, and they have met their financial obligations without delay. In a practical sense, therefore, access to long-term credits would simply mean that China could either lighten her current annual debt burden by converting her present obligations or that she could service, at the current rate or yearly debt payments, a much larger credit.

Whether China could obtain sufficient economic benefits from this access to induce her to pay a political price for it is difficult to forecast. On the basis of experience, it would seem rather doubtful unless, perhaps, the economic gain to be derived were indeed of major proportions. The history of Sino-Soviet relations, for example, would suggest that the Chinese were not prepared to sacrifice what they considered to be vital objectives even if they had to suffer the economic consequences of a break. In her relations with the West, therefore, China probably cannot be expected to give up or modify any of her important foreign policy objectives even though such decisions might benefit her economy. This judgment, however, does not necessarily mean that there may be no chance to obtain concessions in a mutual bargaining situation—at least concessions as to timing, relative priorities, and direction. For several years, for instance, the Chinese Communists maintained that they would not carry on trade with Japan unless the latter accorded them *de facto* recognition. Yet since 1962 trade relations, partly because of the Sino-Soviet split, have been reactivated and broadened essentially on Japanese terms.

As I have indicated, the U.S. embargo is practically of no economic significance, for China has been and is currently able to obtain virtually all the goods she needs from other countries at no significant additional cost. Therefore, the embargo has only a symbolic meaning. It stands as a symbol of our determination to isolate China, to treat her as an outlaw, and to refuse to have any dealings with her.

The embargo also serves, however, to maintain the illusion at home that we are somehow inflicting serious damage upon the Chinese Communists through it. Moreover, the embargo and our general policy on trade with China have three other consequences. They separate us from our allies, who do not see the point of our policy on either theoretical or practical grounds. They contribute to frictions between ourselves and our allies whenever we attempt to press them to bring their policies into line with ours. Finally, they deprive our businessmen of their potential share, however modest, of the China trade now carried on by other countries.

This analysis really indicates that a trade control policy inflicts costs not only on China but on other countries as well. The more important trade with China may be to the country concerned, the greater these costs tend to be. Actually, the costs imposed are likely to be minimal in most cases just as the costs imposed on China appear to be small. Nevertheless, to the extent that embargoes and controls reduce the gains in international trade it is far from clear which side incurs greater losses, Communist China or its potential trading partners.

Removal of the embargo may be peculiarly well suited to serve as the first step on the road to normalization between the United States and China. It can be initiated unilaterally without resort to negotiations, and it can be implemented without any economic cost. If the move is made, it should be carried out as a low-key measure and as a signal that other overtures might possibly follow if the Chinese respond to it.

Just as the embargo now stands as a symbol of our determination to isolate Communist China, its removal could symbolize a new policy posture on the part of the United States. At the maximum, such a move, possibly coupled with other similar measures, might widen our channels of communication with China and maybe even improve the general atmosphere of U.S.-China relations. At the minimum, a complete rebuff to our overtures would place the onus for implacable hostility at the door of Communist China.

In the same general vein, it may be worth considering some experimentation in the field of credit policy. A rigid policy of credit limitation ties the hands of our allies and deprives them of any bargaining power. On the other hand, a policy which would leave credit terms vague and unpublished would make it much easier to obtain a *quid pro quo* not only in economic terms but perhaps in political terms as well.

Ultimately the crux of the problem is: What should be the overall character of our policy toward China? Should we assume a new posture and take new initiatives, or should we permit ourselves to remain preoccupied with the difficulties of change rather than with the penalties attendant upon holding a fixed position? These problems, of course, range well beyond the economic realm; they encompass the totality of our policy in Asia. In this realm, economic considerations and economic instruments can and should play only a subsidiary and supporting role.

9

FOREIGN PROBLEMS AND POLICIES

By Donald S. Zagoria

United States foreign policy, and all considerations of it, must bear in mind a crucial fact of international life: that the Chinese Communist regime today faces the most serious and far-reaching foreign policy crisis it has ever confronted. This crisis is largely the outgrowth of rigidly dogmatic postures assumed in recent years by Mao and his closest collaborators. The crisis is of such magnitude as to have seriously weakened Peking's influence in the underdeveloped countries, cast doubt on the legitimacy and viability of even the regime's reasonable international aspirations, and greatly sharpened existing divergencies among Communist movements all over the world. It is a crisis which will not be resolved without basic changes in Chinese Communist policy — changes which may not come until after Mao's death, but which could occur sooner and, in any case, are bound to happen in the foreseeable future.

The dimensions of this crisis are global: Indonesia, Cuba, Kenya — wherever we look in Asia, Latin America and Africa, the Peking regime stands accused of unwarranted intervention and arrogance, its representatives are asked to go home, and its intentions are viewed with growing suspicion.

Within the international Communist movement, where Peking a year or two ago could count on some 20 allies and sympathizers, and seemed ready to set up a new Communist international alliance of Afro-Asian-Latin American parties, Chinese influence is now at an all-time low. Even the intransigent Albanians are beginning to have second thoughts about the wisdom of Mao's strategy and doctrine. Meanwhile, the split with Moscow deepens.

The current crisis in Communist China's foreign policy has its roots in 1957 when Mao, incorrectly assuming that the development of Soviet ICBM capabilities had wrought a decisive change in the world balance of power, abandoned Peking's previous caution and embarked on a more militant course to achieve his primary foreign policy goals: elimination of U.S. military power from Asia, repossession of Formosa, and international recognition of Communist China as a great power.

It soon became clear that the Soviet Union, on whose support Mao had unquestionably counted, was unwilling to back Mao's ambitious aims at the risk of war with the United States. Quite to the contrary, it soon made overtures for a detente with the United States. The "spirit of Camp David" and Khrushchev's subsequent efforts to persuade Peking to accept a modus vivendi envisaging Chinese Nationalist control of Formosa pressed home to Mao the fact that the Russians could not be depended on to help push the United States out of Asia. This difference of approach to the U.S. presence is among the fundamental causes of the Sino-Soviet split and explains the bitterness of Chinese feelings toward the Soviet leadership.

Peking then turned to the underdeveloped countries, encouraging nationalist and local Communist leaders in these countries to join in an anti-American alliance. Mao's plans could not be carried out without replacing Soviet by Chinese authority in the Communist and leftist groups of Afro-Asia and Latin America. However, Mao's gambit has fallen flat all along the line: radical nationalists receptive to Peking's game are disappearing from power, and Communist parties in Africa, Asia and Latin America are deeply divided and increasingly disenchanted with Mao.

What amounts, then, to effective containment of Communist China has been accomplished primarily by the Peking leadership itself. In a few short years, the Chinese leadership has split with the only other major Communist power in the world, it has alienated itself from the international Communist movement and from the emergent nationalist forces of the developing countries, and it has not only failed to attain most of its pressing national goals but it has even prejudiced them. The rumblings of discontent with Mao's policies are plainly audible in China today.

Loss of Influence. China's failures are essentially the result of its erroneous assessment of the forces at work in the Afro-Asian world. National self-realization rather than instant social revolution or an anti-American crusade is the immediate goal sought by the new countries, and Peking's product mix of subversion, helpful revolutionary hints and polemics on the evils of imperialism has inevitably found only a limited market where economic development and nation-building are the primary concerns. By the same token, Peking cannot compete with Russia or the United States when it comes to economic and military aid.

Similarly, Peking's loss of influence in the international Communist movement is the direct consequence of Chinese intransigence, which even the most radical Communist parties have come to regard as unrealistic. Mao's failure last year to cooperate in a Soviet plan to send a limited number of Russian troops into North Vietnam and to station Soviet fighter planes in southern Chinese airfields provides a striking example of Peking's unwillingness to accept realistic alternatives in a situation of deep concern to the international Communist movement. With such a move Moscow had hoped to reassure China as to its physical security, discourage U.S. bombing of North Vietnam and, at the same time, exert pressures for negotiations on all participants in the Vietnamese fighting. Peking promptly charged that the Soviet leaders were out to make a "deal" with the Americans, and suggested that, instead, Soviet supplies to Vietnam be sent by sea and that the Russians open a "second front" in Europe, preferably in Berlin. Moscow countered by accusing the Chinese of unwillingness to help take united action against imperialist aggression — an accusation which found a wide echo in many Communist parties. The suspicion is growing among them that Peking is willing to fight the Americans to the last Vietnamese.

The extent of the crisis facing the Chinese Communist leadership in the field of foreign policy is dramatically pointed up in the now-notorious statement made by Marshal Lin Piao last September. Ironically, there are two — and only two — countries in the world where Lin Piao's revolutionary smörgasbord is regarded as some kind of magic weapon: one is China, the other is the United States.

Two, in my opinion, equally erroneous interpretations of Lin Piao's statement are current, and both miss the point. On the one hand there are those who dismiss it as Fourth of July rhetoric. On the other are those part-time Pekinologists who call this Lin Piao's "Mein Kampf," blithely ignoring the fact that it is basically a rehash of what Chinese Communist leaders have been saying on and off since at least 1949.

The analogy with "Mein Kampf" comes, therefore, a little late, to say the least, but, more importantly, it is harmful and misleading because it equates Maoist and Nazi ideology in such a way as to evoke the spectre of overt Chinese Communist military and territorial expansion in Asia. Neither in the Lin Piao statement nor in the multitude of similar statements made in the past is there any suggestion of Chinese Communist intentions to engage in direct, Hitler-style expansionism.

Rationalization Regarding Vietnam. In fact, a cardinal point of Lin Piao's message is that Viet Cong and other Communist revolutionaries throughout the world must make their revolutions on their own, that they should not count on Chinese or any other outside assistance. Far from giving notice of any intention to intervene aggressively, Lin Piao is rationalizing Peking's unwillingness to go to the aid of the Viet Cong in a struggle which — let there be no doubt — the Chinese Communists regard as just and which is taking place on their very borders.

The difference between Hitler and Mao, then, is that "Mein Kampf" was a blueprint for what Germany herself, under Hitler, would do; Lin Piao's statement, on the contrary, is designed to tell other Communist parties what they should do. It is, thus, not simply July the Fourth oratory.

However, most of the Communist parties now recognize that Lin Piao's advice is largely inappropriate to their local situations, and they are not about to act on it. The ingredients of the Chinese Communist revolutionary model — long put forward as a "do it yourself" model for foreign Communists — are well-known: a disciplined Communist party, a broad united front, a protracted guerrilla struggle originating in the rural hinterland and based on armed peasantry — the whole led by Communists right from the outset.

How many foreign Communist parties are in a position to implement the model? With the exception of Vietnam, the answer is none, as of this moment, and for very good reasons: not one Communist party in Africa, Asia or in Latin America has a strong base either in the society in general or among the peasants in particular — an indispensable prerequisite for launching a Maoist-style guerrilla war. The one party which came closest to having such a mass base, the PKI in Indonesia, has recently been decimated by the Indonesian army and is unlikely to recover in the foreseeable future. In India, Communism is strong in certain areas but it has not been able to generate a mass basis of support among peasants in the countryside. In Africa, Communist parties are for the most part nonexistent, and Peking had

to build on a variety of the most unlikely patchwork of local oppo-
sitionists, at least one of whom took $70,000 from them and then
opened up a bar at which, we may assume, instruction in Marxism-
Leninism is not regularly supplied.

This is, of course, not to argue that the appeal of revolutionary
Communism has been entirely unsuccessful in the underdeveloped
countries. Apart from the startling conquest of mainland China, it
has been able to generate mass movements in Vietnam, Cuba and until
recently in Indonesia. But the factors that account for its gains in
these areas are not paralleled in other underdeveloped countries of the
world. The single most important element in the advance of Communism in Vietnam, as in China itself, was that the local Communist
party captured a nationalist movement during and after World War II
in the course of a national struggle against a foreign invader. Second,
the nationalist opposition to the Communists both in China and
Vietnam was divided, unimaginative and without effective organization at the rice-root level. Current Viet Cong success in South Vietnam
is inextricably related to the fact that Ho Chi-minh, like Mao, was
able to capture a weak nationalist movement during the last war.

Failures in Afro-Asian Countries. Communist success in China and
Vietnam should not, however, obscure the more fundamental fact
that the Communists have been unable to seize control of a nationalist
movement anywhere in Asia, Africa or Latin America since the start
of World War II. (Castro was not a Communist when he took power;
he converted to Communism afterward in order to obtain Soviet
protection against American attack.) This is not a mere historical
accident. It suggests that the Chinese and Vietnamese successes are
not easy to duplicate even in the favorable circumstances of an anti-
colonial armed struggle. Witness the fact that in none of the recent
or current instances of such a struggle — Algeria and Angola, for
example — have local Communists played a leading role.

In those Afro-Asian countries which have already achieved independence — and these, of course, constitute the vast majority — it is
exceedingly difficult for local Communists to exploit nationalism to
their advantage or to outmaneuver the nationalists and the army in
the post-independence struggle for power. In the one instance where
they were able temporarily to exploit nationalism, namely Indonesia,
they could not convert this into lasting power. Even in the many
new countries which have been torn by strife at the top or have failed

to solve the problems of modernization, the Communists are nowhere close to power.

It is ironic that both Peking and Washington have in the past seemed to share the view that somehow nationalists in the developing countries would prove to be a pushover for the disciplined Communists. This has turned out to be a completely wrong assessment. On the contrary, the containment of Communism in the underdeveloped areas has been accomplished in the main not by Western military action, economic aid or the attractions of Western democracy but rather by the growth of a variety of nationalist regimes who have no particular desire to imitate either Western or Communist economic and political institutions.

Since the Chinese Communist leadership has in the past shown itself flexible enough to adjust policies when they go wrong, I see no reason not to expect that they will be able to recognize their plight and adapt accordingly. True, what we have thus far seen from Peking is not the sign of change in direction but rather the rationalization of past mistakes. But this cannot suffice. The Chinese will not stay indefinitely in the corner they have painted themselves into.

Options. What options do they have? They could try to reach a rapprochement with the Soviet Union. But so long as Mao lives, this is unlikely. They could improve relations with the United States. It is interesting in this respect to note that a recent French emissary to Peking was told that the Americans were, after all, only an enemy, and a respected one, whereas the Russians were traitors, and traitors could never be forgiven. The clear impression was that it might eventually be easier to adjust relations with the U.S. than with Russia. Thirdly, Peking could try to revive the "Bandung spirit" of the mid-1950s when it sought to portray itself not as a revolutionary power but as a friend of the entire Afro-Asian world. But is is not likely to do any of these things until the issue of Vietnam is decided because the old guard still cherishes the hope that a success there could turn back the tide.

It nourishes this hope despite deteriorating relations with Hanoi. Let me at this point clarify certain things about the relationship among Peking, Hanoi and the South Vietnamese Liberation Front:

There is, I believe, general agreement among informed observers that Hanoi is fully independent of Peking. The precise relationship between Hanoi and the Liberation Front is a more controversial matter. It is clear that the Liberation Front is controlled by a South Vietnamese Communist party called the People's Revolutionary Party. It is also clear that the People's Revolutionary Party is a branch of the parent Lao Dong Communist Party in North Vietnam. What is not clear is how much the South Vietnamese Communists and the Liberation Front have emancipated themselves from North Vietnamese control. Important tactical differences between Hanoi and the Front have been apparent for some time. In general, Hanoi shows greater flexibility than the Front, whose position is closer to the intransigence of Peking. It is quite likely that the South Vietnamese Communists, having been abandoned by the northern comrades at the Geneve conference in 1954, are extremely fearful that Hanoi may do it again. The Communists, and especially the South Vietnamese Communists in the firing line, have their own Yalta complex.

Peking and Hanoi, I want to stress, have both overlapping and conflicting goals in South Vietnam. They share an interest in eliminating American power and influence from South Vietnam but Peking has a much greater interest in a protracted war. For Peking, the war in South Vietnam which, to be sure, it did not itself start, nevertheless provides a test case for its "liberation war" strategy. More important, it provides an opportunity to humiliate, divert and to weaken the United States without any cost to itself. This is why Peking, although concerned about the possibility of an American attack on China, is nevertheless not eager for a negotiated settlement in Vietnam. Hanoi, on the other hand, has a clearly more limited interest: namely, the unification of Vietnam under Communist hegemony, a goal that might — under certain conditions — be achieved through negotiations rather than through protracted war against a determined and superior enemy.

These different perspectives have resulted in differences in emphasis on the possibility of negotiations and the preconditions for them — differences that have gone largely unnoted in most of the American press. Peking has repeatedly been at pains to warn against U.S. deceit and far more vehemently than Haonoi has denounced all proposals to end the war in Vietnam short of U.S. disengagement. Moreover, Hanoi's conditions for negotiations have in general been more ambiguous and flexible than Peking's.

The crucial and, as far as U.S. policy is concerned, complicating factor is that Hanoi's leadership is itself divided. Hanoi has its own version of hawks and doves. Hanoi's hawks — who remain predominant — seem to believe that the massive introduction of American power into South Vietnam has not greatly diminished Communist prospects for success, while the doves believe that it has. Peking has consistently sought to strengthen Hanoi's hawks and the Chinese Communists have recently expressed considerable apprehension that the Hanoi dove faction is, with Soviet backing, on the rise.

American Alternatives. In this situation there are some things the U.S. can, and in my opinion, should do. First, it seems to me imperative that we recognize — even if the Chinese Communists do not — that Communist successes in South Vietnam are not easily duplicable. They are the product of conditions that are extremely unusual in the former colonial world. This is not an argument for precipitate withdrawal from South Vietnam, a course of action that would under no circumstances be consistent with the best interests of the United States. But the price we are willing to pay, and the risks we are willing to accept for an eventual settlement will depend in part on whether we regard South Vietnam as the first of a series of dominoes or as an exception to the general rule that the heyday of Communism in the underdeveloped areas has passed.

Second, it appears that our best hope in Vietnam is to strengthen those groups in Moscow and Hanoi who have a more flexible approach to negotiations against the bitter-enders supported by Peking. These moderates can be strengthened by two complementary lines of American policy. First, our words and our actions could substantiate their realistic assessment that the United States cannot be forced out of South Vietnam and that a military victory for the Viet Cong is in fact impossible. Second, our words and our actions could assure them that the United States is not insisting on unconditional surrender. On the first count, we have already made significant progress. A year or two ago Peking, Hanoi and even Moscow seemed to believe that the United States would tire of the war and withdraw. It is now apparent that the moderate groups in the Communist world have revised their estimates. In my view, more effort must now be expended on the second line of approach.

While on the subject of Vietnam, I want to make a specific proposal for neutralizing mainland southeast Asia after the Vietnam war is concluded. We can ensure genuine neutralization of the area only if the smaller countries concerned believe that their security is provided for. If we merely talk about neutralization while withdrawing our military power, they will obviously be forced to accommodate to China on Chinese terms. We must convince all of these countries that the United States, preferably in conjunction with international authority and with the Soviet Union, will help them to resist any threat to their security by an ouside power. To do this, I think we need two things: first, the continued physical presence of effective American power even if it takes the form of the Seventh Fleet; second, bilateral contingency plans which will set down the conditions for American action and the manner in which such action will be undertaken. I do not believe that it is practical to talk about such neutralization, however, until after the Vietnam war is concluded. Too much emphasis on neutralization at this point, before adequate preparation is made with the countries involved, would be bound to have a disquieting effect on them.

Finally, I would like to endorse enthusiastically the changes in our policy toward China recommended to the Senate Foreign Relations Committee by Professors Barnett and Fairbank. As I indicated, it seems to me likely that Peking's failures in foreign policy must inevitably lead the Chinese Communists to undertake a painful readjustment of their strategy and tactics that have brought them to the brink of international bankruptcy. If Mao were a British prime minister, he would by this time have been "elevated" to the House of Lords. There are credible reports that the Chinese leaders are increasingly divided on foreign policy and when Mao dies, it is quite likely that we will witness as furious a succession struggle in China as we saw in the Soviet Union after the death of Stalin. I think it is now generally recognized that we missed the opportunity to strengthen the hand of the moderates in the Stalin succession struggle and we should not repeat the same mistake in our policy toward China. A change in our policy toward China now could provide an alternative to those Chinese leaders who believe that Mao's policy has been too rigid.

It might be countered by some that if China is in such serious difficulty, why is there any need for a change in our policy? I believe such a change is necessary at some point if we are ever to achieve stability in Asia and to solve a host of international questions that cannot be resolved without Chinese participation, including arms control and disarmament. In the past, objections have been raised to a change in U.S. policy on the grounds that it would be interpreted as weakness by the other side. But if this is the case, what better time is there for such a change when it is clear that we are not leading from weakness?

Moreover, there are many countries and people, particularly in Asia, who believe that Chinese intransigence and militance is largely the result of isolation by the U.S. We can prove that they are wrong only by ending our policy of isolation. If the Chinese continue, as they have done in the past, to isolate themselves by their own inept policies, at least the onus will be on them.

Finally, and not least important, our only hope to achieve a stable and tolerable relationship with China is to do all we can to promote not a change of the system — which can be done only by war — but a change within the system. The kind of evolution that is already transforming Russia and the East European Communist countries will have to come one day in China too. We can help to hasten its growth.

10

QUEST FOR GREAT POWER STATUS

By Harold C. Hinton

The Chinese Communist Party came to power in 1949 determined not only to wipe out China's past humiliations at the hands of what it called foreign "imperialism" but to make China the leading state in Asia and a model and source of support for other Communist revolutions in Asia. The scope of its ambitions was soon broadened to include the whole of the underdeveloped areas and even the attainment of the status of a world power. The United States, which was tentatively moving toward diplomatic recognition of Communist China in the last months of 1949, found its intentions frustrated by the Chinese Communist determination to cast the United States in the light of the major enemy for reasons both foreign and domestic, including a desire to isolate Western-oriented Chinese and facilitate their reindoctrination.

A first step in Communist China's quest for influence was the acquisition of all territory claimed as Chinese. In 1936 Mao Tse-tung had said that Taiwan, or Formosa, should be independent after its liberation from Japan, but he changed his mind as the United States and Britain promised Taiwan to China in 1943, the Chinese Nationalists made it their main base and refuge after 1949, and the United States began to protect it after 1950. Shortly afterward Communist China intervened in the Korean conflict in order to keep American ground forces away from its Manchurian frontier. It succeeded in this, but its intervention, together with the developing Sino-American confrontation in the Taiwan Strait, led the United States to shift the emphasis of its military policy in the Far East from containment of the Soviet Union to containment, or as the Chinese would say, encirclement of Communist China.

Thus Communist China's overeager promotion of its own security and influence, although it enhanced its influence somewhat by creating in many quarters an exaggerated impression of its readiness to resort to force, also created a greater and continuing threat to Chinese security. Much the same is happening now as the United States constructs major air bases in Thailand in response to a Vietnamese crisis in which Communist China has chosen to involve itself to a limited degree. Since 1950 a major deterrent to hostile action against Communist China by the United States or anyone else is the widespread belief that China's large conventional forces, which it refuses to reduce under any international disarmament agreement, hold the non-Communist countries of mainland Asia hostage for the good behavior of its enemies. To a degree, therefore, Communist China can count on Asian countries as well as others to exert restraining pressures on the United States. In reality, Communist China's ability to invade other Asian countries is severely limited by logistics and is almost canceled by the threat of American retaliation and the political liabilities that would follow an actual invasion, as distinct from a mere threat or assumed capability to invade. At various times in the past year and a half, Communist China has said that it would fight the United States on the ground in Indochina if the United States attacked China, whether on land or merely in the air is not clear, if the United States invaded North Vietnam or northern Laos, or if the National Liberation Front with Hanoi's consent requested Chinese intervention. Since none of these preconditions is likely to materialize, direct Communist Chinese intervention in Vietnam is also unlikely, except in the highly improbable event of some major miscalculation or irrational decision on the Chinese side.

Alliance With the Soviet Union. For a number of reasons that included its determination to confront the United States in Asia, the Chinese leadership chose to ally itself with the Soviet Union in 1950. The alliance was seriously strained by the Korean crisis and still more by the massive retaliation doctrine and the entry of West Germany into NATO, which riveted Soviet attention on Europe more than ever and reduced almost to the vanishing point Soviet willingness to take serious risks on behalf of China, even in defense of its security and still less in support of its offensive ambitions such as the taking of Taiwan. In 1956, therefore, Communist China decided that it must have nuclear weapons and delivery systems of its own. It succeeded in getting substantial Soviet technical aid and equipment toward this end in exchange for acquiescence in Soviet efforts to achieve a test ban agreement. A Chinese demand for the turning over of finished Soviet nuclear weapons as an interim measure seems to have foundered, however, on a Soviet counterdemand for joint defense arrangements that would have amounted to Soviet controls. The Soviet Union canceled its nuclear aid, and China in return withdrew its support for a test ban agreement, its objections rising to a crescendo when the Soviet Union actually signed such an agreement in 1963. Over and above the specific issue of the test ban, China objects to any sort of American-Soviet detente, because it diminishes still further the Soviet incentive to give China active support against the United States without reducing Sino-American tension in any way.

Nuclear Ambitions. Undaunted, Communist China has continued its drive to become a nuclear power. Indeed, there is strong evidence that it is the only country in the world that is seriously trying to join the United States and the Soviet Union as a thermonuclear super-power. The current Chinese leadership apparently intends to use whatever pressures and exact whatever sacrifices are necessary to put China at least over the hump on the way to thermonuclear weapons and suitable delivery systems, just as Stalin did for the Soviet Union, and is greatly worried that younger Chinese may not share its taste for hardship and nuclear status symbols. The Chinese quest for nuclear weapons, as well as Chinese pressures on the Soviet Union within the framework of the international Communist movement that are at least partly in retaliation for what the Chinese regard as Soviet betrayal of the Sino-Soviet alliance, have contributed heavily to a deterioration of Sino-Soviet relations that since 1963 has occasionally taken on dramatic proportions. One manifestation of this deterioration has been a border dispute that has sometimes approached the level of at least local war.

Relations With Non-Communist Countries. China has done fairly well in its recent relations with the developed non-Communist countries, including Japan and excluding the United States, primarily because its revolutionary activities there are minor and ineffectual and it gives priority to its national interests, which stress trade and the acquisition of technological information. China's trade with these countries, and with Japan and West Germany in particular, is trending upward. On the other hand, Chinese interest in the developed countries is by no means entirely economic. China hopes to lure them away from the United States, and keep them away from the Soviet

Union, in order to use them if possible against both. French recognition in January 1964 was a major diplomatic feather in China's cap, and shortly afterward the Chinese gave signs of an interest not only in signing a trade agreement with West Germany but in establishing diplomatic relations with it, not for the sake of harming East Germany but for the sake of putting pressure on Khrushchev, with whom their relations were almost unbelievably bad at that time. Nothing came of this Chinese interest in relations with West Germany, as it turned out.

Communist China's policy toward the underdeveloped areas consists essentially, although not entirely, of overtly inciting and covertly aiding Chinese-style armed revolutions, not necessarily Communist-led but aimed at "imperialist" influence in the country in question, within the limits of supposed feasibility. The purpose seems to be twofold: not only to promote eventually the spread of communism but to weaken the United States and distract it from the Far East by involving it in crises and brushfire wars elsewhere in the underdeveloped areas. The best known formulation of this strategy is Marshal Lin Piao's article of September 3 last on "people's war," in which he says that the Japanese army in China produced its own defeat by driving the Chinese people into the arms of the Communists, that the United States is now doing in the underdeveloped areas as a whole exactly what the Japanese did in China, and that the peoples of the underdeveloped areas therefore can and should imitate the Chinese people's example, without relying for decisive aid from Communist China or any other external source. So central to Lin's argument, and yet so fantastic, is the analogy between imperial Japan and the United States that one is tempted, even before examining the evidence, to conclude that the Chinese hope for widespread anti-"imperialist" risings in the underdeveloped countries is poorly founded.

If the year 1964 had witnessed such Chinese gains as French recognition, the fall of Khrushchev, and the first Chinese nuclear test, 1965 saw the beginning of a series of major Chinese setbacks in the underdeveloped areas.

Of these setbacks the first in point of both time and importance was the massive American escalation in Vietnam beginning in February 1965, which tended to cast China in the role of a paper dragon unable and unwilling to intervene effectively in a struggle that is of great political importance to it and is being conducted almost on its doorstep.

In the Kashmir crisis of late 1965, China intervened loudly but ineffectively on behalf of Pakistan in a way that tended to distract international attention from Kashmir, where Pakistan wanted it to rest, without giving the Chinese enough leverage to accomplish their objective of obstructing Pakistani acceptance of the United Nations ceasefire resolution and of Soviet mediation.

It appears that the Chinese gave some aid and advice to the Communist coup that was attempted in Indonesia last September 30, and regardless of whether such was the case they have suffered enormously from the bloody losses inflicted on what had been the largest Communist Party in the non-Communist world and one that seemed to stand a good chance of coming to power in a mood to be cooperative with China.

In sub-Saharan Africa, the Chinese have been expelled to one degree or another during the past year from Burundi, Dahomey, Upper Volta, the Central African Republic, and Ghana because of their energetic efforts to promote subversion on the theory that Africa is "ripe for revolution." Farther north, the Chinese have also been caught in subversive activities in Egypt, and more serious still they helped to torpedo the Afro-Asian Conference at Algiers rather than attend it together with the Soviet Union and Malaysia and in the probable absence of resolutions that would condemn both American policy in Vietnam and the receipt of aid by Afro-Asian countries from non-Afro-Asian countries, meaning mainly the United States and the Soviet Union.

In Latin America, the standing of Communist China in left-wing circles has suffered greatly because Castro has been moving away from the Chinese and toward the Russians since late 1964. This trend, which the Chinese only aggravated by putting pressures on Castro, has resulted in a loud and open quarrel in the early months of this year.

Major Rethinking. Communist China's setbacks in the underdeveloped areas in the past year have been so serious that it may well be that a major rethinking of Chinese foreign policy is in process, such as occurred in the Soviet Union after the Cuban missile crisis. If so, the outcome is likely to be less rather than more Chinese pressure on other countries, since it does not appear that China has any rabbits in its hat in this field. In fact, a long-term mellowing is the most likely outlook for future Chinese policy, unless the United States gives China reason to act differently by relaxing its containment policy, which has already contributed substantially to moderating Chinese foreign policy much as it did Soviet foreign policy during the last years of Stalin's life, and for that matter as it has since. There is no compelling reason to assume that American persistence in containment of Communist China, notably by giving it reason to stay out of Vietnam even if the military situation there continues on balance to develop adversely to the Communist side, will put the United States on some sort of collision course with China. Nor is there any reason to think that the possession of more than token nuclear power, which will accrue not to the present Chinese leadership but to its successors, will pose a mortal threat to peace in the absence of formal disarmament. In the nuclear age, power confers vulnerability as well, and therefore tends to lead to responsibility and the acceptance of at least tacit arms control agreements. It is still less likely that Communist China will ever be able to equal or surpass the United States or the Soviet Union in strategic military power. Communist China will remain a problem, and at times perhaps a threat, but not an unmanageable one so long as the United States is willing to do what may be necessary to keep it manageable.

11

RECENT AMERICAN POLICIES

By Walter H. Judd

Twenty-seven years ago I was given the opportunity to testify before this Committee on essentially the same subject as today: how to get and keep freedom and peace in Asia and thus security and peace for the United States. The threat then was Japan's aggressive military expansionism. After months under the Japanese in China, I had become convinced that our best hope for peace and security lay in stopping the vital aid, assistance and comfort being supplied by us to the aggressor, while doing all we properly could to strengthen and help the free peoples resisting that aggressor. Many considered such a policy too dangerous and costly — a confrontation with Japan might lead to war! Our government was persuaded, until it was too late, to try to placate the aggressor. Perhaps we could change his attitudes toward us and others by carrying on normal trade and showing him our good will. Perhaps that might start an evolutionary process in Japan's military leadership leading to better relationships!

This policy did not lead to peace, it led to Pearl Harbor. The same general approach to aggression in Asia is being advocated today as on that earlier occasion. Communist governments and their fronts are waging war against free peoples world-wide. At the moment the hottest spot, the test case for us, is Vietnam — as at other times it has been Greece, Berlin, Korea, Quemoy, Lebanon, Cuba.

But the *issue* is not Vietnam; it is how are disputes to be settled — by resolution through civilized means? Or by "armed force"? The *stake* is not Vietnam; it is Asia — and ourselves and the world. The *problem* is not Vietnam; it is aggressive Communist expansionism — this time from North Vietnam, backed up by the Soviet Union and Communist China.

No great expansionist movement has ever stopped until it was checked. Our choice — with Red China just as it was with Japan and Hitler — is not between checking and not checking; it is whether to check early, while we can, and with allies — or try to check the aggression later when it is stronger, closer, and we have fewer and weaker friends and allies. The urgent question is *how* to check it — with least risk and cost.

Protecting American Interests. Since the beginning of the Korean War in 1950, America's policy toward Communist China under the Truman, Eisenhower, Kennedy and Johnson administrations has been a hard-headed realistic attempt to protect the security interests of the United States by resisting any steps that would further increase Chinese Communist influence and power. An indispensable part of the policy has been to support and strengthen all non-Communist governments that are trying to preserve their independence and thereby to keep their manpower, territory, bases, and resources out of Communist control.

Some say that policy has failed. Red China is still there, it is as hostile, and as dedicated to world domination by armed force as ever. Yes, it is there; but where would the countries around Red China have been without this policy of containment of the aggressor and support of the free? There are great problems ahead for Korea, Taiwan, the Philippines, Burma, as well as South Vietnam, Malaysia and Indonesia. But *all of them are still free.* And who can believe they would have been free, and with at least the possibility of solving their problems, if it had not been for our firm containment of China?

From what I have seen in the press, most of the changes in American policy towards Communist China proposed by various witnesses before this Committee appear to be based on certain assumptions which do not seem to me to be justified:

1. That the Communist regime now in control of the China mainland is here to stay.

But the same was said of Hitler, of Khrushchev, of Sukarno, of Nkrumah. People are not so sure that Castro is here to stay. Despots generally appear invincible — "until the last five minutes."

2. That the United States is stubbornly keeping Red China isolated and therefore we are responsible for its hostility and belligerence. The reverse is the truth; it is Red China's hostility and belligerence in its international attitudes and actions that are responsible for its isolation.

General George Marshall wrote on January 7, 1947, after he had spent a year trying the very policies now being recommended of friendliness, conciliation, bringing the Chinese Communists into the Chinese Government and into the world community: "I wish to state to the American people that in the deliberate misrepresentation and abuse of the action, policies and purposes of our Government this propaganda (against the United States) has been without regard for the truth, without any regard whatsoever for the facts, and has given plain evidence of a determined purpose to mislead the Chinese people and the world and to arouse a bitter hatred of Americans."

The cause of Red China's hostility is not its isolation, but the Communist doctrine of the necessity for use of "armed force" to achieve world revolution. To remove China's isolation now would prove that the ideology is correct and should be followed even more tenaciously.

3. That there is a better hope of getting Red China to change its attitudes and activities by giving in to it on matters like diplomatic recognition, trade, and admission to the United Nations than by resolute continuance of the policy of containment as long as Red China refuses to act like a responsible member of civilized society.

4. That changing our policy vis-a-vis Red China just might start an evolutionary process there. But, of course, it might just as easily reduce the chances of such an evolutionary process. Everybody desires and hopes for "evolution" in Red China. The debate should be over *what measures are most likely to produce it:*

• Giving Red China greater prestige, influence, entreé, that is, making it stronger? Or keeping it as weak and isolated as possible?

• Concessions from its intended victims — like the United States? Or pressures from its present victims — the Chinese within Red China, those on Taiwan and in Southeast Asia, Muslims in Indonesia and Malaysia, etc.?

• Proving that Red China's truculence and stubborn defiance of the world succeeds? Or showing that it will fail?

• Taking the "mountain" (United Nations) to Mao? Or patiently and non-belligerently insisting that Mao come to the mountain of better international conduct if he wants the benefits to Red China of membership in the international community?

What has caused the reported "mellowing" and "evolution" inside Yugoslavia, Rumania, the Soviet Union? Influences from without? Or failures within? If economic and other pressures from within and without are compelling some Communist governments to moderate their policies, at least toward their own people, shouldn't we keep the pressures up rather than reduce them by helping those hostile governments to solve their problems?

Suggested Changes. Let us now look at the changes in policy toward Red China suggested by some. They are mostly three: official diplomatic recognition by the United States, expansion of trade relations, and admission of Communist China to the United Nations. What would be the probable results of such changes, the gains and losses?

Almost no one so far as I have seen, goes further than expressing the vague hope that after these steps Red China may "mellow, moderate, mature, evolve." But there is no evidence on which to base these hoped-for changes.

What benefits, economic or political, has Great Britain received from her granting of diplomatic recognition in 1950? Or France two years ago?

Prime Minister Nehru of India recognized Communist China in 1950 and worked out with Chou En-lai the "Five Principles of Coexistence." He remarked that Americans didn't get along very well with the Chinese Communists because we are not Asians, implying that he being a fellow-Asian could. I replied that I feared he would find that the Chinese Communists will not act as Asians but as world revolutionists. He was Red China's chief opologist and advocate — at the UN and elsewhere. How did his fellow-Asians in Peking respond to his being their best friend? They invaded India, and left Mr. Nehru a broken man.

It is suggested that with diplomatic recognition we might get more information about conditions in Red China. But we have been getting plenty of information by a variety of means, especially from the thousands of escapees each year. Red China has not allowed any newspaper correspondent of any nationality to travel freely in that land unless it had reason to believe in advance that he was generally favorable. Our trouble is not lack of information but erosion of our steadfastness, our patience, our will — as Mao boasted would be the case.

In contrast, there is no uncertainty as to the losses that would result from the suggested weakening of American policy. Here are some:

1. It would pull the rug out from under our loyal allies on Taiwan. The Chinese are a realistic, even fatalistic, people. With no hope for reunion in freedom with their brethren on the China mainland, they

would have little or no choice but to prepare for the inevitable. Americans who advocate admitting Red China and then add glibly, "Of course we would support the defense of Taiwan," may be salving their own consciences but I think no Asians will be deceived. Twelve million Chinese could hardly maintain indefinitely the will or the capacity to resist 700 million, with the world organization for peace itself rejecting the 12 million and accepting the 700 million!

In 1944 an American foreign service officer stationed with the Communists in North China recommended in a secret memorandum that our Ambassador to China be sent on an official visit to the Communist headquarters. He added, "Public announcement that the President's representative had made a visit to the Communist capital at Yenan would have significance that no Chinese would miss — least of all the Generalissimo." He was right. When Ambassador Hurley was ordered to make the trip to Yenan, millions of Chinese understood that their cause was lost. Without full American support they could not hope to recover after the war and put down the Communist rebellion. Obviously America was not going to give them, its ally, full support.

The result of giving such status to the Communist enemy inevitably was deterioration of our ally's morale. It would be the same on Taiwan. At least some of those now advising such a course understand this psychological factor as well as did the foreign service officer. It enables them to appear resolutely in favor of containing Red China while recommending a course almost certain to lead to that policy's failure.

2. With weakening or loss of Taiwan our Pacific island chain of defenses would be breached. It is doubtful that the Philippines could long resist Communist pressures and blandishments. Filipinos remember that it was from Taiwan that their country was invaded by the Japanese. It would take vast intervention with American forces to save that new nation for which we certainly have a special responsibility in the Pacific. I have not found any responsible Filipino leaders who favor recognition of Communist China.

3. The 15 million or so Chinese living in Southeast Asia would be shaken. They occupy key positions of power and influence in Vietnam, Malaysia, Thailand, Burma, Indonesia, the Philippines. Those countries could not refuse to recognize Communist China once we did. That would mean every Chinese embassy and consulate in Southeast Asia, and in the world for that matter, would become a protected center of Communist espionage, propaganda, sabotage and subversion

of the host government — as recently exposed in Indonesia and Ghana. Through these embassies and consulates the Chinese minorities would be under direct and almost irresistible pressure to support the aggressive policies of the Mao regime.

The stability of the strategic countries of Southeast Asia would inevitably be weakened. Can anyone reasonably expect the governments of these smaller and weaker countries to be stronger and firmer *vis-a-vis* Red China than the great United States is?

4. If the United States were to show that it is not a dependable ally in Asia, our allies elsewhere including those in Europe, would know they cannot count on us either. What would happen to the whole system of collective security we have been building at such cost and effort and which is absolutely indispensable to our own survival as a free nation? Why should any country anywhere stand by us if is not sure we will stand by it?

5. It would tell the neutrals and "uncommitted" nations that they were right all along and that they might as well give in to the winning side at once.

6. Perhaps worst of all, it would tell the 700 million people on the China mainland that we are accepting their subjugation, that we think there is more hope for peace for ourselves in deals with their oppressors than in standing steadfastly with them, the oppressed.

During the war and post-war years the United States relaxed under the skillfully built-up illusions that the Soviet Union was a "peace-loving democracy," eager and willing to cooperate to build a world of order and peace, and that the Chinese Communists were just agrarian reformers. Perhaps our best hope of getting out of our present predicament and peril without a nuclear holocaust lies in the urge-to-be-free that lives in the hearts of a billion human beings behind the Communist curtains. Unless these peoples are able from within to force their Communist regimes to change and eventually to abandon Communist world objectives, there is little hope of our avoiding an ultimate all-out clash. Is it intelligent or realistic to adopt a foreign policy that can cause those millions behind the curtains to abandon hope? If the strong accept the Communist overlords, how long can the weak continue to resist them?

Gains and Losses. What would be the gains from resumption of trade relations? The Communists themselves have made clear on numerous occasions that their unwavering purposes in trade are:

First, to get military and industrial equipment and supplies which they cannot yet obtain within the Communist bloc — not in order that they can trade more with us in the future, but so that they can become self-sufficient and not need to trade with us at all.

Second, to take advantage of a favorable trade situation wherever there is one that they cannot match even by exploitation of their own people and of their satellites.

Third, to induce countries to become more and more dependent on trade with the Soviet bloc, and therefore more and more at its mercy. This applies particularly to Germany and Japan.

Fourth, to divide the free world powers.

Our objectives in trade are to improve the lives of people, to improve relations between the countries involved, to promote peace and prosperity in the world, and in the process earn a profit, much of which becomes capital for further expansion of production and trade with further improvement of living standards.

But none of these is or can be the objective of a Communist regime. All trade is conducted by Communist state organizations and monopolies that have as their single objective the strengthening of the State. They cannot trade under the accepted rules of the free world without ceasing to be Communist. They cannot cease to be Communist without their movement collapsing. Trade is as much a weapon of their expansionism as are missles. It is to be expanded or contracted, to be directed here or shifted there, as those at the top determine to be advantageous in promoting the Communist revolution.

This was dramatically illustrated some years ago when Japan established trade relations with Communist China. It soon found that Red China would not actually carry on trade unless Japan bowed to Red China's political wishes.

In 1953 when Pakistan appeared to be veering toward the U.S.A., Red China cut its purchases of Pakistan cotton from $84 million in 1952 to $7 million in one year.

Where trade between Communist China and other countries does exist, it is only on sufferance of the Communist government and will be extinguished when it has served its purpose. This has never been denied by the Chinese Communist leaders. On the contrary, they have avowed on numerous occasions that complete nationalization of industries and trade and collectivization of agriculture has to come, but in stages — which means just as fast as they feel themselves strong enough to impose it. Would it be in our interest, economic or otherwise, to help them do it faster?

Arguments Against Admission to the United Nations. What would be the result of admitting Communist China to the United Nations? I cannot see any important benefits for us or for the U.N., but the benefits for the Communists would be enormous.

Admission would represent for Red China the greatest possible diplomatic victory. It would give the Mao regime the stamp of legitimacy and add immeasurably to its prestige and power all over the world. Why has every communist government, party, and front in the world worked tirelessly for 15 years for Red China's admission if that would be bad for communism and good for us?

Some say, "But Communist China is a fact. We must be realistic. We cannot hide our heads in the sand and ignore it or pretend it is not there." But that is not a description of our policy. On the contrary, it is just because we recognize that Red China is indeed a fact, and such a powerful and dangerous fact, that intelligent concern for our own and the world's future requires its exclusion from the United Nations until it is willing to meet the qualifications for membership. To admit it prior to that time would only make it more powerful and more dangerous.

The Communist regime in China avowedly is dedicated to the isolation and destruction of the United States. Should Americans help it into a better position to work for that objective?

It is a complete *non sequitur* to say that because "Red China is there," therefore it ought to be admited to the U.N. There are gangsters in some of our cities. We do not argue that therefore the city councils, courts and police force should take the gangsters in. Rather we demand that lawless elements be kept *out* of the forces responsible for maintaining law and order, or "peace and security" — which the U.N. Charter states is the purpose for which that organization was established.

It is said that the 700 million Chinese are entitled to be represented in the U.N. Certainly! But the Peking regime does not represent the Chinese people any more than the Quisling regime in Norway represented the Norwegian people. Whenever the Chinese people have opportunity to choose their own representatives in free elections, these representatives will undoubtedly be admitted promptly to the United Nations. Incidentally, is it not strange that free elections are demanded in Vietnam "to determine the peoples' wishes," even during a cruel internal war, but are not demanded in mainland China?

To keep Red China isolated and weaker than it would otherwise be is not denying or ignoring its existence; it is the realistic way to deal with its existence.

It is said that the United Nations ought to be a universal organization with all existing governments in it. But the Charter makes perfectly clear that the U.N. was never intended to be a universal organization. That concept was discussed at San Francisco — and rejected. Why would the Charter have Article 6, providing for expelling "a member which has consistently violated the principles contained in the present Charter," if the organization was supposed to be universal?

Article 4 reads: "Membership in the United Nations is open to all other peace-loving nations which accept the obligations contained in the present charter, and in the judgment of the organization, are able and willing to carry out these obligations."

What obligations? Article 2 reads, in part, "All members shall settle their international disputes by peaceful means," and "All members shall refrain in their international relations from the threat or use of force against the territorial integrity or political independence of any state, or in any other matter inconsistent with the purposes of the United Nations."

For more than ten years we have been negotiating with the Chinese Communists, trying to get them, among other things, to honor their solemn commitment at Panmunjon to release all American prisoners of war captured in Korea. If they would fulfill this commitment, there would be some justification for going ahead with further agreements. They have adamantly refused either to release or to account for the prisoners we know they had.

We have tried to get them to accept the membership obligations prescribed in the U.N. Charter and agree to refrain from the threat or use of force in their relations with their neighbors. They would then be eligible for U.N. membership. But they have refused.

So it is grossly untrue that the United States is stubbornly, blindly, arbitrarily keeping Communist China out of the United Nations, as is sometimes claimed. Red China is stubbornly keeping itself out. It simply refuses to qualify. I don't know any university that will admit a student without his meeting its entrance requirements — even if he has a gun.

Some ask, "But what's the difference between Communist China and the Soviet Union? The Soviet Union doesn't refrain from the threat or use of force either. Look at the missiles it put into Cuba!" The answer is that the Soviet Union got into the United Nations at the time of its founding when it was pretending to be peace-loving and willing to cooperate for peace in international affairs. Red China does not even pretend. In fact, the essence of its quarrel with Moscow is over its unwavering insistence on the use of force.

It is said that if the United Nations is not to admit Communist China, then it ought to expel the Soviet Union. This is a good logical argument, but it is a useless one. The Soviet Union can veto its own expulsion.

If Communist China were to be admitted, it could not be expelled either, no matter what its conduct.

The fact that there are already some bad actors in the U.N. is all the more reason why we should not, knowingly, bring any more in.

Perhaps it might be useful to establish a new universal organization — a league of all existing governments, lawless as well as law-abiding. But the United Nations is not such an organization. Let us not destroy its character as a union of peace-loving states pooling their strength *against* lawlessness and aggression from whatever source.

It is hard to understand how some can advocate world peace through world law and at the same time advocate brazen violation of the nearest to world law that we have, the Charter of the United Nations. One would expect that those genuinely wanting to build respect for international law and order would advocate amending the Charter according to its own provisions, rather than cynical nullification of it.

If some members of an organization break its rules and standards, that is not fatal to the organization. But if the organization itself votes to scrap its own rules and standards in a vain effort to appease some lawless members, that is starting down the road to its own destruction. I do not want to see the United Nations destroyed by its own action, as was the League of Nations.

It is suggested that if we recognize Communist China and admit it to the United Nations, it might improve the functioning of that and related international organizations. There is far more evidence that it would hamper their functioning. The only time the United Nations has been able to operate as it was intended to on a matter as serious as aggression was in 1950 when the Soviet Union was absenting itself from the Security Council in an effort to pressure the United Nations into admission of Red China — and thus was unable to veto U.N. action against the Communist aggression in Korea. Moscow is not likely to make the mistake of being absent again.

It is clear that Communist governments do not join the United Nations with the same purpose in mind as we and other governments have, namely, help make it an effective instrument for resolving disputes. Obviously the Soviet Union joined in order to make sure the U.N. does *not* work effectively. It has a world organization of its own, the Communist Party, with organized, disciplined, efficient units in every country. The Communists intend to win for *their* world organization. What could be more advantageous than to have seats in the other world organization also, particularly in the Security Council, where perfectly legally under the Charter, they can keep the rival organization crippled and ineffective whenever they wish to. Almost all of the more than 100 Soviet vetoes have been against measures that were favored by the overwhelming majority of U.N. members and were in the direction of peace.

It is contended that it is necessary to have Communist China in the United Nations because no agreement on disarmament can be effective without its participation. But until there is some prospect of an agreement with the Soviet Union, which already has deliverable nuclear weapons, what point is there in including Red China, which most experts believe cannot have the capacity to deliver powerful nuclear weapons in a decade or more? If and when the day comes, and I hope and pray it may, that the Soviet Union will agree to effective disarmament proposals — which means with inspection — there will be some point in negotiating with Red China on this subject.

But it is not necessary to have Red China in the U.N. in order to negotiate with her, on this or any other matter. We have had over 130 negotiations with her in the last 11 years — almost one a month — and more than any other non-Communist government has had.

It has been said that the Chinese Communist regime should be accepted because the Chinese people under it are "better off" economically. Such is not the case, as compared with Chinese in Free China. But even if it were true, it would not prove the point. People were better off economically under Hitler than in any other nation in Europe. Did the groups who now urge acceptance of Red China advocate acceptance of Hitler on that ground?

Then there is the old diversionary argument, "What about Chiang

Kai-shek?" Well, what about him? History will decide his proper place and I predict it will be a high one. But our policy is not and has not been based on Chiang; if he were gone tomorrow, America's interests would be precisely the same. We are trying to help free peoples remain free; therefore, it is to our interest to support all peoples who will make determined efforts in that direction. The free Chinese on Taiwan certainly are making such efforts — and succeeding. They are now ahead of every other country in Asia except Japan. We were able to stop our economic assistance to Free China last July.

So if one examines the results of the proposed changes in American policy toward China, it is apparent that the benefits would be minimal, if any. The dangers to the countries still free in Asia, to the United Nations itself, and to our own security and peace, would be certain and serious indeed. On the other hand, the policy of keeping Red China contained and isolated has proved successful in promoting the vital security interests of the United States.

Men have always found ways to bring down tyrants — and the Chinese will bring down theirs — if only we are not beguiled into throwing the ball game away in the last quarter by failing to stand fast — "five minutes longer." We are called upon by history to prove that free citizens have greater fortitude, stronger nerves and steadier patience and faith than do tyrants — faith in man and faith in God.

Implementing Containment. So the key question for us is how best to keep Communist China contained until it fades or changes. What should we do to implement that basic policy in the period just ahead, and in the most crucial area of immediate contest — Vietnam?

1. We must recognize and state frankly that we are at war, however much it was unsought and unprovoked by us.

2. We must develop a national will to wage that war with greater vigor and skill by all the measures, economic and social as well as military, that are required of us by this enemy's new and different tactics. I will pass over a discussion of the measures most suitable for use in Vietnam. Professor George Taylor, I am sure, will deal with them most competently.

3. We must develop a greater unity in support of the total war effort and the heroic sacrifices being made in Vietnam by our own brave men and by valiant Vietnamese and other allies. It is unrealistic to ask or expect Vietnamese leaders to be more united in support of American policy than American leaders are. It is unreason-

able to expect greater stability on this matter in Saigon than there is on Capitol Hill in Washington.

Furthermore, we cannot expect our allies in Vietnam to sacrifice their lives just to improve the position of the United States for bargaining with their enemy, the Viet Cong. For us to negotiate with the Viet Cong, as has been suggested, would undermine and demoralize the government of South Vietnam as surely as negotiation with the Chinese Communists at Yenan in the 1944-46 period undermined the Chinese government in Chungking.

4. We must remember that the objective of a war is political, namely, to change the will of the adversary, killing as few people as possible. How are we likely to change the will of this adversary in Hanoi? Just by the constantly repeated assurances that we will not make him suffer, no matter what he does? The Administration has publicly stated repeatedly that we have "no desire for the overthrow of Hanoi or Peking." Is it any wonder that Ho Chi-minh has felt no need to negotiate? By going all-out in South Vietnam, perhaps he can win the struggle for Asia by humiliation of the United States. If he does not succeed, then he can go back to the 17th Parallel with no penalty to himself and his regime.

Surely the most effective way to change the will of the enemy is to make him know that his aggression, if continued, will become so costly and dangerous to his own position and power that it is to his advantage to call it off. It is troubles in North Vietnam, not killings in South Vietnam, that are likely to influence Hanoi.

To achieve this objective of changing the will of the enemy I would stress several *main* steps:

First, we must continue what we are doing militarily in South Vietnam — that is, we must *hold,* and then advance, cleaning out Vietcong and pacifying liberated areas.

Second, we must achieve economic, educational, health, and therefore, political improvements, even while fighting a cruel war with every village a potential battlefield. The people of Vietnam are no less important in this "people's war" than the military. Whenever it is shown to the rank and file that there is more for them to gain by supporting their government in Saigon assisted by the United States, more and more of them will support it. To stay in their villages and near their land, as they would like most of all to do, is becoming intolerable. They often are under Government forces during the day and under the Viet Cong at night, with both men and women now being drafted to fight or to carry loads for the Communists. If they go over to the Viet Cong, the latter simply do not have the resources to give the people better living conditions or any kind of security. This is the field in which we can run rings around the Communists more easily than in any other. Even in refugee camps, the people can have better food and medical care and hopes of some education for their children than they can under the Communists . . . Relieved from fear of Communist reprisals, the people can give the government the vitally important information they have about Communist bases, hideouts, and planned operations. This could start a tide that in shorter time than most now believe possible could force the Viet Cong to pull back from their present positions and induce thousands of them to give up.

General Edwin F. Black, whom I have known for several years as one of the most astute workers in this field and who has served two tours in Vietnam, has written, "The end to the peoples' war will come when the people make their choice."

A third essential step is to do our utmost to interdict supplies coming from or through North Vietnam. The one thing that seems unjustifiable is to ask an American or a Vietnamese soldier to risk his life for freedom, unless his government is doing everything it possibly can do to cut down the supply of men and weapons which enable the enemy to take his life. Whatever the risks here, they must be taken.

Fourth, we should openly let the South Vietnamese do what they can to make trouble in North Vietnam, as they have wanted all along to do. It would give an enormous boost to morale to let South Vietnam conduct even a small "liberation front" in North Vietnam, making it more difficult for North Vietnam to operate its fraudulent "liberation front" in South Vietnam.

Fifth, should we bomb cities in the North? Not as we did in Germany and Japan. But we should bomb war plants, power plants, oil tanks, whatever is important to North Vietnam's war. Why not openly announce to North Vietnam and the world a list of military targets that are going to be destroyed sometime in the next few weeks or months. Won't Ho Chi-minh please get his people out of those plants or away from those areas because we don't want to kill North Vietnamese people; we want only to reduce his capacity to kill South Vietnamese people and American and other allied forces. There would be criticism. But the cheers in our country and around the world for such action would make the jeers sound feeble by comparison.

Why haven't we done these things? Because an almost hysterical *fear* has been built up that, among other things, it might lead to war with Red China and "we must not get into a land war with Red China's masses."

Well, all things are possible; and there is no course without risks. But let us weigh realistically the small likelihood of such intervention against the absolutely certain dangers involved in going on as we are.

1. Red China would be justifying and inviting destruction by us of her nuclear facilities — her greatest trump in this world power struggle. There is nothing in South Vietnam that is a fraction as valuable to Red China as those nuclear facilities.

2. How would Red China supply "masses" of troops in South Vietnam? A Communist army, just like Napoleon's, moves on its stomach. The Communists are having all they can do to supply the Viet Minh and Viet Cong forces already in South Vietnam.

3. Red China cannot forget for a moment the presence on her own flank of powerful air and military forces on Taiwan. Most of mainland China's lines of communications run north and south and are within easy reach of air bases we have helped free Chinese build on that island for the very purpose they are now serving — a powerful deterrent to Red China's entering the war and getting itself too far extended to the south. Some 700,000 to a million Red Chinese are tied down opposite Taiwan, on guard against possible action from that base. Red China also has to keep large numbers of troops on the long border with India, the longer border with the Soviet Union, on the borders of Korea, and hundreds of thousands of soldiers are required to maintain order in Tibet, Mongolia and at home.

4. If Red China were to get involved in Southeast Asia, she would have to concentrate on it to a degree that would almost certainly make her lose her bitter struggle with the Soviet Union for control of the world Communist movement. That struggle is enormously more important to Red China than anything in Vietnam.

"Confrontation" and Escalation. Despite powerful considerations like the above, many in Washington seem almost paralyzed by two words — "confrontation" and "escalation." They assert, without evidence to support it, that a firm confrontation with Communist ag-

gression will lead to escalation into nuclear war — " and we must not have nuclear war!"

Just to say that, of course, makes more likely the nuclear war we want to avoid. It encourages the Communists to believe we will surrender rather than have nuclear war, and that therefore at the right moment they can cow us into submission by the threat of it. It may well be that the outcome of this world struggle will be determined by which side appears to be less afraid of nuclear war.

Let us, however, look not only at reasons like the above, but at the record:

Eleven times in the last 20 years under three administrations we have accepted a confrontation with Communist expansionism — this is the twelfth. Eleven times the United States has simply said, "No! This we cannot take." Did any one of those 11 confrontations lead to escalation, as was threatened by the Communists and feared by us? No, each led to de-escalation. Each led to improvement of the situation, not worsening. Each time the Communists said in effect: "So sorry. We just wanted to know." And there followed a lessening of tensions.

What has led to escalation? Not confrontations, but hesitation, indecision, division, vacillation, appearance of fear. From the standpoint of inviting or prolonging war, it is as dangerous to look like a paper tiger as to be one.

So I have no difficulty in deciding which is the wiser and safer course for the United States to follow with respect to Communist China. How foolish and shortsighted it would be to abandon the policy of patient firmness and strength in support of human freedom and of our commitments to friends and allies, the course which when consistently followed has brought peace, in order to make changes in policy which would inevitably weaken our friends and allies — the very advocacy of the changes has already shaken some of them — and would inevitably strengthen our enemies. Can we really believe that for us to prove to the Chinese Communists that their tough, unyielding belligerence gets results is the way to get them to abandon that belligerence?

Particularly would it be shortsighted and foolish to give such a smashing and unnecessary victory to Red China right now when it is in such trouble worldwide. Does it make sense to accept its representatives into our country and into the United Nations just when its representatives are being exposed and expelled from countries in

Africa, Latin America and Asia, countries that followed the very policies toward Red China we are now being urged to adopt?

Each year since 1954 it has been confidently predicted that Red China's admission was "inevitable," probably at the next session of the General Assembly, and many came to believe it. Well, a dozen years have gone by and it has not happened. Last year saw the high water mark of support. But in these very last months the tide has been turned against Red China by its own actions. Countries that voted for admission are having their eyes opened. This is no time for us to close ours.

Administrations change, but facts do not. And the facts with respect to Red China's lack of qualifications for membership in the U.N. remain the same under President Johnson as under Presidents Truman, Eisenhower and Kennedy.

May I quote three points stressed before the U.N. General Assembly by Ambassador Adlai Stevenson, who can hardly be called a blind reactionary?

Saying that "the whole future of the United Nations may be at stake," he urged the members to consider with great care the fact that "the step advocated [admission of Red China] once taken, is irreversible. We cannot try it and then give it up if it fails to work. We must assume that, once in our midst, the Peking representatives would stay — for better or worse.

"Secondly, there are ample grounds to suspect that a power given to such bitter words and ruthless actions as those of the Peking regime, far from being reformed in the United Nations, would be encouraged by its success in gaining admission to exert, all the more forcefully, by threats and maneuvers, a most disruptive and demoralizing influence on the organization at this critical moment in its history.

"Thirdly, its admission, in circumstances in which it continues to violate and defy the principles of the Charter, could seriously shake public confidence in the United Nations — I can assure you it would do so among the peoples of the United States — and this alone would significantly weaken the organization."

Illegality and Immorality. In summary, seating of Red China in the United Nations would be *illegal.* It would require violation of the organization's Charter.

It would be *immoral.* It would almost certainly mean removal of a member that abides by the Charter to seat a non-member that brazenly refuses to abide by the Charter. It would abandon 700 million people to Communist subjugation. It would properly be regarded as an attempt to buy peace for ourselves by sacrificing our principles and other peoples' freedom.

And it would bring *no practical benefits*. On the contrary, there would be certain and disastrous losses — with our allies; with the neutrals; with the peoples in Asia and everywhere else who desire to retain their freedom; and with the long-suffering millions now under communist rule who long to regain their freedom. Do not break the hearts of the oppressed and their continued will to resist from within by accepting their oppressors.

Free Asia will crumble once it believes the Communists are winning. Admission of Red China to the United Nations would mean to much of Asia, as it should mean to us, that the Communists have all but won.

Having spent more than $100 billion to strengthen the will and capacity of free nations and peoples to resist Communism, does it make sense now to strengthen Communism?

The whole Communist movement worldwide is in serious trouble today. Why change the policies that have contributed to its difficulties both external and internal, and thereby provided the free world its first ray of hope in years? We must always keep the door open to any genuine change on their part — as proved by deeds. We must keep the door resolutely closed to Communist threats, tricks, or promises not supported by performance.

This is the time to stand fast for the basic containment policies that have proved sound and more successful during the last 15 years than most people believed possible. There is no course that does not involve serious risks; we are dealing with a ruthless and resourceful enemy. But such a course as outlined involves, I believe, far less risks.

Until someone can suggest policies that offer better prospects of success, based on something more substantial than speculation, wishful thinking or just hope, I can see no sound, sensible or logical reason to change present policies and every reason to continue them, always being flexible in our tactics as required by developments as they come along. The true way to influence our enemies is to let them see that the United States stands steadfastly by its friends.

12

CONTAINING AGGRESSION

By George E. Taylor

I am honored by the opportunity to appear before the Senate
Foreign Relations Committee to discuss some aspects of U.S. relations
with Communist China. Since I speak as a member of the academic
profession, it might not be out of place for me to refer briefly to the
basis of all academic work, the availability of information and
materials.

The high quality of the testimony which has been heard by this
committee stems, in my view, from the fact that the United States
is better informed about Communist China today than is any other
country in the Free World. Our government provides daily transla-
tion of the Mainland press and periodicals for general use, it trans-
lates for its own purposes a great variety of specialized Chinese printed
material, some of which it puts at the disposal of scholars. There are
about a dozen major universities with libraries and staff sufficient
to provide the student with advanced graduate training on China.
Courses in the Chinese language can be taken at hundreds of universities and colleges. The financial support provided by private
foundations and by the National Defense Education Act has been
instrumental in providing us with hundreds of scholars well trained
in the Chinese language and one or more of the disciplines. Our
library holdings on China are very extensive and we probably publish more studies of Communist China than all other non-communist
countries put together. The combined resources of England, France
and Germany, both human and material, are small indeed when
compared with those of the United States.

The American scholar, it has been pointed out, cannot go to Communist China and therefore loses a valuable asset. This is true; the
Communists will not allow him. There is no substitute for being on
the ground, but in some cases there is no great advantage in being
there either. Most of the correspondents of other countries who have

resided in Peking are quite frank about the difficulties and frustrations facing the journalistic profession in that country. Hong Kong is a far more valuable source of information about Communist China than is Peking. Ironically enough, an American journalist, Edgar Snow, has written a comprehensive book on Communist China containing very unusual information because he had access to men in high positions and had written about the Communists before the war. So if going to Peking is of any advantage, the Americans have already taken as much advantage of it as any of those who have recognized Communist China. Japan does not recognize Communist China but as many Japanese have visited there, probably, as have citizens of the Soviet Union. Recognition is not necessary for scholars, journalists and politicians to visit a Communist country if the country so wishes.

The main difficulty of getting information about China stems not from the fact that Americans are not allowed to visit there, but from the extraordinary efforts made by the Communist regime to prevent both its own people and other peoples from knowing those things it wishes to conceal. I would not be surprised if Peking found our economic studies to be more accurate than their own. I wish to mention this point about information because there are those who feel that we would be much better informed if we recognized Communist China and could send our scholars and journalists to that country. Unless there were a radical change in the attitude of the Communist regime the evidence does not suggest, considering the price we would have to pay, either that access to the Mainland would make that much difference or that access depends upon recognition.

I am not suggesting that we have sufficient information about Communist China, merely that we [probably] have more than anyone else. In the academic profession, while we all read the same materials, we do not arrive at the same conclusions. I find myself in general agreement with the descriptive material presented in this testimony — that Communist China's domestic problems are serious and exacting, her military as well as economic resources are not those of a great power, her adventurous excursions in foreign policy have been costly and discouraging, and that she is not getting along very well with the Soviet Union in either party or state relations. But I cannot follow some of the policy recommendations of my colleagues because I think that they are based on debatable premises, and it is the premises that are crucial.

Brittle Stability. Much is made of the assumption that we have stabilized our relations with the Soviet Union and that the same can be done with Communist China. The Soviet model is so much taken for granted that it is never clearly defined. It is asserted that we now have a stable and tolerable relationship with the Soviet Union and that this has come about through an evolutionary process marked by changes within the Communist system. There certainly have been considerable changes and there is a sort of stability. But in my view the present stability is brittle in the extreme and is based mainly on the superior military power of the United States and its allies and on a common interest in avoiding one kind of war, and one only, nuclear conflict between the U.S. and the U.S.S.R. Moscow still favors subversion and "just" wars of national liberation. The balance can change because it does not rest merely on a counting of nuclear bombs. There are other factors in the balance such as the state of economy, the state of our alliances, the quality of our leadership. As we showed at the time of the Cuban crisis, a shift in the nuclear balance of power can be prevented by the use of conventional weapons. Nor can we fail to note that the present stability includes a war with the Soviet Union by proxy, in Vietnam, and Soviet cooperation with Cuba in an effort to subvert Latin America, whose governments are so alarmed by Cuban activities that many have broken off diplomatic relations.

Two sets of reasons are usually given for the new Soviet behavior. There are those who think that the stability of our relations with the Soviet Union is due to changes in the mode of production which have been reflected in changes in the ideological superstructure. They would phrase it differently but it is still vulgar Marxism. As the Communists put on fat, according to this theory, they acquire a democratic dislike for muscle. Such scholarly investigation as we have of this subject, to say nothing of the record, suggests that the question of whether or not there have been basic changes in the political objectives of the Soviet Union is still open to serious question.

Then there are those who think that present Soviet behavior arises from the fact that we followed a policy of containment combined with recognition and membership in the U.N. The same formula applied to China should produce the same results. It is proposed to continue the containment, offer recognition, and cease to block the way into the U.N. This is a doubtful analogy on which to base action. Nor is there any real parallel between Communist China and the U.S.S.R., or surety that the same techniques will bring the same results. But the U.S.S.R. could be used as an interesting case study of what happens when a communist party is treated with generosity and goodwill (as during World War II) and allowed to operate within an organization for the maintenance of peace.

In my view it is safer to proceed on the premise that there is no world community, as the phrase goes, into which we can induce the Chinese to enter. Unfortunately we live in a world in which there are at least two violently opposed concepts of international relations, of political and social organizations, and of world order. The dialogue between them is still minimal. Everything we do with Communist China has to be seen in this context. Whatever the relations between Peking and Moscow, as far as the world community is concerned, they share the same outlook. The problem then is one of how to define our relations with the Chinese section of the Communist world. It is clearly necessary, in this dangerous world, to do this.

Further to clarify my premises, I do not think, for example, that the evidence supports the fashionable view that the Communist world is falling apart and that Communist states have the same sort of foreign policy objectives as any other nation state or can be expected to pursue them in the same manner. The social and political content of nationalism is determined by the institutional power configuration and this is what is new and lasting about communism. It is because it is the nature of power that determines foreign policy — to put the matter very briefly — that I feel so little hope of any changes in Chinese Communist policies that are not forced on her. It is necessary to mention this because there is a great reluctance on the part of China specialists, perhaps because they love the Chinese so much, to admit that the Chinese Communists are really Communists.

The agrarian reformers of the 1940s are now the aging paranoids of the 1960s, to be handled, it would seem, by group therapy. If they were really nationalists masquerading as communists, then Chinese tradition as well as the humiliations of 19th century imperialism would be relevant to their mood, but in my view the Communists represent a complete break with the past. Their world view is not conditioned by the imperial past although they are willing to exploit it. A comparison with some real nationalists will point up the differences. It was the National Government that won the ending of imperial privileges in 1942 and lost the chance of building up a modern China largely as a result of the Japanese invasion. We might have difficulties with them if they were in power on the mainland, but I doubt they would be sponsoring the Viet Cong or fomenting trouble over the rest of the world. There is nothing about Chinese nationalism that calls for the hate campaign of the Chinese Communists against the United States, for the militarization of a quarter of the people of the earth, for the racial invective that pervades so much of their propaganda, even in Hong Kong, or for the support of revolutionary movements in Southeast Asia, Africa and Latin America spelled out in the Central Committee decisions of 1963 and reaffirmed in the Lin Piao statement. A true nationalism would call for attention to domestic problems and would certainly avoid a quarrel with a powerful neighbor.

Pragmatic American Policy. In conducting this very valuable review of our relations with China we have to reckon with a commonly held view that U.S. policy has been doctrinaire, rigid, uncompromising, emotional and unrealistic, even that it was manufactured not in the State Department but in the China lobby. An examination of the record shows that this is not very good history. American policy towards communist states in general and China in particular has been pragmatic and flexible. In this regard we may note the rapid adaptation to Tito in 1948, the opening of cultural exchange with the U.S.S.R., and our carefully graduated responses to East European satellites. With Communist China we were about ready for recognition when the Korean War broke out. More recently we have offered to discuss disarmament, negotiate a settlement of Southeast Asia, and permit Americans to travel to the mainland. In this connection I admire the temperate tone and placid reasoning of the position paper signed recently by some of my colleagues. It is good to have debate and to differ as honest men.

The policy problem is how to regulate our relations with Communist China in such a way as to provide for the peaceful and independent development of Southeast Asia and to secure her cooperation in the maintenance of world peace.

Containment and Isolation. Like most witnesses [before the Senate Foreign Relations Committee], I am strongly in favor of containing Chinese Communist aggression. We do not all agree on what we are containing; in fact one gets the impression that some witnesses think that there is almost nothing to contain. Most have referred to the most recent statement of Chinese Communist political goals, the Lin Piao position paper of September 1965, but it is variously interpreted. The Aesopian dialogue of the communist world is not always easy to follow and this effort was clearly designed to achieve several purposes at the same time. In my view it should be taken seriously as a general indication of the objectives and strategy of the Peking wing of the movement. It is not impossible that this strategy could be made to work. It is based on the assumption that the revolution is not going to occur in the great industrial states, that the Achilles heel of the West is the Third World, that the promotion of wars of national liberation in Africa, Latin America and Southeast Asia will distract and waste the energies of the Western powers, confuse their peoples and demoralize their leaders. Some believe that Communist China is too weak to carry out such a grandiose strategy, that in fact she is now reeling from shattering defeat. When the Soviets came to the assistance of the Chinese Nationalists in 1923 they were not a strong power, but they almost succeeded in taking over the Nationalist movement at a cost of 1,000 advisers and about $3 million. The Chinese Communists were not very strong when they provided the Viet Minh with the heavy weapons that made possible the conquest of Dienbienphu, nor when they intervened in North Korea, nor when they promoted a Communist attempt to take over Malaya in 1948. May I also suggest that the Chinese Communists were involved in the attempted *coup d'état* in Indonesia last October and that it came very close to succeeding? If it had succeeded it would have been followed by an intensification of the war against Malaya, Thailand would have been caught in a pincers, and our position in Vietnam would have been very precarious.

The main question that leaders and peoples of Southeast Asia are asking is *who is going to win?* Under the above conditions it would have seemed that the Chinese brand of Communism was in the ascendant; Lin Piao's statement would have looked like a curtain-raiser rather than noisy bragging or defensive defiance. China is obviously in no position to seek a head-on collision with the United States and is most unlikely to give us the opportunity to declare war on her, but she is quite capable of fostering wars of national liberation wherever opportunities are provided. We have chosen to assist in blocking one of these wars in South Vietnam, under the most unfavorable conditions for us that could have been selected. If we succeed there it will not stop the Chinese from aiding others to promote similar wars of national liberation; if we fail we do not necessarily lose the whole of Southeast Asia but it would be that much harder to defend.

How do we contain this sort of threat when the rich countries are getting richer and the poor, poorer; when population growth outstrips economic growth in most of the underdeveloped countries? Certainly not by denying its existence. In the Philippines, made to order for Mao's strategy, American help and advice was of decisive importance; in Malaya British forces and political programs preserved the country from a Chinese Communist takeover. India, Burma and Indonesia took care of the problem themselves and arrived at their own compromises. In Vietnam the Communists were not stopped until 1954 when they had half the country and the nationalist movement split into two opposed camps. In Japan the Communists are far from weak, but they were robbed of an agrarian base by land reform measures undertaken during the occupation. The answer is clearly to assist in building up viable states in the many parts of the world that might come under communist pressure, Chinese or Soviet. To do this is going to require not force backed by a political program, but a political program backed by force, the sort of program that was given some substance recently at Honolulu. It is best to start before massive force is required but if we come in late, as we have in Vietnam, then force is necessary to hold the line so that the real war — on the intellectual, economic and social fronts — can be won.

To bring stability and prosperity to the Third World requires a combination of tremendous human dedication, enormous technical and economic help, and far-reaching social and political changes. To disrupt the process takes comparatively small material resources when they are combined with a forceful and appealing program. Peking has such a program, expects reverses, and has persuaded several Communist parties in other nations that it has the right answer for the future shape of communist expansion.

Containment. How far should containment go? Clearly far enough to prevent the exploitation of wars of national liberation. What is the ultimate purpose? I have argued that it is naive to expect containment to reform a Communist country. We must obviously make it clear to Peking that we welcome and are always ready to accept any overtures directed towards improvement of relations. But the real problem is the future of the National Government of the Republic of China. We are the only great power involved in the Chinese civil war. But there are other civil wars in the world today which have been created or intensified by Communist action — two Germanies, Koreas, Mongolias, Vietnams — that are of equal if not greater urgency and magnitude. They also raise problems of representation. The difference is that one of the Chinas has a permanent seat on the Security Council and the other China has, in effect, been at war with the U.N. since 1950. If the civil conflict cannot be resolved, the problem of policy comes down to the question of what sort of international status we are willing to accord to the National Government and to the People's Democratic Republic. The U.S. will not allow the Communists to take Taiwan by force or assist the Nationalists in returning to the mainland unless we are at war with Peking, so the status quo is what we have to live with, as do the Koreans, Germans, Mongols and Vietnamese, to say nothing of the Irish.

Some day, some time, the international status of the two parts of China must correspond to the facts of power, but there is no hurry. At the present time there is no advantage to the United States in talking about recognition or admission to the U.N. and there are a great many disadvantages. Why help the Peking regime when it is in trouble? What conceivable interest do we have in assisting this regime to become a great power?

It is said that we should not isolate Peking. It is Peking that is trying to isolate us. Communist China is far from being isolated; she has diplomatic relations of a sort with about 40 countries and is trading with many she does not recognize, such as Japan and Canada. She is very much in the international community where it counts, in fact, much too much. The terms she has announced for taking a seat in the U.N. are so outrageous that they must have been designed to show her contempt for that organization. Her terms for accepting recognition are humiliating in the extreme, although she would be delighted to have us help her finish off the civil war by reducing or eliminating the international status of the National Government. If the Chinese Communists really want to live in peace with the world they are quite capable of making a move in that direction.

In the meantime, it should not be beyond the wit of man to devise ways and means of putting the burden of proof, as far as peaceful intentions are concerned, on the Peking regime, so long as nothing is done to damage American credit in Asia and our willingness to stand by our friends and our principles.

13

THE CHINA PROBLEM

By David Nelson Rowe

Why does this problem exist? The Korean War proved that Communist China was willing to fight the Free World in order to achieve Communist expansionist aims in Asia *vis-a-vis* Korea (Japan was the real objective and the most important one). The formula has been repeated in:

- Tibet — anti-India and Nehru.
- Laos — 250,000 Chinese Communist troops massed on the Laos frontier in 1961-62 to bring a settlement favorable to Communist China.
- Indian frontier — this involved an actual Sino-Indian war, with Communist Chinese troops fighting Indian troops.
- Communist Chinese support for North Vietnam aggression against South Vietnam. The Sino-Russian ploy: North Vietnam (the North Korea of this episode) is immune from destruction at the hands of the United States and its allies because of its joint Sino-Soviet backing. Communist China stands behind North Vietnam's aggression militarily, to prevent such military action against North Vietnam as is necessary to the attainment of our military objectives in and for South Vietnam. Thus, Communist China achieves for North Vietnam immunity from the consequences of its aggression in South Vietnam which the previous Sino-Soviet techniques and strategies of support for North Korea failed to achieve, and this without any cost thus far in Communist Chinese manpower.

Thus, Sino-Soviet "indirect" aggression in South Vietnam depends upon their joint success in preventing the United States from taking military action against North Vietnam adequate to achieve the defense of South Vietnamese independence.

The chief Sino-Soviet weapon in this psychological warfare struggle is the threat of massive Chinese manpower intervening as "peoples volunteers" in the Vietnamese war.

How did we deal with this threat and fact in the Korean War? By making no direct attacks on the Chinese Communist home base and by application of massive firepower to Communist Chinese mass attacks in Korea, resulting in such heavy Communist Chinese casualities as to make them insupportable indefinitely. This led to truce talks of great length, so long that most United States casualties were incurred during the truce talk period.

The difference this time is that we have publicly announced that never again would there be a privileged sanctuary in Communist China in case we got into another war directly with Communist Chinese military forces under whatever guise and in whatever circumstances. Thus, the risk to the Communist Chinese regime is incalculably greater this time than in the case of Korea, albeit the current actual costs to them are negligible. This pattern fits the current picture of China perfectly:

• Internal economic crises prevent Communist China's incurring real costs, particularly in manpower (for political reasons).

• Lack of logistical support to Communist China from the Soviet Union means poverty of Chinese Communist military means. All material from the Soviets in the Korean war was purchased by Communist China in exchange for food and agricultural raw materials sent to the Soviet Union.

• The internal crisis in Communist China demands external action, for internal mobilization, diversion of attention, and internal political and military and economic pay-off with the victory that is confidently counted upon for the Communist forces in Vietnam.

To mitigate the risks of Communist China's Southeast Asia policy today is the aim of all true friends of Communist China in the U.S. today. Many others aid and abet this aim for a variety of reasons. Thus, almost immediately after the Johnson policy of heavy, direct United States military involvement in the Vietnamese war was initiated, the friends of Communist China began to emerge from the relative obscurity into which they had been forced by the Communist Chinese attack on us in Korea and to start openly supporting Communist China again and attacking the United States' Far Eastern policy at the same time.

These movements, so patently anti-anti-Communist, seem to have forced the Administration to speak as though Communism by and large was not involved in the Vietnamese war, thus robbing us of one of the chief psychological supports and chief political bases of the war in Vietnam and the whole war against Communist aggression everywhere. This is clearly seen in President Johnson's Baltimore speech (see my analysis in the *Congressional Record*) and even more so in his recent speech at Freedom House, New York, where he uses "Red" and "Communists" just once each in the whole speech, thus playing down Communism as an issue in the Vietnam war.

By contrast, on January 12, 1966, the Ambassador from Vietnam to the United States, in a speech of only about 1,000 words (about one-fifth as long as that of President Johnson cited above), used the term "Communist" nine times, for a frequency thus 22 times greater than that of President Johnson. This is a useful index of the importance of the Communist issue in the Vietnamese war to the government and people of South Vietnam. The purpose of the anti-anti-Communists is clear, namely to try to show that the war in Vietnam has no valid ideological basis and thus to depict it as naked United States aggression without any justifications. Who sold President Johnson the line of deemphasizing Communism as an issue in the Vietnamese war?

Paralleling these movements are the hearings in the Senate which seem to aim at two main effects:

• To align selected civilian propagandists uniformly against the main lines of United States foreign policy in Asia and then to bring to rebut them the main Administration figures such as the Secretary of State and Secretary of Defense (much of whose testimony has to be classified). This show then goes on radio and TV (highly edited toward the left). The whole effect is to depict public "experts" as at odds with the Administration. This not only persuades the Communists in Hanoi, Peking and Moscow of divisions of opinion in the United States that do not exist in fact, it also seems to drive the Administration toward public positions on Communist China that contradict its public position that the war in Vietnam could soon be ended if only Communist Chinese attitudes and measures would change. It also seems to lead members of the Administration to start softening its policy of resistance to Communist China by talking "containment without isolation" and to that extent undercutting its own experts such as Secretary of State Rusk Rusk and Assistant Secretary for Far Eastern Affairs William Bundy.

• To have a main effect of softening our resistance to Communist

China. Senator Fulbright himself stated that the main aim of his hearing on China was a political aim, namely to prevent a war with Communist China.

In fact, the prevention of a military showdown now between the United States and Communist China is the main aim of Communists everywhere. Why?

If such a showdown came soon it would destroy Communist China as such and constitute the single most catastrophic setback in history to the course of the Communist world revolution. In the course of such an event, however, the Soviet Union would assuredly grab both Manchuria and Sinkiang in order to have those Chinese areas available as bases to start over again the job of communizing East Asia. But the rest of China could be saved, without doubt.

If such a showdown can be prevented for five to ten more years, the pro-Communist China and anti-anti-Communist elements in this country count on the development of Communist Chinese thermonuclear power to produce a standoff and make Communist China then invulnerable to United States destruction by means of the retaliatory threat. They count on this stage lasting ten to twenty years during which either one and probably both of two things would happen:

• The United States would prove unable to develop any effective deterrent to so-called "indirect aggression" and "peoples wars" with the result that all of Asia would come under Chinese Communist domination and control and the impact on Africa and Latin America would be disastrous.

• Under the deterrent of terror, the political and psychological pressures toward a "detente" with Communist China similar to present illusions along that line with the Soviet Union, would engender a thorough and complete "co-existence" policy vis-a-vis the Communist Chinese.

The Communist Chinese need "co-existence" much worse than do the Russians. Why? The lack of massive external support and their huge and insoluble internal problems doom them forever to weakness and mediocrity and complete totalitarianism and military adventurism. They are trying their hardest now to soften our approach to them under the blackmail of aggression and war to gain *at no cost to them politically* what they need in outside economic and technical support from the West and particularly from the U.S. This is why their friends in the United States are trying so hard to soften the American approach to Communist China.

What are the main themes now being pushed by the pro-Communist China and anti-anti-Communist elements along this line?

The historical causation line. The Communist Chinese foreign policies are merely a logical result of China's frustrations and suffering at the hands of the outside world for the last century or more:

Question: Why are these frustrations and hostile reactions focused on the U.S., the one nation with the longest and best record of pro-Chinese aims and actions for 125 years? Answer: Because our past pro-Chinese policy and our present anti-Chinese Communist policies are identical. Both involve (as with our war against Japan, 1941-45) the defense of the territorial integrity and sovereignty of small and/or weak countries in Asia. The Chinese Communists today are the chief declared opponents of this policy of ours, as Japan was previously.

Question: In this framework, why should anyone react emotionally to the word "Munich" when it is used similarly to evoke a hostile reaction to any sell-out of our friends in Southeast Asia. (Was a surrender to Fascism appeasement and surrender; a surrender to Communism neither?) Answer: Is this reaction hypocritical, merely naive, or knowingly wrong-headed?

The "inevitable softening of the Communist Chinese." This line is pushed hard by all the pro-Communist China and anti-anti-Communist elements. Even Fidel Castro gives them aid and comfort by blasting the current Chinese Communist leaders as "senile" and anticipating a less dangerous Communist Chinese leadership to come with the demise of Mao.

Question: Was Khrushchev better than Stalin, and is the present leadership of the Soviet Union better than Khrushchev? Answer: No.

The "two-Chinas line." This is tantamount to saying we can play with enemies without alienating friends. Whatever the distant future holds we cannot know. But for the responsible policy-making future there can be no two-Chinas policy for the United States or anyone else. For example, the United Kingdom has tried to adopt a two-Chinas policy: recognition of Peking and trying to do business with Taipei. Result: it has neither China. The Communist Chinese have never entered full diplomatic relations with the United Kingdom, and the United Kingdom cannot really cooperate with the Republic of

China on Taiwan, the single most rapidly advancing and developing area in Asia. By contrast the United States, without recognition of Peking, has much higher level diplomatic contacts with the Chinese Communists than Britain, and is the main ally and collaborator with the Republic of China on Taiwan.

Question: Should anyone believe there can be any formal United States - Communist China diplomatic relationship without United States' abandonment of the Republic of China? Answer: No.

Question: Can any United States Administration advocate abandonment of the Republic of China without committing political suicide? Answer: This is what two-Chinas policy advocates really are urging the Administration toward, some knowingly and others unwittingly; *i.e.*, the two-Chinas policy means, to start, full diplomatic and other relations with Communist China and, with a trend toward this once set in motion, we can more easily abandon the Republic of China on Taiwan, particularly since it would break relations with us if we recognized Communist China.

The "they don't mean what they say" line. Anyone who believes in drawing the lessons of history should not object if we say the world would have been better off if more people had taken seriously such historical documents as the Marxist Manifesto, Hitler's *Mein Kampf,* or the pre-World War II utterances of the Japanese imperialists. The current utterances of the Communist Chinese leadership seem just as dangerously unrealistic today as the previously cited ones did then. They are therefore hard to give credence to. They are, in fact, filled with nonsense, but then of course so too was *Mein Kampf!* But this is merely to say that all madmen are dangerous, to a great extent precisely because they are *mad.*

For example, in the same March 19, 1966, issue of the *New York Times* in which witnesses before the Fulbright Committee were quoted as describing Communist China as being "fundamentally weak" and "inward-looking" and "desirous of avoiding a military confrontation with the United States," the *Times* carried (on the last page in the upper right-hand corner) a statement by Kuo Mo-jo, Vice Chairman of the Standing Committee of the National Peoples Congress, as follows: "Listen, U.S. imperialists! The 650 million people of China are prepared. If you insist on another trial of strength, suit yourselves. Come whenever you like, alone or with others. We will not shut you out; we will wipe you out, as many as you come."

Question: When men talk madness (as the Communist Chinese

do) would it not be wise to assume they mean it until and unless they prove otherwise by their acts? Yes. Are the Communist Chinese proving otherwise by their acts? No. They do just the opposite. Witness: Korea, the Taiwan Straits, the Indian frontier, Laos and Thailand, as well as Vietnam.

The "simultaneous hard and soft" line; "containment but not isolation." The friends of Communist China and the anti-anti-Communists are constantly describing our post-World War II policy toward the Soviet Union as combining these two features and advocating that we adopt such a policy toward Communist China.

What is the truth?

Our immediate postwar policy toward the Soviet Union was not one of containment, but of surrender. Eastern Europe and Outer Mongolia were surrendered to the Soviets with the connivance of the U.S. and even with highest pressures being brought to bear by the United States on our allies to surrender to the Soviet Union land grabs, as in the case of Nationalist China and of Mongolia. This was an effort to appease Stalin and get him to accept this as his price for cooperating with us. He took the price, but did not cooperate.

The containment policy was then resorted to and it has prevented further territorial takeover. However, this whole policy is now threatened by French action regarding NATO, and the chief deterrent to armed action by the Soviet Union in Europe is now the mutual thermonuclear threat.

Accordingly, we have generally not applied the policy of surrender of territory to Communist China, and in every case but one, have resisted Communist Chinese efforts to push outward. This case was Laos in 1961-62, and much of our trouble in Vietnam stems from the application to Laos of the formula of appeasement and surrender through the device we tried to use in China (1946-47) to prevent a Communist Chinese takeover pure and simple; *i.e.*, the coalition government with Communists in it. Sino-Soviet cooperation helped bring about the surrender in Laos and thus to mark out South Vietnam and Thailand as the next Communist targets.

As far as Communist China is concerned, containment means isolation; the two are one and inseparable and the crux of this problem is Taiwan. The Communist Chinese price for non-isolation (which is a two-sided matter, not solely under our control) is the handing over of Taiwan to them, *i.e., destruction of containment. Any United States*

Administration which would even suggest any such thing would commit political suicide by producing a major catastrophe in Asian affairs.

Question: Do those who suggest the ending of Communist China's isolation in relation to the U.S., the United Nations, etc., know what they are saying? Are they merely stupid? Or hypocritical? Or are they trying to be "smart"?

The line "we have no support among our allies" for our Southeast Asia policy. This line was, for example, advanced in relation to the Japanese by that great authority (?) on Japanese affairs, Mr. George Kennan. Mr. Kennan today seems to know even less about Far Eastern affairs than he did 17 years ago when I asked him what Asia would mean in our future struggle with communism. He replied then that the struggle with Communism would be settled somewhere along a line drawn between Stettin in the north and Trieste in the south. Of course, since then we have had Greece and Turkey in Europe; Korea, the Taiwan Straits and the 17th parallel in Vietnam, not to mention Laos and the Indian frontier, in Asia.

But today Mr. Kennan is our latest "Johnny-come-lately" on Japan. He resembles his colleague as a Soviet specialist, Ambassador "Chip" Bohlen, who in 1958 while U.S. Ambassador in the Philippines, assured me personally that the U.S. would not support the Republic of China in its defense of the offshore islands against the then current Chinese Communist attack. I told him we would, and we did.

Mr. Kennan now says we are seriously alienating our Japanese friends by our military actions in Vietnam. He thus shows his profound ignorance of the Japanese people, who suffer as we do ourselves in this country, from the presence of a lunatic fringe of cowards, pacifists, appeasers and just plain simple Communists and pro-Communists. In spite of this they basically understand and respect what we are doing in Vietnam. They know their own security depends upon us, and our resolution and will to suffer and die for what we believe in. Despite their "lunatic fringe" problem, the Japanese people are sound and sensible. They understand the need of armed defense. Their own small "self-defense" forces are slowly, but steadily, growing in strength and improving. Even business firms today are sending their new employees for short periods of living and working with the armed forces before starting work in order to bolster their morale and acquaint them again with the spirit of disciplined organization so lacking in upper-level educational institutions today both there and elsewhere. They increasingly support their defense arrangements with us, and this is because of, not in spite of, the war in Vietnam. In the past two years, the number of Japanese who support their alignment with the West has increased materially, and the number advocating so-called neutralism has decreased. This "new mood" is the result, I believe, of our firmness in Southeast Asia, an area vital to Japan from an economic point of view.

The Japanese people will respect and honor success on our part in Vietnam. Like others, they view with apprehension any irresolution, lack of determination or willingness to pull out and surrender on our part. This is generally true of all Asians, from Japan clear around through Korea, Taiwan, the Philippines, Southeast Asia and South Asia. This is one of many reasons why we cannot and must not fail in Vietnam.

Other friends and allies, including Korea, the Republic of China, the Philippines, Australia and New Zealand are all helping in various ways in Vietnam, and will doubtless help still more in the future. If and when the need arises, the arrangements have no doubt already been worked out for the Republic of China on Taiwan to become directly involved. But whether this will be required only time can tell.

As to allies and friends in Europe and elsewhere, the vast preponderance of them approve what we are doing whether they say so or not. Secretary Rusk is right on this.

The line "if we can get to know enough about China and the Chinese people we can promote better relationships with the Chinese Communists." This is the opposite of the truth. Actually, the more we study Chinese history and culture the more we can see that the Chinese Communists are reversionists who have chosen to re-emphasize the worst that can be found in the Chinese tradition instead of the best. What are some of these things? Totalitarianism, authoritarianism and autocracy, conspiratorial politics, dogmatic subjectivity, the perversion of education into sheer indoctrination, the exaltation of political dogma and the corresponding debasement of technology, true science and scientific expertise. They have chosen these emphases, and allied them with the religious subjectivism of Marxism, which appeals to them because it demands so little in the way of abandonment of those reprehensible features of the Chinese tradition that they have seized upon in their fanatical desperation and urgency to change China and the Chinese overnight. This latter characteristic they assert over and over again in such terms as "The Great Leap Forward," "Socialism Within Five Years," "Do Twenty Years Work in Two," etc., etc.

Such hopeless and futile experiments at doing something with nothing (as the backyard steel furnace debacle) are also illustrative of this trend, as well as of the subjectivist dogmatism of the upper level Chinese Communist leadership. No wonder the Chinese intellectuals reacted in such a hostile way to this leadership in the brief interval of the so-called "Hundred Flowers" episode when they were encouraged to express their opinions, only to be ruthlessly suppressed by Mao Tse-tung when he realized the truth, namely that they were not for him but against him. With true subjective self-deception he had convinced himself that the intellectuals were on his side! But they were not, and are not today. In the last two years 160,000 intellectuals have been seized by the regime and forced into so-called "reform through labor" camps. This means for most of them merely slow death by overwork and starvation. This has gone virtually unnoticed in the West, at a time when even some European Communists are openly rebelling at the recent arrest, "trial" and condemnation to forced labor of only *two* Soviet intellectuals!

Indeed the notion that to know the Chinese Communists better will make it easier for us to tolerate them is no more true than if we were to say that to know Italy better would make it easier for us to tolerate the Mafia. The fact is we already know enough about both the Mafia and the Chinese Communists to know one thing, and that is that we do not need to know any more in order to justify our policies of opposition and hostility. Of course we can always use more knowledge on what can be described as a tactical level, such, for example, as is being supplied by U-2 overflights from Taiwan. But we are not likely to learn much from proposals to allow our scholars and students of China to visit Communist China, and for two reasons: (1) The Chinese Communists are not going to allow anyone to come there unless they are convinced that he is a dependable friend of Communism and of Chinese Communism, in particular. They have been following this policy for years. (2) Under these circumstances what knowledge is brought back is likely to be either superficial or biased along pro-Chinese Communist lines.

Even in the Soviet Union, as my colleague Professor Barghoorn could no doubt testify, efforts at objective fact-gathering by foreign scholars are not without their risks! The hazards to life involved in even minor contacts with the utterly incompatible are clear from the recent death of an innocent American traveler while in the hands of the Russians. The subsequent warnings to such potential travelers by the State Department were well deserved.

The campaign, along the lines analyzed above, is being carried out in this country at a pitch of intensity unmatched in recent propaganda history. The so-called "teach-in," more extensively used in the earlier phases of the anti-Vietnam war campaign, has not been emphasized in this one. Instead, full-blown new organizations have been established on a nationwide basis, including "Americans for a Review of Far Eastern Policy" (ARFEP). This organization was started on the Yale campus by a group of students and faculty members. It has been spread across the country from there by a well-manned organization of promoters and organizers. Recently a large advertisement advancing its views appeared, for example, in a San Francisco newspaper, as emanating from the "Northern California Chapter" of ARFEP.

Certain features of this organization appear very clearly. For example, what they mean by a "review" of our Far Eastern policy usually turns out to be nothing but propaganda in favor of Communist China in the shape of support for its admission to the United Nations, United States recognition of the Red regime, full United States relations in trade, cultural relations, etc., well calculated to advance the aims, purposes and interests of Communist China. This propaganda also, at times, is heavily in derogation of our ally, the Republic of China, President and Madame Chiang Kai-shek, etc.

Secondly, the main centers of organization and the main personnel involved are the colleges and universities. I do not know how many ARFEP centers and branches there are, or how many persons have "signed up" or are otherwise formally or informally affiliated with them. Nor can we fully know at present just what activities they engage in. The following is a no doubt incomplete list of activities: signing petitions and placing advertisements in newspapers; holding small and unadvertised "seminars" conducted by faculty members on China and China policy; sponsoring open debates on China policy questions, with both sides represented (a minor feature); conducting what amounts to a speaker's bureau to supply speakers from one campus to another.

What we do not know is the extent to which ARFEP is behind the second main feature of the current campaign, that is the current rash of conferences on various aspects of China and United States policy toward Communist China being held on college and university campuses from coast to coast.

For example, in Portland, Oregon, two such conferences, involving a number of educational institutions on a cooperating basis, are being held within a month of each other this spring. At these and other such meetings, speakers are brought in from long distances for substantial honoraria plus travel costs, necessitating very substantial budgets in the amount of thousands of dollars. Where does this money come from?

At a "National Conference on the United Nations and China" to be held next month at the University of Pennsylvania, the fee and travel cost paid to one speaker alone will approximate $1,000. At this conference, where they hope for a maximum of 800 registrants, a $10 registration fee is being assessed toward expenses. But it is doubtful that the cost of the conference can be met in this way. Where will the balance come from?

It should be noted that at the University of Pennsylvania conference not one single academic expert on China will be present to speak on the program in favor of the official United States policy toward Communist China. This defense is relegated to official representatives of the United States Government and of the Republic of China. This repeats the pattern so clearly seen elsewhere of putting up as academic "experts" on China only those in opposition to the official policy, and "balancing" them with "official spokesmen" who can be discounted in advance as such. Thus the false impression is created that the "public," represented by the academic experts, is uniformly opposed to the policy of our Government at this time. This is false, and utterly false.

At a conference at Harvard under the auspices of the Collegiate Council for the United Nations on March 25-27, Professor Owen Lattimore of Institute of Pacific Relations fame was scheduled to speak on "The Chinese Revolution: Causes and Consequences."

Also, from an organizational point of view, new and political uses are now being made of an organization that predictably would be used for pro-Chinese Communist purposes if and when the time came to do so. This is the Association of Asian Studies. When I say its current political uses were predictable, I mean just that. I refer you to my statement on this organization made in testimony under oath before the Internal Security Subcommittee of the Senate Committee on the Judiciary on March 27, 1952 (pp. 4010-4013). I referred then to the Far Eastern Association, which is now the Association of Asian Studies, and I characterized it as designed, at least in part, to take over the political propaganda functions of the Institute of Pacific Relations in case the latter institution came to grief, as I believe it subsequently did, over questions of the pro-Communist bias of its activities.

Well, my prophecy on this matter in 1952 has taken almost exactly 14 years to prove out, but prove out it has. We now see (on March 21, 1966) that "all the signers" of a pro-Chinese Communist position paper published on that date in the *New York Times* are from among the about 2,700 member of the Association of Asian Studies. Of these 2,700 persons, 198, labeled (in many cases incorrectly) by the *Times* as "China experts," signed the statement which now places the Association of Asian Studies squarely in the policy-making arena. Of the total membership of 2,700, some 300, *i.e.*, about one-ninth, "responded to the paper" signed eventually by 198 of them, *i.e.*, about 7.3 percent of the total membership. To the views of this small minority of the total membership, the *New York Times* of March 21, 1966, devoted a full column on its front page and nearly an entire inner page (p. 12)! In an editorial on March 23, 1966, the *Times* stated that "this shows where the weight of informed American opinion lies." This is at the very least a gross distortion of the meaning of the statistics. Such are the distortions of propagandistic journalism.

The least the *Times* could do would be to give equal weight and coverage to the some 330 signers, as of January 1966, of the "Declaration in Opposition to Any Concessions to Communist China" sponsored by The Committee of One Million (not 2,700) Against the Admission of Communist China to the United Nations. I say this in view of the fact that all of those 330 signers are Senators or Representatives in Congress, representing I do not know how many millions of American voters! But the *Times* would not even print a letter submitted to it in February 1966 by two U.S. Senators in opposition to a *Times* editorial on the subject of China and the United Nations. The two Senators wrote as members of the Steering Committee of the Committee of One Million, which no doubt accounts for the failure of the *Times* to print it.

What the *Times* will print is well exemplified by the letter in its columns for March 18, 1966, by Professor Vera M. Dean of New York University. In this letter the lady professor, while expressing her views on various policy matters, also expresses her hopes. Among these, as she puts it, is that the "ghosts," as she describes them, of "Senator McCarthy and the Committee of One Million on China" should be "exorcised," and that former "China experts" who she says were driven from the State Department by "McCarthyism" should be sought out to advise the President and Secretary Rusk. Leaving this latter point aside, the lady professor should be informed that before she can exorcise the "ghost" of the Committee of One Million it will have to die and produce such a ghost. Far from dying, the Committee is very much alive today, and shows no signs of dying. All reports to the contrary are highly premature, to say the least. As time goes on I am sure the Committee will do everything in its power to continue its efforts by all means at its disposal. It should see to it that Professor Dean is aware of these efforts. Or is she merely whistling to keep up her courage?

In this situation and from this background, in what policy area should our best and strongest efforts be made to counter the current attempts to support Communist China and its program for Asia and the world? We are talking here, of course, of United States policy alternatives.

I do not believe the matter of possible United States recognition, trade and cultural relations, etc., is central. It is quite doubtful that, under current circumstances, any adminstration in Washington would move toward such policies. More real is the danger that we will succumb to the folly of supinely accepting the supposed "inevitability" theory, and submit to the admission of Communist China to the United Nations. In fact, so central do I believe this whole question to be to the problem of "standing up to Communist China's grandiose demands" in world affairs, as Professor John Fairbank puts it, that I believe here is where major emphasis should lie in respect to China policy today. Therefore, I propose to devote a considerable part of my presentation to analyzing the problem of Chinese representation in the United Nations.

Let us see why the Chinese Communists should not be admitted to the United Nations. First, let us sketch in the background of the problem.

What was the origin of the United Nations? The United Nations originated as an association of victors in World War II. It excluded the soon-to-be-defeated powers, Germany, Italy and Japan. In its very origins it was thus exclusive, not universal. The essential feature was the wartime association of the wartime allies, the "United Nations," and the community of interests that that alliance embodied.

The United Nations: what for? The United Nations was founded in the hope for peace and the search for it. The functional approach was adopted, *i.e.*, cooperation wherever possible, in whatever measures possible. Measures were to be taken for common and mutual security. The problem of expanding the United Nations membership arose at the United Nations Conference of 1945. Exhaustive debate at San Francisco in 1945 produced the decision that the organization should not be based on universality of membership, but there should be qualifications for membership. In the Charter these are: (a) Only peace-loving nations are eligible. It may be difficult to define and determine what is meant by a peace-loving nation, but it is not hard at any given time to determine what nations are breakers and disturbers of the peace. (b) Only those nations are eligible for membership that are willing to assume and live up to the obligations of the Charter. (c) Members who violate the Charter may be expelled.

This opened the way for the defeated nations in World War II to enter, if and when they qualified, and also for new states to enter. But the United Nations, unlike the League of Nations, has never expelled a member, although a member has voluntarily withdrawn.

The United Nations: how has it done? It has been almost swamped by the worldwide results of the breakup of the wartime alliance and the worldwide contests between the U.S. and the Soviet Union, the Free World countries (divided as they may be) and the Communist countries (divided as they may be). Its whole future has been put into the balance by a gross increase of its membership drawn largely from nations newly emerged as independent and many of which are themselves caught up in internal and international problems threatening constantly their very existence. Having (many of them) recently emerged from colonialism, they are now, willy-nilly, dragged into the worldwide contest between Communism and freedom.

Korea after 1945 is a perfect case in point. Emerging after the defeat of Japan from 35 years of Japanese colonialism, it was divided between the U.S. and the Soviet Union for post-surrender administration. The United Nations tried to unify it by peaceful means, but the Soviet Union thwarted this at every point. The Russians tried to unify it by indirect war in 1950, but U.N. forces thwarted this. Then the U.N. tried to unify it by war, but Communist China thwarted this and was branded by the United Nations as an aggressor for its armed

invasion of Korea. This act by Communist China firmly and irrevo-
cably established that regime as a full-time, highly activated part of
the Communist side of the worldwide struggle between the Free World
and the Communist countries.

How did the United Nations representation issue on China arise,
and why does it exist? The Republic of China was a founding member
of the United Nations in 1945. On November 18, 1949, shortly after
Communist China set up a new regime on the mainland, Communist
China notified the United Nations that the Republic of China's delegation to the U.N. was illegal. The United States upheld the right
of the Republic of China to continue to represent China. The Soviet
Union supported Communist China. The basis of the United States
position was not Communist China's Communism *per se,* but its lack
of qualification. But can these be separated? On January 13, 1950,
the Security Council voted 3 to 6 against Communist China's claim
to represent China at the United Nations. Norway and the United
Kingdom abstained, the United Kingdom on the basis that action
should be deferred until the majority of the United Nations recognized Communist China. On March 9, 1950, Secretary General
Trygvie Lie issued a memorandum on this, saying that representation
and recognition should not be linked in the United Nations. He stated
that representation should be based on a United Nations determination of which government is in the position to carry out the obligations
of the United Nations Charter, to exercise effective authority and
to employ the resources of the state.

On November 6, 1950, Communist China's forces invaded Korea,
thus forcing the United Nations to brand Communist China "guilty
of aggression in Korea" and disqualifying Communist China by Secretary Lie's criteria, for United Nations membership. Since then the
China representation question has arisen frequently, but Communist
China never secured approval for U.N. membership.

What are the main elements of the United Nations situation in
regard to this issue? (a) Growth of the functions of the General Assembly, due to multiple impasses in the Security Council. The Assembly tends to argue the case, but the Security Council authority in
this matter is still present and available on the basis of the 1950
precedent. (b) A large increase in Assembly memberships has taken
place. This has produced a struggle to secure the votes of African
nations, for example. (c) The "important question" issue. Is the

question of China's representation an "important question" at the
United Nations? It has several times been decided to be.

What are the issues today? Communist China's record as to aggression. This is overwhelmingly relevant to the question of its accepting
the "obligations of the Charter." This is not just a matter of Korea.
In February 1950, five months after the Chinese Communists established their regime, it began its aggressive course. This was predictable: Mao says every good thing comes out of the barrel of a gun.
In February 1950 the Chinese Communists issued a call to all people
of Southeast Asia to overthrow their governments. Was this merely
a move against colonialism? No. It called for revolution against
independent governments also. Then there came the Chinese Communist 1950 Korean aggression and the United Nations resolution
(still outstanding) which branded Communist China as an aggressor.
The Chinese Communist philosophy is: "Ours is a policy of fight-fight,
stop-stop, half-fight, half-stop. This is no trick, but a normal thing."
This is a philosophy of alternating war and subversion. This was
followed by direct Chinese Communist aggression in Southeast Asia
(Laos and Thailand), India, and indirect aggression in Vietnam.

In view of this, in order to admit Communist China to the United
Nations, the United Nations Charter would have to be changed and
the relevant qualifications for membership removed. The Communist
Chinese know this and themselves say the Charter must be revised as
a prerequisite for their accepting a seat there.

Communist China's position on this and the United Nations is as
follows: (1) "All countries should review the United Nations Charter
together." All "independent countries" should then be admitted and
all "imperialist puppet states should be driven out." It wants to
expel some members even before its own admission. Clearly the
Chinese Communists neither want nor plan either universality or "co-
existence." (2) They openly state what kinds of changes would have
to take place in the United Nations:

• As a prerequisite to Communist China's accepting a seat, the
United Nations would have to openly declare that the United Nations
resolution condemning Communist China for aggression in the Korean
war was "wrong," and brand the United States as the aggressor in
Korea. As Chinese Communist "Foreign Minister" Chen Yi said on
September 29, 1965: "Calling China an aggressor and then asking the
aggressor to join, would not the United Nations be slapping its own
face?"

- The United Nations is nothing but a United States-Soviet Union medium of cooperation.
- Another United Nations should be set up as a rival to the United Nations now extant.

Thus, there is no more argument possible about what the necessary effect of the United Nations admission for Communist China would be: it would destroy the United Nations as we know it. The United States could not any more be a member under these conditions and would have to withdraw.

The current issue today is that of the war in Southeast Asia. (1) The Communist Chinese show complete obduracy here and hold to a hard line of demanding total United States-South Vietmam surrender. (2) Can we change this by admitting Communist China to the United Nations? On September 1, 1965, the New China News Agency authorized broadcast stated: "The Vietnam questions have nothing to do with the United Nations." (3) But we'd better believe that once Communist China was in the United Nations and a permanent member of the Security Council it would veto all acts by the Security Council which sought to promote peace by curbing Red Chinese aggression. Even the thus-far futile efforts of U Thant to mediate the war would be impossible.

The current issue today is the Taiwan issue. Communist China demands that we abandon a loyal ally, an excellent partner in economic, social and political development, and a strategic strength close up, by insisting that the United Nations throw the Republic of China out of that body as a prerequisite for its own entry. This would mean we would tell everyone else: "Go make your settlement with Communist China; become its vassal." Is there a way out of this in the so-called two-Chinas policy? No. This policy is utterly infeasible because both the two main parties to it, Communist China and the Republic of China, reject it totally and absolutely.

The general issue today in regard to the Western Pacific is: can we have any security if the whole area falls under control of such a hostile power as Communist China? No. We tried withdrawal between 1922 and 1941, but it just led to a greater war.

Can we hope for change in Communist China? It is often said that we can make the United Nations a reform school for Communist China. I would like to quote on this Edgar Snow in *The Nation*, September 12, 1953, when he said: "A Chou En-lai showing us his posterior from Peiping and uttering slanderous statements or carrying out irresponsible or warlike actions against us is not necessarily less a threat than the *same infidel* seated in full view of the United Nations and answerable to a body of world judgment" (my italics). But, of course, the answer is that if the United Nations is made over on the Communist Chinese model, Communist China won't have to change, will it? Since *we* can't change that much, we will have to get out if they come in on their terms.

The overriding policy question is the growing United States-Communist China confrontation in Southeast Asia and what it may mean to Communist China: destruction at our hands. In view of this, it is natural that more interest in United States China policy should develop. The possibility is clear that *this time* another major United States-Communist China confrontation may destroy Communist China.

Finally, Pope Paul VI has been widely quoted (October 4, 1965) as urging Communist Chinese United Nations admission by saying to the United Nations that it should "study the right method of uniting to your pact of brotherhood in honor and loyalty, those who do not yet share in it." But here is what *L'Osservatore Romano*, the official organ of the Vatican, said on this on October 18-19, 1965. In an editorial under the title "The Church and the Universal Community of States," it takes note of the fact that there are people who have "given a precise political meaning" to those words of His Holiness. Then the editorial declared: "But true universality does not mean the arithmetic sum of nations; it presupposes the convergence of everybody on the effective recognition of and respect for natural law, which is the foundation of the United Nations." That is to say, the rule of law is primary; expanding United Nations membership is secondary.

The Pope is thus saying what we all know to be true, namely that any form of political association must be founded on some measure of agreed-upon community of values, and that for such associations to tolerate as components thereof those elements which deny and forcefully flaunt the agreed-upon community of values will seriously endanger and probably eventually destroy the association. Thus, limitations upon membership and upon participation in political action are common to all political communities. The United Nations, weak as it already is, is no exception. It cannot be an exception.

To sum up, I quote in full the leading editorial in the *New York*

Herald Tribune for November 8, 1965, as follows. It is a welcome antidote to the columns of the *New York Times*. It reads:

RED CHINA OVER THE U.N.

"If the United Nations were administered by completely rational men, there would be no reason to doubt the outcome of this week's General Assembly debate on the issue of admitting Communist China as a member of the world organization. But reason does not always rule. Not infrequently it is clouded and weakened by set positions which, as in the case of Soviet Russia and India, have become so hardened as to imprison those who have assumed them; or by misleading arguments, such as the contention that Peking's effective control of the Chinese mainland automatically entitles it to China's seat; or by wishful thinking, such as the suggestion that admission to the U.N. will convert Peking overnight from a war-making into a peace-loving country.

"Therefore it cannot be taken for granted that the United States and its allies will again succeed in turning back the attempt to seat Peking. The two sides appear to be more closely balanced than ever before. This throws a still greater burden on the handful of countries which have acquired the power to decide the issue one way or another. How could they better discharge it than by exercising the rational process?

"On moral, legal and constitutional grounds, Peking is ineligible for admission. It is an aggressor; its leading spokesmen, beginning with Mao Tse-tung, insist on their right to commit aggression so long as it advances their Communist, international, revolutionary aims. The U.N. Charter, on the other hand, clearly disqualifies an aggressor by stipulating that a candidate for membership must be a peace-loving state.

"The question must then be considered on what are called "realistic" grounds. The main argument is that Peking, once inside the the U.N. and exposed to its civilizing, restraining influence, will be less aggressive than if it remained outside the U.N. — an unhappy and rebellious outcast.

"These who advance this argument forget one very crucial point. If Peking were admitted to the U.N., it would become a permanent member of the Security Council. As such, it would acquire the power to veto any act by the Security Council (and, according to the Soviet view, by the General Assembly, too) which sought to produce peace by curbing Red Chinese aggression. In other words, admission of Peking, in its present frame of mind, could very well tie the hands of the United Nations and thereby advance, rather than inhibit, Red Chinese acts of aggression.

"In view of this possibility — one which has yet to be disclaimed, or even aired in the General Assembly — admission of Red China this year would be carrying irrationality dangerously close to the edge."

In the time and space available to me I cannot well deal with all the other aspects of positive policy which should be dealt with. However, I wish to call the attention of the Committee, the Congress as a whole and the country at large to what I consider a very excellent presentation of these matters from an official source. I do not believe this cogent and learned statement has been given anywhere near the attention it deserves, either in the public media of communication or by the body of our citizens who are so actively concerning themselves with questions of China policy today. In order to help, I hope, in securing general circulation for it and what it says, I enter it here, as the final section of what I want to present to this honorable Committee and through it, I hope, to the Senate, the Congress, and the public at large.

14

STRIKING A BALANCE

By Robert A. Scalapino

I would like to believe that we are entering a new era in the United States, one which will be marked by much more intimate, frank, and continuous exchange between government officials and public office-holders on the one hand, and private scholars and specialists on the other. There are some individuals on both sides who fear that such contact will be corrupting. They would impose a policy of isolation, or limit communication to confrontation. Personally, I regard these approaches as more likely to be corrupting since they restrict both perspectives and knowledge. Hence, I welcome expanded contacts of many types.

In approaching the issue of American policy toward China, I should like to set forth very briefly certain premises which I hold concerning China that are germane to any consideration of policy.

The question is often asked, "Can we anticipate major changes in China in the near future?" If by major changes, one means on over-throw of the Communist Party, the chances seem to me remote, barring global war or some other major and unforeseeable crisis. This is not because dissidence is absent in China. We have no accurate method of measuring such dissidence, but I am inclined to believe that if one could measure the total spectrum of opposition — from the most passive "grumblers" to the active or potential "subversives" — it would be relatively high, despite the fact that certain groups have clearly benefited from the revolution and are grateful.

The point, however, is that Communists, more than most modern rulers, have mastered the science of power. Consequently, dissidence can be relatively high and still pose no serious threat to a regime such as that of Peking because the dissidents cannot find or develop an organizational outlet. Without depreciating the significance of ideology or policy, I regard organization as still the most important weapon of the Communists, especially when it can operate in an unorganized or disorganized environment.

Thus if change is to occur in China, it is most likely to come through communism, and via top party circles. Any American policy should be based upon this assumption. It is possible, of course, that at some point, the Red Army can pose a threat since it represents the one organizational alternative to the party of any significance, and the trend toward modernization is more likely to separate the military and the party than to bring them closer together. In the era of guerrilla warfare and its immediate aftermath, the party has dominated the military via the type of political-military leadership represented by Mao Tse-tung himself. That era is coming to a close.

There is a growing struggle which in its essence posits the primitivism implicit in Maoist political-military doctrines against the professionalism that is implicit in the whole modernization program. Already, some military men have been placed in major opposition to party leaders. As it unfolds, however, this struggle will involve the bureaucracy in all of its aspects, civilian as well as military, and it is likely to be settled within the party, especially since most of the key disputants will either be in the top echelons of the party or have access to these. I cannot easily envisage a situation where the military and the party would enter into struggle as separate, self-contained units.

Thus, in all probability, the most meaningful question is that so frequently posed, "Will a younger generation of party leaders diverge considerably from the group of old Bolsheviks currently holding absolute power, so that the resulting changes while taking place within the party, will nonetheless be profound and, in general, in the direction of realism and moderation?

This is a crucial question, and one that cannot be answered with any complete certainty. My own belief is that such changes will occur, but that the critical element of timing will depend heavily upon both the internal and the external environment. Even under the best of circumstances, I am inclined to feel that the struggle for a more pragmatic, realistic, and moderate political elite in China will be long and arduous, extending considerably beyond one generation. But the rate and nature of change will certainly be affected by the degree to which a wide range of subtle external pressures and alternatives can be developed.

In certain terms, we are conducting a holding operation in Asia, and one of the variables with which we must contend is the race in China itself between the acquisition of power and the acquisition of responsibility. Our policies and those of other foreign states, while not representing the sole determinants of this race, are vitally important elements.

One final point regarding change in China might be added. No political regime can be totally rigid and survive. Clearly, current Chinese leaders have been forced to make substantial adjustments to various programs that have failed, at home and abroad. That will continue. Indeed, just as the Maoists had to retrench in the aftermath of the failure of the Great Leap Forward at home, so now they are engaged in a reassessment of the Great Leap Forward abroad which has also failed on a major scale. No democratic regime, incidentally, could possibly have survived the colossal failures in foreign policy suffered by Peking in the last few years.

Thus, tactical adjustments and modifications will be made because there is literally no alternative. One must distinguish, however, between belated responses to inescapable realities and the frame of mind which is bound to a minimum of dogma, the mind fundamentally responsive to a wide range of alternatives. China is still ruled by hardcore idealogues who hold to the thesis that being "red" is more important than being "expert," and who have now been driven to the deification of Maoism as the repository of all significant truth. Even a casual reading of Chinese journals today reveals the staggering degree to which ideological rigidity has produced a cult of irrationality centering on Mao. Is crop failure threatened? The answer lies in Mao's writings, asserts *Hung Ch'i*. Is the student having trouble in solving a mathematical equation? Read Mao's collected works, suggests *Jen-min Jih-pao*.

Perhaps a basic fragility is revealed in a regime that is forced increasingly to rely upon the omnipotence of one man and descend into such irrational depths in the process. But the current scene in China has universal implications. In most emerging societies, a broad and supremely important conflict ensues at some point between elements we may roughly call ideologues and pragmatists. First generation revolutionaries are generally strongly ideological, high politicized, possessed of certain "charismatic" qualities, and lacking in most advanced technical skills. Their primary task is nation-building, often via mass mobilization. At some point, however, they must give way to an elite who are more pragmatic than ideological, more bureaucratic than charismatic, and more concerned with the technical and administrative skills essential to progress in economic and social terms. The implications of this process for American foreign policy, I would suggest, are far-reaching.

The era of the ideologues is likely to be at once dynamic and disappointing — disappointing in the sense that many of the broad goals projected will not be realized. Expectations will be high. Performance will generally be low, with the means employed often not in accordance with the ends sought. Consequently, mounting pressures upon the elite in power will ensue. The temptation on their part to engage in irrational, distractive behavior will increase. But there will also be ultimate pressures for realistic policies that can achieve results.

Extremism and Moderation. It is certainly incumbent upon the United States in these circumstances to take a positive position in the affirmation of the broad goals constantly voiced in this era: nationalism; the acceptance of, and involvement in the world community; democracy; social justice and economic development. It is equally important that we devise policies that in concrete terms will discourage extremism and encourage moderation, primarily by making clear the risks of the former, and setting forth the opportunities of the latter. And these opportunities must involve precisely the types of interaction and assistance that would abet the movement from ideological rigidity toward pragmatic experimentalism. This general approach, I would submit, is appropriate to our China policy, as to our policy elsewhere, because it relates to the general nature of change.

There are two other general questions relating to China upon which I should like to comment prior to discussing the specifics of our China policy. There has been some debate over the nature of Chinese Communist power and intentions. Some emphasize the thesis that China is essentially a weak nation, one thoroughly frightened by the massive power and encirclement policies of the United States, and most likely to respond to us only in a defensive sense — hence constituting no basic threat to us, our allies or the neutrals. Others argue that we should treat China as a major power and one that clearly has aggressive, expansionist aspirations threatening the whole of the non-communist world.

In my opinion, the truth is approached as one combines these two views, treating them as more complementary than in conflict. China is weak in a variety of ways. Her economic recovery from the disasters of a few years ago is scarcely complete, and despite remarkable feats in certain areas of production and distribution, overall increases — particularly in agrarian production — appear to be modest, especially when measured against population growth. Moreover, the changing of the political guard is at hand and even if the resulting changes may not be dramatic, some internal tension must be present in the Chinese Communist Party at this point, heightened by the significant setbacks in foreign policy. Finally, China is scarcely a military match for the United States, and she undoubtedly fears American power.

American power confronts China on the east and south. Soviet power lies on the west and north. Without question, the existence of this power contributes to a psychology that is at once fearful and blatantly defiant. It would be extremely unwise, however, to deduce from this that such power being removed, Chinese foreign policy would subsequently be characterized by passivity or moderation. Were it not for American and Soviet power in Asia, the Chinese Communists would almost certainly have advanced much further toward their basic goals there, although I do not believe for a moment regard American and Soviet interests and objectives in the area as identical.

What are the Chinese goals? Three have been oft-proclaimed: to remove all Western influence from Asia; to encourage by a variety of means an ideologically-politically uniform Asia cast in the image of "the new China"; and to enlist this "progressive" Asia in the global struggle against both the "revisionists" and the "imperialists."

These are scarcely the goals of an elite that is primarily oriented toward defense, and posing its objectives in very limited terms. It is quite true, however, that these goals — and some of the actions that have accompanied them — have triggered a reaction, not alone from us but from many others as well. Thus today, China must calculate defensively because the United States, and in some degree the Soviet Union, will not permit her to calculate offensively on any significant scale.

Her defensive calculations undoubtedly include a determination in each specific instance as to what she can and cannot tolerate from the standpoint of her own national interests, and what risks, correspondingly, she is prepared to run. Personally, I do not believe that the Chinese Communists are prepared to take the risks of an open war with the United States at this time except under the most extraordinary of circumstances *or* under conditions where they misinterpret

American signals. Specifically, I regard it as highly unlikely that
China will intervene fully in the Vietnam war unless the obliteration
of North Vietnam is threatened. Even then, it will be an extremely
difficult decision for Peking because she knows she would be subjected
to massive destruction, and such a war would run completely counter
to her basic policy which has been aimed at provoking an American-
Soviet confrontation in the course of involving the United States simultaneously in a series of "national liberation wars."

The fact, however, that China is forced to react defensively and
partly from fear at this point should not obscure the very strong commitment which the current generation of Chinese leaders have had
to global revolution and global influence. From the moment they
emerged into full control, these leaders committed themselves and
their society to the cultivation of power in all of its forms: military,
political, psychological and economic. Contrast their attitude toward
power and their actions, for example, with those of Nehru and Nehru's
India. Nehru eschewed armaments, avoided alliances, and on occasion, seemed to shun even active political diplomacy. Mao and his
comrades, on the other hand, were prepared to make major sacrifices
for the sake of political and military power, including the development
of a nuclear arsenal.

Since the Communist era began in China, no Asian state has been
capable of matching Chinese power unaided, and it is wise to remember
that there is not a pacifist bone in a Maoist body. The Chinese Communists, moreover, have consummated alliances large and small,
undertaken aid and technical assistance programs far beyond their
economic capacities, and engaged in a range of political activities
throughout the world that caused most nations — friend and foe —
to label China "major power designate." That is a significant accomplishment because such a status grants certain rights without con-
veying the requisite responsibilities.

When all of these activities are surveyed, I do not understand how
anyone can regard Chinese actions or goals of the past decade as
defensive, either in character or intent. The recent major failures of
that policy, indeed, are due to precisely the opposite problem: the
Chinese Communists sought to force the pace, undertaking actions in
Asia, Africa and Latin America that were interpreted by others as
aggressive, ultra-nationalistic and dangerous. As noted earlier, it is
quite likely that Peking will now be forced to retrench in foreign policy
as they have previously been forced to do in domestic policy. The

basic ingredients — the fundamental source-springs — of Chinese foreign policy, however, are likely to remain. It will be important,
therefore, to distinguish between short-run tactics and long-range
goals.

Major Source-Springs of Policy. What have been the major source-
springs of Chinese foreign policy under the Communists? Three forces
are of central importance: tradition, nationalism and MLM — Marx-
Lenin-Maoism. In certain respects, the current Chinese leaders still
think of their problem as how to handle the barbarians. They still
divide the world into those who accept Chinese culture (now to be read
"ideology") and those who live outside the pale. The former are the
"civilized" or the "progressive" people; the latter are barbarians, be
they "revisionists," "imperialists" or "neutrals." The barbarian must
be handled by a combination of persuasion and coercion. One uses
visits to the imperial capitol, exchanges of gifts and many other de-
vices to awe and impress; and one uses strong words and, when necessary and possible, strong actions to cajole and coerce. Some of China's
difficulties today are unquestionably due to a continuance among her
present generation of mandarin rulers of an "imperial complex," an
engrained sense of cultural superiority and the attitude of condescension toward other peoples that invariably accompanies this.

The nationalist quotient in Chinese foreign policy is, of course,
extremely high. In many respects, China is behaving in much the
same fashion as have other major societies en route to power. First,
she has sought to define and defend her boundaries as she interprets
these; secondly, she has sought to create a buffer state system around
her; and finally, she has sought hegemony in the worlds in which she
lives: the Asian world, the non-Western world, and the Communist
world.

In pursuit of these objectives, the Chinese Communists have been
no more able to follow a totally consistent foreign policy than the
leaders of other major states. The main thrust of Chinese Communist
foreign policy, as suggested earlier, has been characterized by revolutionary fervor, global commitment, and a relatively inflexible division
of the world into comrades and enemies. The line has been hard,
advanced by practicing ideologues fiercely impatient with the existing
order and anxious to challenge it in radical fashion. And yet, for
tactical reasons and out of necessity, these leaders have adopted
a great variety of approaches. On occasion, they have not hesitated

to consort with "feudalists" and support "reactionary" regimes; sometimes, they have used the soft line, as at the time of Bandung; not
infrequently, they have been caught in such un-Marxian stances as
making an appeal to race. Indeed, one is forced to conclude that the
one element of major consistency is that which runs through the
policies of all nations: the consistent expression of what appears to
the political elite as in their national interests. And it is precisely this
fact that offers hope of some flexibility, even among hard-core
ideologues.

At its roots, the Sino-Soviet dispute itself is closely connected with
the phenomena of nationalism. We now know that nationalism has
not only survived communism, but in many respects triumphed over
it. The Sino-Soviet cleavage illustrates the fact that two nations
supposedly sharing a common ideology but differing substantially in
cultural traditions, timing of revolution, stage of development, generation of leadership and degree of power are almost certain to have
different views of the world and of their own needs. Hence, they
will have different concepts of national interest which, in the case of
Marxists, will be translated into different interpretations of what is
truth, namely what is orthodox Marxism-Leninism. (In fact, of course,
all modern Marxists are revisionists of the highest order.)

The Sino-Soviet dispute centers upon the issue of how to treat the
United States, although there are other significant issues as well. The
Soviet Union basically believes in nation-to-nation competition with
the United States, counting upon the ultimate superiority of Soviet
productivity and power. Thus it argues that the appropriate method
of confrontation is peaceful co-existence, meaning all-out economic,
political and social competition but the avoidance of war. There is,
to be sure, an element of ambiguity in the Soviet position surrounding
its defense of national "wars of liberation," which may be variously
defined and supported. Nevertheless, its standard criticism of the
Peking line is that the Chinese leaders have rejected peaceful co-
existence, and pursue a left-adventurist policy that risks global war.

China, on the other hand, not being able to conceive of the possibility of nation-to-nation competition with the United States in the
near future, and having no basic responsibility for the maintenance
of peace or the prosecution of a nuclear war, argues the classical Bol-
shevik thesis that America must be challenged by the technique of
unfolding the world revolution. The Chinese theme is that primary
emphasis must be placed upon mobilizing the non-Western world for

a rapid, continuous assault upon the "capitalist West, led by the United States." Thus, the Russians are rebuked for their refusal to take massive risks on behalf of global revolution, and they are now charged by Peking with active collaboration with Washington for purposes of world domination. At the moment, China asserts that Vietnam is the supreme test of the validity of her position and her principles. The United States is a paper tiger which, if challenged resolutely and in accordance with Maoist principles, will collapse as a result of internal and external pressures. Maoism will be vindicated on the battlefields of Vietnam — and in the streets of the United States — against the combination of American imperialism and Soviet sabotage.

Striking a Balance. As the nationalist component in Chinese foreign policy is surveyed, I would suggest that the following conclusions pertinent to policy might be advanced. One critical problem is that of striking a balance between providing Chinese nationalism with legitimate outlets and guarding against those aggressive potentials that lie embedded in any nationalist movement, and particularly one possessed of active messianic goals like that of China. There are some who argue that Chinese domination of Asia is appropriate, or in any case, inevitable. Their thesis is that Asia is the legitimate sphere of influence for China, just as the Western hemisphere is for us. I am not prepared to accept this argument in any of its major conclusions, as it is usually advanced. The simple "spheres of influence" concept is misleading in terms of fact, unrealistic in terms of current political trends, and untenable in terms of basic morality.

There can be no question that the United States, of all modern nations, has had the greatest unchallenged preponderance of power historically in its own region. Yet even the United States has lived for various periods of time with hostile states in this hemisphere, and with states having intimate ties with foreign powers — from the time of British Canada to the time of Moscow-oriented Cuba. Certainly, the Russians have never had any total dominance of their near neighbors — witness the existence of Finland, Turkey, Greece and Iran, among others. My own belief, indeed, is that the existence of some elements of competition and neutrality in the vicinity of a major power is healthy. A major state totally secure in its own region may not only be oblivious to the problems of its neighbors, but may also be unduly free to undertake expansionist activities afield. Thus,

I do not believe that Chinese dominance of Asia is either inevitable or desirable — and neither, I suspect, do the peoples of India, Japan, Indonesia and the Soviet Union, among others.

This is not to say, however, that China should be denied — or can be denied — all elements of security. Already, China has a certain buffer state system: North Korea shields the Manchurian complex, at least from the East; North Vietnam stands in front of the Kwantung area; China now controls Tibet; and many of the border states of South and Southeast Asia, notably Afghanistan, Pakistan, Nepal, Burma and Cambodia can either be accounted neutral or friendly. Over time and under conditions where a general balance of power in Asia had been achieved, it might be possible to extend that belt of neutrality to other states. Indeed, nothing should be ruled outside the range of future possibility, including large-scale disarmament and a reliance upon collective security agreements by the major Asian states. Progress on any of these fronts, however, now depends primarily upon China: her willingness to renounce force as a means of effecting international change; her preparedness to enter into negotiations on a wide range of issues; her capacity to accept compromise as an essential ingredient in international agreement; and her ability to abandon the thesis that the destruction of the United States as it is presently constituted takes priority over all other foreign policy objectives.

The final source-spring of Chinese Communist foreign policy I have labeled MLM. The Maoists think of themselves as orthodox Marxist-Leninists, indeed, as the only legitimate leaders of the world Marxist movement. At the same time, however, they pride themselves upon having "applied Marxism-Leninism creatively" to the conditions of China. Perhaps it is accurate to define the Maoist element in Chinese Marxism as the practical development of a five-stage revolutionary progression which places heavy reliance initially upon intellectual leadership and a peasant-based radical movement that has its roots in the countryside.

The Maoist revolutionary formula begins with the creation of a Communist Party which must never lose control of the revolutionary movement. That party proceeds to guide the creation of a united front, using nationalist and socio-economic appeals, but relying heavily upon organization, and using freely the instruments of coercion as well as those of persuasion. When the front has been prepared, the movement into guerrilla warfare is the next stage, and then the advance to positional warfare. When military victory has been attained, the so-called People's Democratic Republic is established under the complete control of the Communist Party.

Long before Lin Piao's speech of last summer, it was clear that the Chinese Communists regarded this revolutionary formula broadly applicable to the world scene — from the Congo to Vietnam. In very high degree, indeed, the old Bolsheviks of China, so strongly isolated from world reality, have seen the world mirrored in their own ideological-revolutionary image and history. The need for a *true* Communist Party means that one must fight such false Marxist-Leninists as the Russians. The united front with its emphasis upon a union of peasants, workers, intellectuals and national bourgeois under the leadership of the vanguard party spells out the Chinese determination to unite the world peasantry (the Afro-Asian societies) and certain susceptible bourgeois elements (clearly France was once in mind) under Peking's banners.

Thus, MLM makes Chinese Communist foreign policy something more than merely another expression of nationalism in action. It defines both the scope and the techniques of policy in a unique way. China is interested in Albania as well as Korea; in Mali as well as in Vietnam. The definition of national interest, the conceptualization of problem, the vocabulary of dispute are all colored by MLM. It would be as dangerous to underestimate the Marxist quotient in Chinese foreign policy at this point as to accord it total influence.

Broadly Gauged Policy Needed. The above considerations seem to me germane as we examine American policy toward China. Nearly six years ago, I had the privilege of writing the Northeast Asia section of a report on United States Foreign Policy in Asia which was submitted to the Senate Committee on Foreign Relations. At that time, I defined our current policy as one of attempted containment by isolation, and I suggested a variety of reasons why, in my opinion, we should move away from such a negative, inflexible approach to an admittedly complex, difficult problem.

Naturally, I am gratified to note that in recent months and weeks, there have been increasing signs that our government is seeking a more broadly gauged policy. Some of the steps which I advocated in 1959 are now being initiated or at least actively contemplated. These include a willingness to allow American scholars, scientists, journalists and certain other citizens to travel to China; positive steps to seek the involvement of China in international negotiations on such problems as disarmament, nuclear weapon control and similar issues of world importance; and the establishment of terms under which mainland China might come into the United Nations.

Because these steps, and others which should follow will be strongly debated, I should like to reiterate the reasons why I believe such actions, on balance, are highly desirable. A policy of containment by isolation robbed the United States of initiative or leverage, and tended to posit our rigidity against that of Peking. This in turn served to separate us from our allies and the neutrals, making collective thinking and action with respect to China vastly more difficult. It also rendered far less effective the type of multiple external pressures that are essential if the element of extremism in Chinese foreign policy is to be effectively curbed or countered.

Our past policy has been insufficient in certain other respects. To foster isolation is to foster fanaticism. Isolation, indeed, is one of the major weapons of a police state, and there is no reason as to why we should be a party to its support. On the contrary, a truly sophisticated American foreign policy will always aim at complicating the decision-making processes of a totalitarian state. To be able to engage in selective diplomacy and to bear negligible responsibilities in the world community represent significant tactical advantages which we should not bestow lightly. Such a situation also encourages a purist, uncompromising and irrational attitude, an air of complete unrealism.

A policy of containment by isolation, in short, not only provides an inadequate approach from the standpoint of international political realities, but it is also highly unsatisfactory from the standpoint of its impact upon the Chinese nation itself. In immediate terms, therefore, we must move from such a policy toward one that heightens the element of choice for the Chinese political elite by providing additional incentives for moderation and firm, explicit deterrents to extremism. We must find a way of making peaceful coexistence the only conceivable path for the next generation of Chinese leaders and we must do this without abandoning any of the basic rights or requirements of the non-Communist world.

I do not claim that this will be easy or that it can be done quickly. The thrust of my earlier analysis was that we face a China both militantly nationalist and strongly ideological at present, a China whose leaders have committed a series of excesses from which they must now beat some retreat, but who still appear to be intent upon cultivating power in all of its aspects and quite prepared to use violence to effect revolutionary change throughout the world. At this point, presumably, the Chinese leaders are sufficiently realistic to want to avoid war with the United States, and even with less powerful forces. The time may not be too long, however, before China's military capacities come closer to matching her political visions. We must prepare for that eventuality now.

There are a few individuals who would argue that we should forcefully remove the Chinese military threat before it becomes serious. But preventive war, in my opinion, is politically impossible even if one were to waive all questions of morality. We are a democratic society, and neither our people nor our officials would sanction such a policy. Moreover, preventive war by its very nature would fail because it ignores the response of the world community as well as of the people most immediately affected, and provides therefore no basis for erecting a meaningful world order.

Opportunities and Deterrents. The only realistic approach is the complex one of creating an elaborate structure of opportunities and deterrents, and in this task we must have the cooperation of other nations, particularly those of non-communist Asia. Our first steps seem clear enough. Progressively, we must make it clear by concrete actions that if China is isolated, the initiative lies with her, that we are prepared to enter into cultural relations with her, engage in trade on the same basis as with other Communist nations, and negotiate with her on all matters of international importance. At the same time, we should accept in principle the desirability of universal membership in the United Nations, a principle which among other things would make natural the acceptance of both China and Taiwan as *de facto* states deserving international representation. Bilateral recognition between the United States and China is not, in my opinion, a first priority item under the present circumstances. Once again, however, I believe that we should move toward the establishment of a general principle, namely the complete divorcement of recognition from the question of moral or political approval.

Having supported the above actions, let me make it emphatically clear that I am under no illusions about the initial Chinese response. Peking will not help us develop a new Chinese policy because basically she likes our old one, and does not want us to change. As has already been implied, she believes that our present policy isolates us more than her; makes the United States available as a perfect scapegoat both before her own people and before others; and prevents or at least mitigates the types of pressures developing upon her from the outside that might otherwise be created.

Thus, we can assume that the torrent of abuse against us will continue to flow out of China, and that initial responses to our overtures will be almost completely negative. As in so many other situations today, this will test our patience and our sophistication. We must neither be driven back into rigidity nor panicked into making unwarranted concessions. Suppose, for example, that at this time, China does not permit American scientists or scholars other than those prepared to support the Peking regime into the country. Upon whom does this onus lie, if our doors are kept open? Suppose China refuses to accept a United Nations seat once terms such as those suggested above have been established, and that seat lies vacant for a time? Upon whom will the pressures mount?

Thus far, however, I have advanced and defended only one side of the policy proposed earlier. But it is my firm belief that moderation will be encouraged only if the risks of extremism are made both credible and clear. When the history of this era is written, it may be recorded that the two Asian wars in which we have been engaged since 1950 were both the products of Communist miscalculation for which we must assume some share of responsibility. When the Communists planned their aggression in Korea, did they have any strong reason to believe that the United States would act to protect South Korea, given the manner in which we had recently stated our Asian defense commitments? And when the Communists planned their military campaign in South Vietnam, did they have any real reason to believe that the United States would undertake major military efforts to aid South Vietnam, in view of the statements of numerous American leaders about land wars on the Asian continent? Let us not make this type of mistake again. Let us make clear our definition of aggression and neo-aggression, and make clear also our commitments and resolves so that miscalculation can be reduced to an absolute minimum.

At this point, for example, we should make it absolutely clear that any attempt to change the status of Taiwan or South Korea by means of the use of externally directed or assisted force will be resolutely countered by the application of American force. We should also continue to make it unmistakably clear that we do not intend to allow these tactics to succeed in South Vietnam. In my opinion, nothing would be more calculated to pump life into the extremist movement within China and within the Communist world than a Maoist victory in Vietnam — and nothing would lead us more quickly into the awful choice between precipitous retreat everywhere and World War III. The Chinese have repeatedly emphasized the fact that Vietnam is a supreme test of Maoist principles in statements to their own people, to other Asians, and to fellow Communists. We can be certain that the path toward moderation and peace will be infinitely longer and more painful if extremism pays in this crucial test.

If we are to be successful in gradually developing a new approach to China, we must also look closely at our total Asian policy, because obviously there must be a close interrelation between our approach to China and our approach to Asia as a whole. Time permits only the suggestion of a few basic long-range considerations which I believe to be of importance in this respect. First, if we look at the present political situation in its broadest dimensions, two powers largely external to Asia — the United States and the Soviet Union — are each in somewhat different ways playing a critical role in balancing the thrust of China, primarily because no Asian nation — or combination of nations — is currently prepared to play that role. It is recognized on all sides, however, that ultimately a balance of power must be developed within Asia, if diversity and peace are to be rendered possible, and our most basic planning and support must be directed toward this end.

Second, a major world power like the United States is destined by virtue of its strength and resources to be somewhat apart from other nations. In this era, we are required to bear heavier responsibilities, be subjected to heavier criticism, and on occasion to make grave decisions, the execution of which falls primarily upon us, or upon us alone. In many cases, moreover, the decision not to act is at least as fateful as the decision to act. Thus, we cannot escape from a powerful element of unilateralism, and I see no point in naively or romantically railing against this fact. We are going to do certain things alone, or almost alone, if they are done at all. At the same time, it is incumbent upon us — now more than ever before — to develop programs and also an attitude of mind soliciting international opinions and support, especially from nations like Japan and India, nations that should be taking more responsibility in world affairs and in the affairs of Asia than is currently the case.

Third, until we find better methods of enabling freedom and socioeconomic development to go together, we will be under substantial handicaps in the struggle to preserve open societies. I am personally convinced that we have the brains and much of the data needed to make significant progress on this problem, and in the course of making that progress, providing answers to a host of crucial questions that relate to certain basic aspects of American foreign policy. At the present time, for instance, we are not posing the critical questions in very precise or meaningful terms. I regard such questions as "Should we be policeman — or Santa Claus — to the world?" as very crude expressions of problems that should be raised in much more precise manner. Obviously, we should not be and we are not involved equally in every nation of the world — or even in every region. But under what conditions — assuming that the initiative is largely ours — should we be involved, and how? If we can mount at great cost an Apollo project to reach the moon, I would suggest that we should mount a similar project to reach our own planet in this, the most critical century since life first evolved here. We should have in operation now a high-level group of scholars, scientists and officials probing the basic questions of development and change, peace and war, forms of effective national and international interaction, and this group should be established with some type of permanence so that its hypothese can be tested and periodically revised.

Status and Responsibilities. I should like to conclude with two final observations that relate to our status in the modern world and our responsibilities. Perhaps we have underestimated the psychological and intellectual problems of moving from a position of regional influence to one of global power. Our intellectual center of gravity, for example, and also the center of our decision-making process continues to evidence strong Europocentric tendencies. I would not for a moment depreciate the ability or the values of those in the scholarly and governmental community whose interests, training and knowledge relate primarily to the Western world. I would, however, suggest that in an age when our responsibilities are global and when a region like Asia is so crucial to our own national interest and that of the rest of the world, some redress in the power of internal authority in this country is desirable. For example, I would suspect that when the testimony of the Asian scholars heard during these hearings is reviewed, it will reveal a somewhat different emphasis — and on certain issues a different thrust — than would have been the case had European specialists been the primary witnesses.

Finally, I cannot avoid the observation that perhaps our gravest problem today is the fact that our culture conflicts in certain significant respects with the requirements of our status and power. To some extent, incidentally, this is also true of our main competitors, the Russians and the Chinese. Whereas power in the mid-nineteenth century was held by small states which had come to the industrial revolution early and had accumulated their resources externally, power in the mid-twentieth century is held by continental-mass societies whose resources lie largely within themselves, and each of whom has had a long history of relative self-sufficiency, a reasonably high quotient of ethnocentrism, and a strong commitment to isolation not easily removed. Whatever our political and ideological differences, we, the Russians and the Chinese share these traits.

Beyond that, ours is a culture that has placed an enormous premium upon speed and efficiency. I suspect that the critical test of American success or failure in world leadership in the years that lie immediately ahead will hinge upon whether we can modify those cherished qualities in accordance with the dictates of the world in which we live. This requires patience and, more than patience, an appreciation of the signal importance of being able to move from 10 to 11, or 8 to 7, in the broad range of policy alternatives, rather than being forced to operate only on the basis of 0 or 100. I regard this as the single most important test of American maturity. If we continue to live by the All or Nothing philosophy — either "all in" or "all out" — we cannot possibly sustain our values or our interests. This is to use a neolithic approach to the problems of a nuclear age.

This problem merits the most searching scutiny particularly because our mass media too frequently encourages the 100/0 approach by focusing upon the extremities of every issue, thus heightening the sense of crisis and making proper timing and appropriate means to ends so difficult. The time has come, in short, to explore in the greatest possible depth the relation of both the mass media and government to foreign policy formulation in an age when we must preserve democracy at home and, at the same time, undertake the massive obligation implicit in being the world's greatest power. In the process, we might be able to redefine our responsibilities as well as our rights, both as citizens and as officials.

I am aware that such an inquiry would go far beyond the issue of

China, or even Asia, but it seems particularly appropriate to suggest it as I conclude. In no theatre of the world is a correct sense of timing and the capacity to utilize effectively the most minute gradations of policy more critical to our future and that of others.

15

FUNDAMENTAL INTERESTS AND POLICIES

By Hans J. Morgenthau

China poses for the United States three fundamental issues, which can be separated for purposes of analysis but in practice blend into each other. First, China is the most powerful nation of the mainland of Asia and potentially the most powerful nation in the world. Second, China has been for at least a millenium a great power of a peculiar kind in that her outlook upon, and relations with, the outside world have been different from those of other great powers. Third, China is today the fountainhead of the most virulent kind of Communism, proclaiming the inevitability of armed conflict and instigating and supporting Communist subversion throughout the world.

As a great Asian power, China seeks to restore the position she occupied before she was reduced to a semi-colonial status about a century ago. That goal has been proclaimed by the Chinese leaders, and the policies actually pursued by them with regard to the offshore islands and Taiwan, Korea, Vietnam, Burma, Cambodia, Tibet and India conform to a consistent pattern: restoration of the territorial boundaries and of the influence the Chinese Empire possessed before its modern decline. These boundaries are likely to comprise Taiwan and the offshore islands, Outer Mongolia, and the Asian territories claimed by China and annexed by the Soviet Union during the nineteenth century. Physically, considering the distribution of power on the Asian mainland, China could go much farther, she could go virtually as far as she wanted to. But she has never done so in the past, and she is not likely to do so in the future. The reasons are to be found in the peculiar Chinese outlook upon the world.

According to Professor C. P. Fitzgerald, one of the most eminent experts in this field, "Rather more than a thousand years ago, the T'ang dynasty thus fixed the geographic limits in which the Chinese people were to live until modern times. Instead of conquering neighboring states, which she could have conquered without undue risk,

China has been traditionally satisfied with the establishment at her southern and southwestern borders of friendly governments, whose political identity was left intact and whose friendliness was assured and symbolized through tributary relationships of different kinds and degrees.

These subtle and indirect relationships are the result of the traditional Chinese conception of China as the center of the political universe, the only sovereign power worthy of the name, to which all other nations owe tribute. This extreme ethnocentrism goes hand in hand with contempt for, and ignorance of, the outside world, which from the Chinese point of view really does not need to be understood and to be dealt with on terms of equality with China. As the present relations between China, on the one hand, and Cambodia and Burma, on the other, can be regarded as a modern version of the tributary relations of old, so the present ignorance of the Chinese leaders of the outside world, their verbal assaults upon it, and their ineffective policies with regard to it can be understood as a modern version of China's traditional ethnocentrism.

China as a Communist Power. The quandary which the United States faces in its relations with China is created by the addition to these traditional elements of Chinese foreign policy of a new and unprecedented one: the sponsorship of a militant world communism. That quandary is similar to the one the United States dealt with successfully in the immediate aftermath of the Second World War when we had to distinguish between the great-power and world-communist aspirations of the Soviet Union. The Soviet Union modified and mitigated its world-revolutionary fervor when it began to realize, starting in the '20s, that the risks it ran for its own survival on behalf of world revolution were out of all proportion to the chances to achieve that revolution. It is likely that China will undergo a similar process of adapting world-revolutionary aims to political and military realities. The chances for such a development must exist, provided China has a rational government, and they are enhanced by Mao Tse-tung's intellectual characteristics and the nature of his past policies, both at home and abroad.

Mao Tse-tung's approach to the political and military problems at hand is characterized by two main interrelated qualities, as revealed in his writings and actions: a radically independent interpretation of Marxism-Leninism and a highly undogmatic pragmatism. The classic example of the former is the reliance upon the peasantry as the spearhead of the Communist revolution, in spite of the teachings of Marxism-Leninism and Soviet advice to the contrary. Both Mao Tse-tung's writings and political actions abound in examples of the latter. In reading Mao Tse-tung, one is time and again reminded of a Confucian peasant, shrewd, patient, and infinitely adaptable to changing and adverse circumstances. These same qualities mark the foreign policies Mao Tse-tung has pursued in Asia. Their caution and limitation to the traditional national objectives of China stand in stark contrast to the militant rhetoric of the Chinese leaders, in which an ethnocentric disregard for the realities and contempt for the interests of the outside world manifest themselves.

Marshal Lin Piao's famous manifesto of September 2, 1965, provides a particularly impressive but by no means unique example of this ethnocentrism, which is intellectually absurd and politically impractical. The Marshal tries to apply the lessons of the Communist revolution in China to the world scene. As the Communists conquered the countryside, isolating, surrounding, and finally conquering the cities, so, the Marshal suggests, the Communists will conquer the rural areas of the world, and isolate and finally conquer the cities of the world, by which he means the capitalistic nations of the West. To take these geopolitical metaphors as a program for political and military action is to completely misunderstand their ethnocentric source. Marshal Lin Piao's manifesto is not the Chinese equivalent of *Mein Kampf*, for the simple reason that even a Chinese Hitler would be incapable of putting it into practice. Completely lacking in even the most elementary understanding of the outside world, it rather reminds one, if one needs a historic analogy, of the eccentricities of German geopolitics.

China's Future Policies. It can thus be expected that both the present and the coming generation of Chinese leaders will continue to learn from experience and to adapt their policies to the real world. It is also quite possible that the coming generation will be less given to militant Marxist-Leninist rhetoric and to the instigation and support of subversion throughout the world. But it would be futile to expect that the new generation will be more accommodating than is the old one when it comes to the restoration of China's traditional domain in Asia. In this respect, Mao Tse-tung and Chiang Kai-shek see eye to eye, and so must Mao Tse-tung and his successor, whoever he may be. To mention only the most crucial issue where the traditional Chinese national interest is at stake: both Mao Tse-tung and Chiang Kai-shek consider Taiwan to be an integral part of China, they only disagree as to who shall rule China. Regardless of its ideological commitment, no patriotic government of China can be expected to give up the claim to Taiwan, and any Chinese government which believes to have the power will try to recover it. The issue of Taiwan has indeed proven the main stumbling block in the Warsaw negotiations between the United States and China, and it bound to do so in the future. That it has proven to be no more is due to China's temporary military weakness. Once China has realized its military potential, the issue of Taiwan, if it has not been settled in the meantime, will be the most likely *casus belli* between the United States and China.

The Interests and Policies of the U.S. What are the interests of the United States with regard to China, and what are the policies most likely to serve those interests? The United States has two such interests: maintenance or, if need be, the restoration of a viable balance of power in Asia and the maintenance of a world balance of power. We have tried to serve these interests for more than 15 years through two policies: the isolation and the peripheral military containment of China.

The policy of isolating China seeks the downfall of its Communist government. It is intimately connected with the recognition of the Chiang Kai-shek government as the legitimate government of China and with the expectation of its return to the mainland. By maintaining close relations with the Chiang Kai-shek government and none with the Communist government, a policy in which we expected our allies to participate, we tried to destroy the legitimacy of the Communist government. By interdicting all personal and commercial relations with mainland China we expected to make it impossible for the Communist government to govern. This policy has obviously failed. Chiang Kai-shek will not return to the mainland and his government survives only by virtue of the presence of the Seventh Fleet in the Straits of Taiwan. The Communist government of China enjoys diplomatic, cultural and commercial relations with many nations, among which there are many allies of the United States, and it is the United States rather than Communist China which has been isolated in consequence of its policy of isolation. Insofar as China is isolated, as it is in the Communist world, that isolation is in good measure self-inflicted, and our policy of isolation has nothing to do with it.

Thus from the point of view of China, our policy of isolation is no longer an important issue. Therefore, no favorable response can be expected from China if the United States should give up this policy. The real issue is not isolation but containment. This is the crucial point at which the traditional national interests of China and the policy of the United States clash. The slogan "containment without isolation" obscures that crucial issue. It is a formula for continuing the unsuccessful policy of peripheral military containment by making it appear that the abandonment of the policy of isolation portends a significant change in American policy. It tends to make the policy of military containment palatable by tying it to an apparently real and benevolent change in our China policy. It also carries a suggestion of condescension — "We are going to be nice to you from now on" — which is not likely to impress a China that is mindful of its humiliations, past and present.

Similar considerations apply to the proposal to end the isolation of China by engaging in trade with her. The existence and the volume of trade between the United States and China are irrelevant to the basic issues that divide the two nations. Furthermore, China looks at foreign trade not as a series of transactions undertaken for commercial gain, but as an instrument of national policy. To engage in indiscriminate trade with China, apart from an overall political settlement, is self-defeating, for such trade strengthens China politically and militarily without giving an equivalent political or military advantage to the other partner.

Finally, the seating of the Communist government as the representative of China in the United Nations is not likely to be successful if it is conceived merely as the liquidation of the policy of isolation and not also and primarily as a settlement of the issue of Taiwan. It is virtually inconceivable that a representative of the Communist government should set foot in the United Nations while a representative of the Chiang Kai-shek government is present; for the idea of "Two Chinas" is as repellent to Mao Tse-tung as it is to Chiang Kai-shek. If the General Assembly should vote this fall that the representative of the Chiang Kai-shek government, the latter would no longer be represented in the General Assembly but would still occupy the seat of China as a permanent member of the Security Council. It is here that the issue would be joined.

If the Security Council should decide to emulate the General Assembly and install the representative of the Communist government in the permanent seat of China — a decision the United States could nullify by vetoing it — the Chiang Kai-Shek government would be deprived of any representation in the United Nations. In consequence, its claim to be the legitimate government of China would be destroyed, and its claim to be the legitimate government of Taiwan would be considerably impaired. Thus our policy of containing Communism, which we could continue behind the military shield of the Seventh Fleet, would be politically undermined. For by weakening Chiang Kai-shek's claim, Communist China would have taken the first step towards achieving the recognition of its own. Thus it becomes obvious again that the real issue is not isolation but containment.

The Policy of Peripheral Military Containment. We thought that the policy of military containment which worked so well against the Soviet Union in Europe would work equally well elsewhere, and so we applied it to the Middle East through the Baghdad Pact and to Asia through SEATO, and have followed it in our policies *vis-a-vis* China. Yet what succeeded in Europe was bound to fail elsewhere. The reasons for that failure are two-fold.

First, the threat that faced the nations of Western Europe in the aftermath of the Second World War was primarily military. It was the threat of of Red Army marching westward. Behind the line of military demarcation of 1945 which the policy of containment declared to be the westernmost limits of the Soviet empire, there was an ancient civilization, only temporarily weak and able to maintain itself against the threat of Communist subversion.

The situation is different in the Middle East and Asia. The threat there is not primarily military but political in nature. Weak governments and societies provide opportunities for Communist subversion. Military containment is irrelevant to that threat and may even be counter-productive. Thus the Baghdad Pact did not protect Egypt from Soviet influence and SEATO has had no bearing on Chinese influence in Indonesia and Pakistan, to speak of Asia only.

Second, and more important, China is, even in her present underdeveloped state, the dominant power in Asia. She is this by virtue of the quality and quantity of her population, her geographic position, her civilization, her past power remembered and her future power anticipated. Anybody who has traveled in Asia with his eyes and ears open must have been impressed by the enormous impact which the resurgence of China has made upon all manner of men, regardless of class and political conviction, from Japan to Pakistan.

The issue China poses is political and cultural predominance. The United States can no more contain Chinese influence in Asia by arming Thailand and fighting in South Vietnam than China could contain American influence in the Western Hemisphere by arming, say, Nicaragua and fighting in Lower California. If we are convinced that we cannot live with a China predominant on the mainland of Asia, then we must strike at the heart of Chinese power — that is, rather than try to contain the power of China by nibbling at the periphery of her empire, we must try to destroy that power itself. Thus there is logic on the side of that small group of Americans who are convinced that war between the United States and China is inevitable and that the earlier it comes, the better will be the chances for the United States to win it.

Yet, while logic is on their side, practical judgment is against them. For while China is obviously no match for the United States in overall power, China is largely immune to the specific types of power in which the superiority of the United States consists — that is, nuclear, air and naval power. Certainly, the United States has the power to destroy the nuclear installations and the major industrial and population centers of China, but this destruction would not defeat China; it would only set her development back. To be defeated, China has to be conquered.

Physical conquest would require the deployment of millions of American soldiers on the mainland of Asia. No American military leaders has ever advocated a course of action so fraught with incalculable risks, so uncertain of outcome, requiring sacrifices so out of proportion to the interests at stake and the benefits to be expected. President Eisenhower declared on February 10, 1954, that he "could conceive of no greater tragedy than for the United States to become involved in an all-out war in Indochina." General MacArthur, in the Congressional hearings concerning his dismissal and in personal conversation with President Kennedy, emphatically warned against sending American foot soldiers to the Asian mainland to fight China.

If we do not want to set ourselves goals which cannot be attained with the means we are willing to employ, we must learn to accommodate ourselves to the political and cultural predominance of China on the Asian mainland. It is instructive to note that those Asian nations which have done so — such as Burma and Cambodia — live peacefully in the shadow of the Chinese giant. On the other hand, those Asian nations which have allowed themselves to be transformed into outposts of American military power — such as Laos in the late '50s, South Vietnam and Thailand — have become the actual or prospective victims of Communist aggression and subversion. Thus it appears that peripheral military containment is counterproductive. Challenged at its periphery by American military power at its weakest — that is, by the proxy of client-states — China or its proxies are able to respond with locally superior military and political power.

Thus, even if the Chinese threat were primarily of a military nature, peripheral military containment would be ineffective in the long run in view of China's local military superiority. By believing otherwise, we have fallen heir to a misconception of our containment of the Soviet Union and of the reasons for its success. The Soviet Union has not been contained by the armed forces we have been able to put in the field locally in Europe. It has been contained by the near-certainty that an attack upon these forces would be countered by the nuclear retaliation of the United States. If we are to assume that the Chinese armies stand, or one day will stand, poised to sweep over Asia, they will not be contained by the armed forces we or our allies can put into the field on the mainland of Asia. They will only be deterred by the near-certainty that China as an organized society will be destroyed in the process of nuclear retaliation.

China is today protected from the full measure of our nuclear retaliation by her own technological backwardness; for she does not possess the number of industrial and population centers whose nuclear destruction would spell her defeat. It is for this reason that China is today more daring in words, and might well might become more daring in action if her vital interests were sufficiently threatened, than would be justified in view of the overall distribution of power between the United States and China. However, in the measure that China develops her nuclear capability, she also becomes vulnerable to nuclear retaliation; for once China has developed into a modern nation with a high technological capability, she will also have developed a large number of vital industrial and population centers and will then have become as vulnerable to nuclear attack as are the United States and the Soviet Union today. Assuming a modicum of rationality in the government which will then govern China, fear of nuclear retaliation must be assumed to have the same restraining influence upon Chinese policies as it has had upon the policies of the United States and the Soviet Union since the beginning of the nuclear age. Thus the nuclear arms race, at least as long as it is carried on among a few great powers, carries within itself its own corrective, however tenuous: nuclear power and nuclear vulnerability go hand in hand, and so does the rational requirement of self-restraint.

Worldwide Containment of China. The peripheral military containment of China, is however, being justified not only in local terms but also, and to an ever greater extent, in worldwide terms. We are told that by containing China in South Vietnam we are containing her everywhere, and that by frustrating a "war of national liberation" in Southeast Asia, we frustrate all "wars of national liberation." This argument has the virtue of simplicity, but it is supported by no historic evidence. It brings to mind the statement which William Graham Sumner made at the beginning of the century: "The amount of superstition is not so much changed, but it now attaches to politics, not to religion.

The so-called "domino theory" is indeed an echo of the Marxist dogma of historic inevitability which asserts that communism will inevitably spread from country to country until in the end it engulfs the world. Nothing of the kind has actually happened. After the Second World War, the nations of Eastern Europe went communist, but Finland to this day has not. After the collapse of French rule in Indochina in 1954, North Vietnam went communist, but nobody else did. By 1960, half of Laos had gone communist, but nobody else followed suit. For almost two decades, the fortunes of communism in Indonesia have fluctuated according to local conditions, not according to what happened or did not happen elsewhere. Can anyone seriously maintain that the fortunes of the guerrilla wars in Guatemala, Colombia or Venezuela will depend upon what happens or does not happen in South Vietnam? It stands to reason that the triumph or defeat of communism in any particular country is not simply a by-product of what happens or does not happen in other countries. What will happen in Vietnam can at the very best be no more than one factor among many, and most certainly not the decisive one, that will influence developments in other countries.

A New China Policy for the U.S. What follows from this analysis for the policies of the United States *vis-a-vis China?* In view of the vital interests of the United States in the Asian and world balance of power, five basic principles ought to guide the policies of the United States with regard to China:

First, the policy of peripheral military containment ought to be gradually liquidated. This policy is not only irrelevant to the interests of the United States but actually runs counter to them.

Second, both the policy of isolating China and the policy of ending that isolation are essentially irrelevant to the issue at hand. One may aggravate, and the other ameliorate, the international climate; but they have no relevance, one way or the other, to the basic issue of containment.

Third, since the expansion of Chinese power and influence, threatening the Asian and world balance of power, proceeds by political rather than military means, it must be contained by political means. To that purpose, it is necessary to strengthen politically, socially and economically, the nations of Asia which are within China's reach, without exacting in return political and military alignments directed against China. We ought to pursue a similar policy with regard to the uncommitted nations in which China in the recent past has attempted to gain a foothold.

Fourth, we ought to be clear in our minds that if we should continue the present policy of the peripheral military containment of China, we will find ourselves in all likelihood sooner or later at war with China. If we want to avoid such a war, we must change our policy. If we do not want to change our policy, we must be ready to go to war. That is to say, either we bring the means we are willing to employ into line with our objectives, or we cut down our objectives to the measure of the means we are willing to employ.

Fifth, the ultimate instrument for containing China is the same that has contained the Soviet Union: the retaliatory nuclear capability of the United States. It must be brought home to China, as it was brought home to the Soviet Union, that in the unlikely event that she should embark upon a policy of Asian or world conquest, she is bound to be at war with the United States.

16

ALTERNATIVES IN VIETNAM

By GENERAL JAMES M. GAVIN

I particularly appreciate the opportunity to appear in an open hearing because I feel strongly these issues are of the utmost importance to our people. They should hear the differing views and out of this discourse will come, hopefully, a coalesced and consolidated national will to get on with the work at hand.

May I say at the outset that in the background of my point of view that I have arrived at and expressed in *Harper's* magazine [February 1966] went two years of service with the Philippine Scouts in the late '30s, and since that time considerable interest in the affairs of Southeast Asia.

At the time of the fall of Dienbienphu, at the direction of the Chief of Staff, I visited Korea, Formosa, Saigon, talked to Diem, talked to General Ely there, General Collins, General Daniels, and others about the problems; went on to Thailand and talked to Mr. Sarit.

Among other things at that time I recommended the construction of a highway from Bangkok to the Mekong, feeling that Thailand was a very sensitive spot and very likely might become a very deeply involved part of the Southeast Asia — deeply involved in our own strategy and affairs.

Since then, perhaps one of the most interesting experiences I have had was with Mr. Kennedy. About a month after going to the post in Paris he asked me to return to talk about the problems of Laos. He was confronted with a very difficult situation, and I speak from memory now. We were supporting Phoumi, a rightist, and the question confronting President Kennedy was to what extent should we become involved in land warfare in Laos.

I do not know, but I would suspect if he had sought the advice of the Pentagon, we no doubt would have committed forces and ultimately more divisions and more divisions. But to Mr. Kennedy this made little sense and, indeed, the more we talked about it, the more I agreed with him; a landlocked country, remote from the immediate application of seapower and somewhat less of airpower seemed to offer a hopeless situation to us.

He asked me, therefore, to go to Paris upon my return and enter into discussions with Souvanna Phouma to see if we could not convince that gentleman that we were interested in a "free, neutral, independent Laos." This I undertook to do.

Admittedly it was with some misgivings at the outset because Souvanna Phouma had a reputation of being then very close to the Communists, and I was not at all sure of how our negotiations would come out . . .

After about eight meetings, and very fruitful and fascinating meetings they were for me, we did arrive indeed at a treaty that, hopefully guaranteed the freedom, neutrality, and independence of Laos.

I was aware then, as I am now, that what our President sought to achieve was a political settlement to what appeared to be a potentially serious military problem. He was absolutely right and we did arrive at that solution.

Interest in Global Strategy. Since then I have continued to devote a great deal of my time to matters of global strategy in our commitments.

Late last spring I was asked by the *New York Times* to do an article on the meaning of the atomic bomb 20 years later. This was for the early August (1965) edition of the *New York Times Magazine*. I had given a great deal of attention to the bombing in 1940, and even then came to the conclusion that urban bombing lacked credibility for a number of reasons perhaps not worthwhile going into here, and I wrote an article that I was denied publication at that time. I felt that the problems of the bomb were quite different than simply escalating World War II experience into more and more applied power.

As the summer of 1965 came to an end, my thinking on this matter formed into real meaning of the changes in global strategy that in my opinion have taken place in the last 20 years, and I did an article on this, and in the midst of this I was exchanging correspondence with Mr. Fisher, talking about air cavalry which was a postulation advanced in the early 1950s, considered far too radical for acceptance at the time, and now has valid and accepted battlefield application.

So I at that time and late in the summer or early fall decided that in view of our total spectrum of global commitments, and the changing nature of global strategy, we had better look hard at our Vietnamese commitment. It was becoming alarmingly out of balance and this was the basis for the letter I wrote which I will be very happy to come back to later.

I might say that all I said in that letter was let's look at (a) where we are today, what our commitments are, what it is costing and what we do; and (b) what the alternatives are, what these costs might be, and having done this, let's make up our mind what we are going to do.

Escalation at Will of Opponents. My feeling was that we were being escalated at the will of opponents rather than at our own judgment, and I based this as much upon the statement of many officials who have been to that war-torn country and who returned with optimistic statements only to find they have had to change them successively thereafter, which suggested to me that in the very beginning they didn't understand what the needs might be to meet those requirements.

In that letter I, too, in passing made reference to Hanoi and Peking and the futility of bombing, pointing out that just more of this would cause more problems, create more problems than it would solve. I referred specifically to "urban bombing." I would like to make that clear.

I have a feeling as our bombing went on beyond what were obviously military targets such as ammunition dumps, tank cars or concentrations of trucks and military targets, to powerplants and such as that, we were slowly creeping to urban bombing. I wanted to lay this at rest for once and for all time.

Just bombing a city per se, for psychological reasons achieves little in the way of military effect and, in fact, today in the court of world opinion could be extremely damaging and we would have nothing to show for it, and I want to be sure to head that off, that in my own opinion just bombing Peking wouldn't serve anything

Concept of Strategy. Now if I may talk a little about the matter of global strategy into which I would like to fit Vietnam. Two of the most significant things that have happened in our time certainly have been the bomb and the space exploration. Both of which have tremendous military significance.

The bomb is a very interesting case in point. The first question we asked ourselves was the meaning of the bomb. Was the bomb the beginning of a new age, in which the atom would solve our military problems that we have been unable to solve in the past by other means, or was it indeed the end?

I suspected at first that it was the end, although this was a very minority opinion and now I am absolutely satisfied that it was. As man has sought to impose his will on an opponent from the beginning of recorded history he has sought to use energy in every form that he could get it, bludgeon, metallic penetrating instruments, metallic pellets fired by chemical charges to the explosion of the fission of the atom and fusion of the atom itself. He finally has succeeded in bringing down to the earth the very explosions that take place on the surface of the sun, fission. He has brought the energy of the cosmos itself to the earth. He no longer can use it because it could destroy a major segment of the human race. He is at the end of the search for energy with which to impose his will on fellow men. He is at the end; that search has terminated. Now he must find more discreet means, more discriminating means. He must find greater mobility, rapid data transmission, he must keep these weapons under control. He must know what is going on everywhere as quickly as he can find out so as to keep under control local conflagrations and thus avoid the major catastrophe that might occur if, thoughtlessly, nuclear weapons were used.

If this is so, and it is purely a concept in which I do not ask you to share agreement but I am grateful for the opportunity of expressing it; if this is so, then for the first time in human history something very unusual is happening in warfare and I believe indeed it is.

Strategy has to do with those measures which taken short of war that makes absolute victory certain. If war occurs inadvertently you are sure to win.

It seems to me the best analysis I have been able to make . . . I might say, if I may, that I have given a great deal of thought and done some writing on the subject. I taught political science at the University of California, four weeks in 1946 on a sabbatical, and I haven't come to these conclusions rather casually. They represent for me, at least, considerable effort and thought.

Strategy Based on Prospering Economy. It seems to me, therefore, that our strategy today should be based upon, first of all, a dynamic and viable prospering economy, an economy that can export entrepreneurial skills, managerial techniques, dollars for acquisition, ventures abroad, to help other people. We have developed a way of life that provides an abundance of means for our people, and we should continue to export this just as aggressively as we can to help other people.

I am not talking about economic colonialism, for the enlightened businessman working abroad today is trying to help other people help themselves. People are not born equal nor indeed are nations born equal and they need help to achieve a place for their people. They need help of many kinds. We have been doing extremely well in this respect.

While I am talking in this context of strategy, it seems to me, for example, if one of these great books on decisive battles, *Fifteen Decisive Battles of the World*, by Sir Edward S. Creasy, were to be rewritten today it would include the demise of Mr. Khrushchev, who sought to coexist with his own totalitarian system organized on the basis of planning and not on market demand, who failed because he simply couldn't get the grain grown, he didn't have fertilizer and his economy just simply couldn't produce, and characteristically as happens in a failing strategy he sought the tactical gambit to recoup. He went to Cuba in a great adventure that, thanks to our great President, and our Secretary of Defense, he was defeated in.

I would say that his demise is one of the decisive setbacks in all history, and I think now in my personal opinion, that our efforts to work closely with the Soviet people should be rewarding, in fact I believe that in the President's State of the Union message the references to making changes in our tariff laws to encourage trade is a very good thing.

We have done a great deal exporting professors, entertainers, and scientists, now export businessmen and their techniques. I think we can go a long way together.

There was a turning point and it was the demise of Mr. Khrushchev.

Well now, I would say further that strategy today is in the realm of science and technology. Out of science and an adequate research program we are producing an abundance of new knowledge that will energize our economy and keep it moving and, very briefly, I think that in the court of world opinion, world opinion itself, we have the area that will have a very great deal to do with what we may do.

Strategy and World Opinion. I would draw a parallel of the use of

energy and power through the many, many centuries of human existence when people were restrained by their fellow men in what they
could do. They may have wanted to do many things. Even cities,
states, restrained what their armed forces could do, and this nation
has shrunk, this world has shrunk to the point today where we simply
can't do all the things we would like to do.

I have always felt that one of our greatest captains of all time was
General MacArthur and yet even he had to come to realize and learn
the hard way that the use of a nuclear bomb, because we had them in
our arsenal, did not permit him under his mandate from the United
Nations to use it. It was simply an intolerable thing.

I have touched on three areas of strategy that I believe are of
overriding importance.

Vietnam and Global Commitments. My concern, therefore, for
Vietnam first became aroused when I found us cutting back in our
global commitments in the realm of economics, for I began to suspect
that the escalation in Southeast Asia would begin to hurt our world
strategic position. If this has significance now it may have tremendous significance in the long run. When we begin to turn back on
what we are doing in world affairs, through our economic endeavors,
to support a tactical confrontation that appears to be escalating
at the will of an enemy we are in a very dangerous position in my
opinion, and for this reason what we are doing there deserves looking at.

There are several areas where confrontations occur tactically. I
mentioned Cuba. Europe is one today, in my opinion.. Our commitments in Europe are far in excess of our needs, not only troop
commitments but logistical support to back up those commitments.

To return to Asia, the Korean commitment is one we must maintain,
and we are maintaining it. The support of Chiang Kai-shek, Taiwan, the offshore islands of Quemoy and Matsu likewise. Southeast
Asia is a very volatile, dynamic area of operations. Vietnam is not
alone. Thailand I look upon as a very, very dangerous area and one
that we should regard most seriously at this time.

First of all, what do we have today and what can they do, and I
simply stated today we have sufficient forces in South Vietnam to
hold areas along the coast where sea and air power can be made fully
effective, and then we can use this power as we see fit to do so, I then
suggested that we might look at the alternatives very realistically.

Are we really trying to seal off Vietnam entirely, extend the 17th parallel all across, all the way across to the Mekong River? This has been considered. One could put a cordon sanitaire across there at considerable cost. It would still be open ended a bit at the end but it is possible.

One could extend the security down to the Cambodian border but to me these appear to be terribly costly in manpower and our national wealth, and I use the word "wealth" to include all necessary material resources.

So I finally came to the conclusion, and I think this is very important in view of the charges that have been made about what I have said, and I quote "We must do the best we can with the forces we have deployed in Vietnam now." Nothing more than that. I did not say "withdraw," "retreat," "go ahead," "attack," do anything else. We must do the best we can with what we have in hand, keeping in mind the true meaning of global strategy in world affairs today.

Economics, science and technology, and world opinion will, in the long run, serve our strategic interests well if we handle our national resources wisely.

On the other hand, tactical mistakes that are allowed to escalate at the initiative of an enemy could be disastrously costly. Since the advent of the space age there has been a revolution in the nature of global conflict. The confrontation in Vietnam is the first test of our understanding of such change or lack of it. The measures that we now take in Southeast Asia must stem from sagacity and thoughtfulness, restraint and an awareness of the nature of strategy in this very rapidly shrinking world, and that is right from the letter that I wrote to *Harper's*.

* * *

A COMMUNICATION ON VIETNAM FROM GEN. JAMES M. GAVIN

(NOTE: In the following letter General Gavin presents the first basic criticism of the administration's policy in Vietnam by a major military figure. As an alternative, he urges the stopping of our bombing of North Vietnam, a halt in the escalation of the ground war, withdrawal of American troops to defend a limited number of enclaves along the South Vietnames coast, and renewed efforts "to find a solution through the United Nations or a conference in Geneva."

General Gavin argues for such a change in policy on purely military grounds. His views on the Vietnam war cannot be taken lightly, since he has established a reputation during the last 30 years as one of America's leading strategic thinkers. At the time of the French defeat in Vietnam, he was Chief of Plans and Operations for the Department of the Army, and his advice is generally believed to be largely responsible for the U.S. refusal to enter the Southeast Asian conflict on a large scale at that time. He enlisted in the Army as a private in 1924 and rose to the rank of lieutenant general before his retirement in 1958; he had a distinguished combat career as a paratroop commander in World War II; and he served for a time as Chief of Research and Development for the Army. After retirement he was Ambassador to France, and is now chairman of the board and chief executive officer of Arthur D. Little, Inc., an industrial research firm in Cambridge, Mass.

He left the Pentagon because of disagreements on what was, in 1958, the basic military policy of the Eisenhower administration. His reasons for such disagreements were set forth in his book, *War and Peace in the Space Age,* published by Harper & Row; as he indicates in the following letter, most of the changes he then urged have since been carried out.

The editors hope that General Gavin's communication may stimulate a searching reexamination of American military and foreign policies by other public figures who are especially qualified by experience and training to discuss them. In the coming months *Harper's* hopes to publish further contributions to such a reappraisal. — *The Editors)*

Last November our Secretary of Defense, while in Vietnam, finally gave battlefield approval to the concept of Sky Cavalry. *Harper's* should take some pride in the fact that it published my article, "Cavalry, and I Don't Mean Horses," in 1954. That was the genesis of the idea for this new form of mobility for our ground forces. It was too revolutionary for acceptance in the Pentagon then, and *Harper's* performed a public service in helping advance the idea.

I would like to comment about the Vietnam situation further. I should emphasize at the outset that I am writing solely from a military-technical point of view. I was Chief of Plans and Operations in the Department of the Army when Dienbienphu brought the French endeavors in Vietnam to an end. The Chief of Staff, Gen. Matthew B. Ridgway, directed that we go into the situation quite thoroughly in case a decision should be made to send U.S. forces into the Hanoi Delta. As I recall, we were talking about the possibility of sending eight divisions plus 35 engineer battalions and other auxiliary units. We had one or two old China hands on the staff at the time and the more we studied the situation the more we realized that we were, in fact, going to war with China, since she was supplying all the arms, ammunition, medical, and other supplies to Ho Chi Minh. If we would be, in fact, fighting China, then we were fighting her in the wrong place on terms entirely to her advantage. Manchuria, with its vast industrial complex, coal, and iron ore, is the Ruhr of China and the heart of its warmaking capacity. There, rather than in Southeast Asia, is where China should be engaged, if at all.

I should emphasize at the outset that there are philosophical and moral aspects of the war in Southeast Asia that are understandably disturbing to every thoughtful person. My comments, however, are based entirely upon a tactical evaluation of our efforts there. At the time of the French defeat, it seemed to us military planners that if an effort were made by the United States to secure Vietnam from Chinese military exploitation, and that if force on the scale that we were talking about were to be employed, then the Chinese would very likely reopen the fighting in Korea.

At the time, General Ridgway thought it prudent to bring this situation directly to the attention of President Eisenhower, pointing out that we should be prepared for a large-scale war if we were to make the initial large-scale commitment to the Hanoi Delta that we were thinking about. I thought at the time that it took great moral courage for General Ridgway to take this action, but he has never been a man to lack such courage. The President decided not to make the commitment and in his book, *Mandate for Change*, he commented that to have gone to war under those conditions would have been "like hitting the tail of the snake rather than the head," which is a good analogy.

Today we have sufficient force in South Vietnam to hold several enclaves on the coast, where sea and air power can be made fully effective. By enclaves I suggest Camranh Bay, Danang, and similar areas where American bases are being established. However, we are stretching these resources beyond reason in our endeavors to secure the entire country of South Vietnam from the Viet Cong penetration. This situation, of course, is caused by the growing Viet Cong strength.

The time has come, therefore, when we simply have to make up our mind what we want to do and then provide the resources necessary to do it. If our objective is to secure all of South Vietnam, then forces should be deployed on the 17th parallel and along the Cambodian border adequate to do this. In view of the nature of the terrain, it might be necessary to extend our defenses on the 17th parallel to the Mekong River, and across part of Thailand. Such a course would take many times as much force as we now have in Vietnam.

To increase the bombing and to bomb Hanoi — or even Peking — will add to our problems rather than detract from them, and it will not stop the penetrations of North Vietnam troops into the south. Also, if we were to quadruple, for example, our combat forces there, we should then anticipate the intervention of Chinese "volunteers" and the reopening of the Korean front. This seems to be the ultimate prospect of the course that we are now on.

On the other hand, if we should maintain enclaves on the coast, desist in our bombing attacks in North Vietnam, and seek to find a solution through the United Nations or a conference in Geneva, we could very likely do so with the forces now available. Maintaining such enclaves while an effort is being made to solve the internal situation in Vietnam, and in the face of the terroristic war that would be waged against them, poses some serious problems, and the retention of some of the enclaves may prove to be unwise; but the problems that we would then have to deal with would be far less serious than those associated with an expansion of the conflict.

I do not for a moment think that if we should withdraw from Vietnam the next stop would be Waikiki. The Kra Peninsula, Thailand, and the Philippines can all be secured, although we ultimately might have heavy fighting on the northern frontiers of Thailand. But we should be realistic about the dangers of the course that we are now on. A straightforward escalation of our land power in Southeast Asia to meet every land-based challenge, while at the same time we leave China and Cambodia immune from attack, poses some very forbidding prospects. I realize that our Secretary of State was recently quoted in the press as having said that "the idea of sanctuary is out." However, the initiative is not ours and there is an abundance of evidence now that both China and Cambodia are sanctuaries for Communist military strength that is used to support the Viet Cong.

To get to the heart of the problem, I doubt that world opinion would tolerate the bombing and seizure of Manchuria. If the Chinse Communists continue their present course of aggression and, at the same time, continue to develop more devastating weapons — and I refer to nuclear weapons — the time may come when China will bring upon herself a nuclear war. But that time is not here yet. In the meantime, we must do the best we can with the forces we have deployed to Vietnam, keeping in mind the true meaning of strategy in global affairs. Economics, science and technology, and world opinion will, in the long run, serve our strategic interests well if we handle our national resources wisely. On the other hand, tactical mistakes that are allowed to escalate at the initiative of an enemy could be disastrously costly. Since the advent of the space age, there has been a revolution in the nature of war and global conflict. The confrontation in Vietnam is the first test of our understanding of such change, or our lack of it. The measures that we now take in Southeast Asia must stem from sagacity and thoughtfulness, and an awareness of the nature of strategy in this rapidly shrinking world.

Referring again to the sky cavalry concept, which we are now employing in South Vietnam, it is the kind of innovation that is generally unpopular in a conservative society, and in the military establishment of such a society. But many more innovations, both technical and in management methods, must be found if we are to continue to survive as a free people. Merely making bigger bombs or using more of them is not the answer. So I hope that *Harper's* will continue to support innovative methods when they are suggested, as you did when you first published the idea of sky cavalry in 1954.

When I retired in 1958, I said that I would be happy to serve as a private in the Army if it were the kind of Army that I wanted it to be. I think it is that kind of an Army now, and I would be happy to serve it in any grade in Vietnam or anywhere else. It is doing a splendid job in Vietnam and needs the support of all of our people.

17

IS AMERICAN INTERVENTION JUSTIFIABLE?

By GEORGE KENNAN

The subject on which I am invited to give my views is . . . the complex of problems connected with our present involvement in Vietnam. I would like to explain, in undertaking to speak on this subject, that Southeast Asia is a part of the world for which I can claim no specialized knowledge. I am not familiar with the official rationale of our policy there except as it has been revealed in the press. I cannot recall that I have ever, either during my official service in government or subsequently, been drawn by the executive branch of our Government into consultation on the problem of our policy in Southeast Asia, or even been made privy to the official discussions by which that policy was decided.

I am sure that there are many data, relevant to any thoroughly founded judgment on these matters, which are not available to me; and this being the case, I have tried in recent weeks and months not to jump to final conclusions even in my own thoughts, to remain sympathetically receptive, both to our Government's explanations of the very real difficulties it has faced and to the doubts and questions of its serious critics.

I have not been anxious to press my views on the public but I gladly give them to you for whatever they are worth, claiming no particular merit for them except perhaps that they flow from an experience with Communist affairs that runs back now for some 38 years, and also from the deepest and most troubled sort of concern that we should find the proper course, the right course, at this truly crucial moment.

Wisdom of U.S. Military Involvement. The first point I would like to make is that if we were not already involved as we are today in Vietnam, I would know of no reason why we should wish to become so involved, and I could think of several reasons why we should wish not to.

Vietnam is not a region of major military and industrial importance. It is difficult to believe that any decisive developments of the world situation would be determined in normal circumstances by what happens on that territory. If it were not for the considerations of prestige that arise precisely out of our present involvement, even a situation in which South Vietnam was controlled exclusively by the Viet Cong, while regrettable, and no doubt morally unwarranted, would not, in my opinion, present dangers great enough to justify our direct military intervention.

Given the situation that exists today in the relations among the leading Communist powers, and by that I have, of course, in mind primarily the Soviet-Chinese conflict, there is every likelihood that a Communist regime in South Vietnam would follow a fairly independent course.

There is no reason to suspect that such a regime would find it either necessary or desirable in present circumstances to function simply as a passive puppet and instrument of Chinese power. And as for the danger that its establishment there would unleash similar tendencies in neighboring countries, this, I think, would depend largely on the manner in which it came into power. In the light of what has recently happened in Indonesia, and on the Indian subcontinent, the danger of the so-called domino effect, that is the effect that would be produced by a limited Communist success in South Vietnam, seems to me to be considerably less than it was when the main decisions were taken that have led to our present involvement.

Let me stress, I do not say that that danger does not exist, I say that it is less than it was a year or two ago when we got into this involvement.

From the long-term standpoint, therefore, and on principle, I think our military involvement in Vietnam has to be recognized as unfortunate, as something we would not choose deliberately, if the choice were ours to make all over again today, and by the same token, I think it should be our Government's aim to liquidate this involvement just as soon as this can be done without inordinate damage to our own prestige or to the stability of conditions in that area.

It is obvious on the other hand that this involvement is today a fact. It creates a new situation. It raises new questions, ulterior to the long-term problem, which have to be taken into account. A precipitate and disorderly withdrawal could represent in present circumstances a disservice to our own interests, and even to world peace, greater than any that might have been involved by our failure to engage ourselves there in the first place.

This is a reality which, if there is to be any peaceful resolution of this conflict, is going to have to be recognized both by the more critical of our friends and by our adversaries.

Expansion of Hostilities is Dangerous. But at the same time, I have great misgivings about any deliberate expansion of hostilities on our part directed to the achievement of something called victory — if by the use of that term we envisage the complete disappearance of the recalcitrance with which we are now faced, the formal submission by the adversary to our will, and the complete realization of our present stated political aims.

I doubt that these things can be achieved even by the most formidable military successes.

There seems to be an impression about that if we bring sufficient military pressure to bear there will occur at some point something in the nature of a political capitulation on the other side. I think this is a most dangerous assumption. I don't say that it is absolutely impossible, but it is a dangerous assumption in the light of the experience we have had with Communist elements in the past.

The North Vietnamese and the Viet Cong have between them a great deal of space and manpower to give up if they have to, and the Chinese can give them more if they need it. Fidelity to the Communist tradition would dictate that if really pressed to extremity on the military level these people should disappear entirely from the open scene and fall back exclusively on an underground political and military existence rather than to accept terms that would be openly humiliating and would represent in their eyes the betrayal of the future political prospects of the cause to which they are dedicated.

Any total rooting out of the Viet Cong from the territory of South Vietnam could be achieved, if it could be achieved at all, only at the cost of a degree of damage to civilian life and of civilian suffering generally for which I would not like to see this country responsible.

And to attempt to crush North Vietnamese strength to a point where Hanoi could no longer give any support for Viet Cong political activity in the South, would almost certainly, it seems to me, have the effect of bringing in Chinese forces at some point, whether formally or in the guise of volunteers, thus involving us in a military conflict with Communist China on one of the most unfavorable theaters of hostility that we could possibly choose.

This is not the only reason why I think we should do everything possible to avoid the escalation of this conflict. There is another one which is no less weighty, and this is the effect the conflict is already having on our policies and interests further afield. This involvement seems to me to represent a grievous misplacement of emphasis in our foreign policies as a whole.

Effect on Confidence of Other Countries. Not only are great and potentially more important questions of world affairs not receiving, as a consequence of our involvement in Vietnam, the attention they should be receiving, but in some instances assets we already enjoy and hopefully possibilities we should be developing are being sacrificed to this unpromising involvement in a remote and secondary theater. Our relations with the Soviet Union have suffered grievously as was to be expected, and this at a time when far more important things were involved in those relations than what is ultimately involved in Vietnam and when we had special reason, I think, to cultivate those relations. And more unfortunate still, in my opinion, is the damage being done to the feelings entertained for us by the Japanese people. The confidence and good disposition of the Japanese is the greatest asset we have had and the greatest asset we could have in east Asia. As the only major industrial complex in the entire Far East, and the only place where the sinews of modern war can be produced on a formidable scale, Japan is of vital importance to us and indeed to the prospects generally of peace and stability in east Asia. There is no success we could have in Vietnam that would conceivably warrant, in my opinion, the sacrifice by us of the confidence and good will of the Japanese people. Yet, I fear that we abuse that confidence and good will in the most serious way when we press the military struggle in Vietnam, and particularly when we press it by means of strategic bombing, a process to which the Japanese for historical reasons are peculiarly sensitive and averse.

I mention Japan particularly because it is an outstanding example, both in importance and in the intensity of the feelings aroused, of the psychological damage that is being done in many parts of the world by the prosecution of this conflict, and that will be done in even greater measure if the hostilities become still more bloody and tragic as a result of our deliberate effort.

It is clear that however justified our action may be in our own eyes, it has failed to win either enthusiasm or confidence even among peoples normally friendly to us.

U.S. Motives are Misinterpreted. Our motives are widely misinterpreted, and the spectacle emphasized and reproduced in thousands of press photographs and stories that appear in the press of the world, the spectacle of Americans inflicting grievous injury on the lives of a poor and helpless people, and particularly a people of different race and color, no matter how warranted by military necessity or be the excesses of the adversary, produces reactions among millions of people throughout the world profoundly detrimental to the image we would like them to hold of this country. I am not saying that this is just or right. I am saying that this is so, and that it is bound in the circumstances to be so. A victory purchased at the price of further such damage would be a hollow one in terms of our world interests, no matter what advantages it might hold from the standpoint of developments on the local scene.

Now, these are the reasons . . . why I hope that our Government will restrict our military operations in Vietnam to the minimum necessary to assure the security of our forces and to maintain our military presence there until we can achieve a satisfactory peaceful resolution of the conflict. And these are the reasons why I hope that we will continue to pursue vigorously, and I may say consistently, the quest for such a peaceful resolution of the conflict, even if this involves some moderation of our stated objectives, and even if the resulting settlement appears to us as something less than ideal.

Agreement with General Gavin's Enclave Theory. I cannot, of course, judge the military neccessities of our situation. But everything that I can learn about its political aspects suggests to me that General Gavin is on the right track in his suggestion that we should, if I understand him correctly, decide what limited areas we can safely police and defend, and restrict ourselves largely to the maintenance of our position there. I have listened with interest to the arguments that have been brought forward in opposition to his views, and I must say that I have not been much impressed with some of them. When I am told that it would be difficult to defend such enclaves it is hard for me to understand why it would be easier to defend the far greater areas to which presumably a successful escalation of our military activity would bring us.

I also find it difficult, for reasons that I won't take time to go into here, to believe that our allies, and particularly our Western European allies, most of whom themselves have given up great territories within recent years, and sometimes in a very statesmanlike way, I find it hard to believe that we would be subject to great reproach or loss of confidence at their hands simply because we followed a defensive rather than an offensive strategy in Vietnam at this time.

In matters such as this, it is not in my experience what you do that is mainly decisive. It is how you do it; and I would submit that there is more respect to be won in the opinion of this world by a resolute and courageous liquidation of unsound positions than by the most stubborn pursuit of extravagant or unpromising objectives.

U.S. Commitment to South Vietnam Bewildering. And finally, when I hear it said that to adopt a defensive strategy in South Vietnam would be to rat on our commitment to the Government of that territory I am a little bewildered. I would like to know what that commitment really consists of, and how and when it was incurred. What seems to be involved here is an obligation on our part not only to defend the frontiers of a certain political entity against outside attack, but to assure the internal security of its government in circumstances where that government is unable to assure that security by its own means. Now, any such obligation is one that goes obviously considerably further in its implications than the normal obligations of a military alliance.

If we did not incur such an obligation in any formal way, then I think we should not be inventing it for ourselves and assuring ourselves that we are bound by it today.

But if we did incur it, then I do fail to understand how it was possible to enter into any such commitment otherwise than through the constitutional processes which were meant to come into play when even commitments of lesser import than this were undertaken.

Now, just two concluding observations: I would like it understood that what I have said here implies nothing but the highest respect and admiration for the fighting qualities of our forces in the field. I have the greatest confidence in them, men and commanders alike. I have no doubt, in fact, that they can and will, if duty requires, produce before this thing is over military results that will surprise both our skeptical friends and our arrrogant adversaries. It is not their fighting qualities. It is the purpose to which they are being employed that evokes my skepticism.

U.S. Should Not Shoulder Political Burden of Other Countries. Secondly, I would like to say I am trying to look at this whole problem not from the moral standpoint but from the practical one. I see in the Viet Cong a band of ruthless fanatics, many of them misled, no doubt, by the propaganda that has been drummed into them, but cruel in their methods, dictatorial, and oppressive in their aims, I am not conscious of having any sympathy for them. I think their claim to represent the people of South Vietnam is unfounded. A country which fell under this exclusive power would have my deepest sympathy; and I would hope that this eventuality at any rate would be avoided by a restrained and moderate policy on our part in South Vietnam.

But our country should not be asked, and should not ask of itself, to shoulder the main burden of determining the political realities in any other country, and particularly not in one remote from our shores, from our culture, and from the experience of our people. This is not only not our business, but I don't think we can do it successfully.

Timely Words of John Quincy Adams. In saying this, I am only paraphrasing and very poorly the words once uttered by one who had at one time been a member of the U.S. Senate, and who, had a Foreign Relations Committee existed in his day, would unquestionably have been a member of it. This was John Quincy Adams, and I would like your permission to recall, before I close, the words of his that I have in mind. They were spoken in this city 145 years ago on the Fourth of July, 1821:

"Wherever the standard of freedom and independence has been or shall be unfurled, there will be America's heart, her benedictions, and her prayers. But she goes not abroad in search of monsters to destroy. She is the well-wisher to the freedom and independence of all. She is the champion and vindicator only of her own. She will recommend the general cause by the countenance of her voice, and by the benignant sympathy of her example. She well knows that by once enlisting under other banners than her own, were they even the banners of foreign independence, she would involve herself beyond the power of extrication, in all the wars of interest and intrigue, of individual avarice, envy, and ambition, which assume the colors and usurp the standards of freedom. The fundamental maxims of her policy would insensibly change from liberty to force . . . She might become the dictatress of the world. She would no longer be the ruler of her own spirit."

Now . . . I don't know exactly what John Quincy Adams had in mind when he spoke those words, but I think that without knowing it, he spoke very directly and very pertinently to us here today.

18

U.S. OBJECTIVES

By General Maxwell D. Taylor

I agree thoroughly with the motivating purposes of these hearings; namely, to analyze the reasons why we are involved in South Vietnam, the importance of this involvement, and the effectiveness with which we are dealing with the resultant problems. If my personal view can assist in clarifying these points, I shall be most happy to present them.

For the purpose of providing a basis for our subsequent discussion, with your permission I would like to make a continuous statement which will undertake to answer three basic questions. First, what are we doing in South Vietnam? Secondly, how are we doing it? And, finally, can we improve upon what we are doing?

What We Are Doing in Vietnam. A simple statement of what we are doing in South Vietnam is to say that we are engaged in a clash of purpose and interest with the militant wing of the Communist movement represented by Hanoi, the Viet Cong and Peking. Opposing these Communist forces, in the front rank stand the government and people of South Vietnam supported primarily by the United States but assisted in varying degree by some 30 other nations.

The purpose of the Hanoi camp is perfectly clear and has been since 1954. It is to absorb the 15 million people of South Vietnam into a single Communist state under the leadership of Ho Chi Minh and his associates in Hanoi. In the course of accomplishing this basic purpose, the Communist leaders expect to undermine the position of the United States in Asia and to demonstrate the efficacy of the so-called war of liberation as a cheap, safe, and disavowable technique for the future expansion of militant communism.

Our purpose is equally clear and easily defined. In his Baltimore speech of April 7, 1965, President Johnson did so in the following terms: "Our objective is the independence of South Vietnam and its

203

freedom from attack. We want nothing for ourselves — only that the people of South Vietnam be allowed to guide their own country in their own way." This has been our basic objective since 1954. It has been pursued by three successive administrations and remains our basic objective today.

Like the Communists, we have secondary objectives derived from the basic one. We intend to show that the "war of liberation," far from being cheap, safe, and disavowable, is costly, dangerous, and doomed to failure. We must destroy the myth of its invincibility in order to protect the independence of many weak nations which are vulnerable targets for "subversive aggression" — to use the proper term for the "war of liberation." We cannot leave while force and violence threaten them.

The Importance of Vietnam to the United States. The question has been raised as to whether this clash of interests is really important to us. An easy and incomplete answer would be that it must be important to us since it is considered so important by the other side. Their leadership has made it quite clear that they regard South Vietnam as the testing ground for the "war of liberation" and that after its anticipated success there, it will be used widely about the world. Kosygin told Mr. Reston in his interview last December: "We believe that national liberation wars are just wars and they will continue as long as there is national oppression by imperialist powers."

Before him, Khrushchev, in January 1961, had the following to say: "Now a word about national liberation wars. The armed struggle by the Vietnamese people or the war of the Algerian people serve as the latest example of such wars. These are revolutionary wars. Such wars are not only admissible but inevitable. Can such wars flare up in the future? They can. The Communists fully support such just wars and march in the front rank with peoples waging liberation struggles."

General Giap, the commander in chief of the North Vietnamese forces, has made the following comment: "South Vietnam is the model of the national liberation movement of our time. If the special warfare that the U.S. imperialists are testing in South Vietnam is overcome, then it can be defeated anywhere in the world."

The minister of defense of Communist China, Marshal Lin Piao, in a long statement of policy in September 1965, described in detail how

Mao Tse-tung expects to utilize the "war of liberation" to expand communism in Latin America, Africa and Asia.

Effect of Success of "War of Liberation." These testimonials show that, apart from the goal of imposing communism on 15 million South Vietnamese, the success of the "war of liberation" is in itself an important objective of the Communist leadership. On our side, we can understand the grave consequences of such a success for us. President Eisenhower in 1959 stressed the military importance of defending Southeast Asia in the following terms. He said: "Strategically, South Vietnam's capture by the Communists would bring their power several hundred miles into a hitherto free region. The remaining countries of Southeast Asia would be menaced by a great flanking movement. The loss of South Vietnam would set in motion a crumbling process which could as it progresses have grave consequences for the forces of freedom."

Now, this view has often been referred to as the "domino theory." I personally do not believe in such a theory if it means belief in a law of nature which requires the collapse of each neighboring state in an inevitable sequence, following a Communist victory in South Vietnam. However, I am deeply impressed with the probable effects worldwide, not necessarily in areas contiguous to South Vietnam, if the "war of liberation" scores a significant victory there. President Kennedy commented on this danger with moving eloquence:

"The great battleground for the defense and expansion of freedom today is the southern half of the globe — Asia, Latin America, Africa and the Middle East — the lands of the people who harbor the greatest hopes. The enemies of freedom think they can destroy the hopes of the newer nations and they aim to do it before the end of this decade. This is a struggle of will and determination as much as one of force and violence. It is a battle for the conquest of the minds and souls as much as for the conquest of lives and territory. In such a struggle, we cannot fail to take sides."

Gentlemen, I think a simple answer to the question, what are we doing in South Vietnam, is to say that for more than a decade we have been taking sides in a cause in which we have a vital stake.

How Are We Doing It? My second question was, How are we doing in the pursuit of our objectives in South Vietnam? Both sides in the struggle have over the years developed the current strategies which are now in confrontation.

During 1964 and 1965, the Hanoi leadership attempted to exploit the political turbulence which followed the fall of President Diem in November 1963. Greatly encouraged by the disorder which marked the political scene in Saigon, the Communist leadership made a massive effort to press on to victory. To meet the growing needs in military manpower, they began the infiltration of personnel of the North Vietnamese army, first as individual replacements, later as formed tactical units. Utilizing this new strength, they intended to make the monsoon offensive of 1965 a major drive for significant military victories.

Concurrently, they increased the sabotage directed at the land communication system in South Vietnam for the purpose of hampering the distribution of commodities and thus adding to the economic stresses in the south.

Terrorism was stepped up and directed with added frequency at U.S. personnel and installations. They apparently hoped to be able to seize and hold politically important localities such as district and provincial capitals, to demoralize the Vietnamese people and government and to demonstrate to the United States that we were backing a cause which must inevitably fail.

Introduction of American Ground Forces. Faced with this growing threat, the Vietnamese government and our American officials were obliged to develop a counter strategy to blunt and defeat the intensified efforts of our adversaries. It evolved out of the experience of the preceding months and years and assumed its full form with the critical decisions in 1965 to introduce U.S. ground forces and to initiate the bombing campaign against military targets in the north. Both of these courses of action had been under consideration at least since November 1961, when I presented my report to President Kennedy following a visit to Saigon to appraise the growing criticality of the situation there.

We did not take either action at that time but my report contained the following comment with regard to the possible necessity of using air power against the source of the Viet Cong support in North Vietnam. I quote:

"While we feel that the program recommended represents those measures which should be taken now, I would not suggest that it is the final word. If the Hanoi decision is to continue the irregular war declared on South Vietnam in 1959 with continued infiltration and covert support of guerrilla bands in the territory of our ally, we will then have to decide whether to accept as legitimate the continued guidance, training and support of a guerrilla war across an international boundary.

"Can we admit the establishment of the common law that the party attacked and his friends are denied the right to strike the source of the aggression after the fact that external aggression is clearly established?"

By February 1965, it became clear that we could no longer tolerate this clandestine support from the immune sanctuary in North Vietnam which served as the external base for the Viet Cong insurgency.

Increasing the Effectiveness of Ground Forces. In brief, the strategy which we have been and are pursuing consists of four components. The first includes the many activities directed at increasing the effectiveness of our ground combat against the Viet Cong and North Vietnamese units in South Vietnam. For this purpose, we have made the utmost efforts to increase the indigenous forces of South Vietnam, always mindful that this is a Vietnamese war in which we should do only those things which the Vietnamese cannot do for themselves or cannot do in time to avert defeat.

From July 1964 to July 1965 the armed forces and police of South Vietnam were increased by some 140,000 trained men, a very creditable effort on the part of this small country where military leadership and administrative experience are inevitably in short supply. As of today, the overall military strength in South Vietnam is approaching 700,000, the largest military force in being among all of our allies, worldwide.

Encouraging though the results have been in increasing the Vietnamese strength, during the year cited, our intelligence authorities believed that the Viet Cong increased their total strength by some 60,000. In other words, we were advancing at a rate only a little better than 2 to 1 in our favor.

Since history has shown that the government forces successfully opposing a guerrilla insurgency in the past have required a much greater preponderance of strength, 10 to 1 or 12 to 1, for example, it was quite clear the Vietnamese could not raise forces fast enough to keep pace with the growing threat of the Viet Cong in time. It was this sobering conclusion that led to the decision to introduce American ground forecs with their unique mobility and massive firepower to compensate for the deficiency in Vietnamese strength. With such forces available, it was felt that the ratios of required strength cited above would lose much of their validity.

Is the Requirement for U.S. Troops Endless? I am thoroughly ... aware of the concern of this committee over the growing requirement for American troops in South Vietnam. Is this an endless requirement in an open-ended war? I do not believe that anyone can give a completely satisfactory reply to this question but I can suggest the consideration of certain limiting factors which have a bearing on the matter.

First, on our side, we are not setting as an objective for our ground forces the occupation of all South Vietnam or the hunting down of the last armed guerrilla. We are in Vietnam to safeguard the people who are the real target of the enemy. Terrain has little meaning except insofar as it supports people. Thus the extent of control and protection of population is the true measure of progress rather than control of territory. By the former indicator we are not doing too badly.

Senator Mansfield estimates, in his recent report, that the government controls about 60 percent of the population, the Viet Cong about 22 percent, leaving about 18 percent contested. When I left Saigon last July, those figures were 53 percent, 25 percent, 22 percent.

The point I wish to make is that when one expresses our military objective in terms of securing a high proportion of the population, the troops requirement loses some of its impression of open-endedness. Under this concept, the prime target of our U.S. forces becomes the main-line enemy units which constitute the greatest threat to population — not the entire guerrilla force wherever found.

Another limiting factor is the logistic difficulty of the Viet Cong in supporting increased numbers of troops in combat. The combination of air attacks on their lines of supply and of increasing ground attacks on their units which must then consume supplies at an increased rate places some kind of ceiling on the forces they can maintain in South Vietnam.

I wish I knew exactly where that ceiling is but our basic data on Viet Cong logistics are too uncertain to permit precision. But the point is that there are factors which tend to keep our troop requirements finite and limit the capability of Hanoi to support large numbers of additional forces in the south.

Airpower Against North Vietnamese Military Targets. The second component of our strategy relates to the use of airpower against military targets in North Vietnam. It is well to remind ourselves the reasons which impelled us to this decision. There were three which we recognized perfectly at the time of the decision and which remain valid today. The first was to give the people of South Vietnam the assurance for the first time of imposing a direct penalty on the source of the aggression. For 11 years they had suffered the depredations of the Viet Cong without exacting any price from the country which provided the direction and support. The morale of the people and that of the armed forces in Vietnam received an inestimable lift from the decision to use the air forces of both our countries against military targets in the homeland of the enemy — a lift which has certainly contributed to sustaining their will to continue to fight.

The second reason for the decision was to use airpower, insofar as it could be effective, to limit and render more difficult the infiltration of the men and supplies from North Vietnam to South Vietnam. It was perfectly clear from the start as it is clear today that airpower would not be able to stop infiltration. We were quite sure, however, that it could impose a ceiling on the forces which could be sustained in combat in South Vietnam. I do not believe that anyone who has reflected on the effect of the destruction of bridges, ports, railyards and similar facilities, and on the effect of the limitation of daylight movement on the roads throughout a large part of North Vietnam can avoid the conclusion that the air campaign has had an important effect in slowing down infiltration and in raising its price. A testimonial to its effectiveness was the feverish activity in North Vietnam during the bombing pause to repair bomb damage and to move transport in daylight.

The third reason for the decision to use our airpower was to provide a sobering reminder to the leaders in Hanoi that progressively they must pay a mounting price for the continuation of their support of the Viet Cong insurgency.

In spite of their defiant statements of determination to endure these attacks forever, I for one know from experience that no one derives any enjoyment from receiving incoming shells and bombs day after day and I have no doubt that the warning message is getting through to the leadership of Hanoi. In a very real sense, the objective of our air campaign is to change the will of the enemy leadership.

We hope that, in due course, the combination of the Viet Cong failure to win victory on the ground in South Vietnam and the effect of continued air attacks will present to the Hanoi leadership a situation so disadvantageous that they will decide that it is in their interest to halt their aggression, redefine their aims, and join with us in discussing ways and means of improving the lot of all Vietnam.

Nonmilitary Activities. The third component of our current strategy includes all of those nonmilitary activities which are so important but which receive too little public attention. It is not that our leaders have been unaware of the importance of better government, better living conditions, and the promise of a better future for the people of this country. Unfortunately, lack of security and governmental instability were for a long time factors limiting the effectiveness of the many programs for development and reconstruction. But now, with the growing military effectiveness of our forces on the ground and the slowly developing maturity of the civil leadership in Saigon and in the provinces, I hope that conditions will permit much greater progress than in the past in bringing the benefits of a comparatively normal life to this war-weary people.

As you know, the recent Honolulu Conference devoted most of its time to a consideration of these nonmilitary activities. If we are to leave a country after the end of the Viet Cong insurgency, it is essential that we make progress even under the conditions of war in stabilizing the government, the society and the economy.

Political and Diplomatic Efforts. The fourth component of our strategy is that which relates to our political and diplomatic efforts to initiate the discussion of a peaceful settlement of this conflict.

The so-called peace offensive is so well known as to require no discussion at this time, as is also the discouraging lack of response from the other side.

I am obliged to feel that the Hanoi leadership is not yet convinced that it must mend its ways. Perhaps they still hope for some kind of military victory in the south. Certainly, they are not convinced that in some way the United States cannot be detached from the support of

South Vietnam. They hope against hope that through international or domestic pressures our government can be forced off course.

They have not forgotten that the Vietminh won more in Paris than in Dienbienphu and believe that the Viet Cong may be as fortunate in Washington. They doubt the will of the American public to continue the conflict indefinitely. In a contest of patience, they expect to win even though North Vietnam like the South has been constantly at war for over 20 years. Until it becomes perfectly clear to them that we are going to stay on course regardless of anything they can do, I am afraid we are not likely to see them at a conference table. Or if they come unconvinced of the inevitability of the failure of their present course, we can expect them to stall, delay and maneuver just as they did at Panmunjon in Korea for over two years.

In summary then, our four-point strategy consists of a complex but coherent package of measures designed to improve the effectiveness of our forces on the ground in South Vietnam, to exploit our air superiority by attacking military targets in North Vietnam, to stabilize the political, social and economic systems in South Vietnam, and to seek an honorable negotiated settlement of the conflict.

It is limited as to objective, as to geographical scope, as to weapons and forces employed, and as to targets attacked.

All parts of it are interrelated; all parts are indispensable; we must be successful on all fronts. The key, I believe, is inexorable pressure at all points, directed at the will, the ability and the means of the Communist aggressors.

Best Strategy to Win U.S. Objectives. It is a fair question to ask whether this is the best strategy to attain our basic objectives. I am the first to concede that we can and must do better in all four categories of our efforts and, unhappily, progress toward peaceful negotiations is a bilateral affair which can progress only with some cooperation from Hanoi. As you know, thus far that cooperation has been withheld.

Having conceded the need and possibility for improvement within the components of our current strategy, I must add in honesty that I know of no new strategic proposal which would serve as a better alternative to the one which I have described; that is, provided we do not sacrifice our basic objective. There are, of course, the two old alternatives which we have always rejected and I hope will continue to reject — to withdraw and give up our basic objective or to widen the war by massive air attacks on the North Vietnamese or even on Chinese targets. These two courses of action appear so to contravene our national and international interests that I shall not take the time of the committee to discuss them here.

Holding Strategy. The only new proposal of which I am aware is the so-called holding strategy which, in its least extreme form, calls for a cessation of U.S. reinforcements and limitation of military operations to those necessary for the security of our forces and for the maintenance of our military presence. On several occasions, I have expressed myself in opposition to such a course of action. To button up our troops in defensive positions and thus to the sacrifice of their unique attributes of mobility and firepower would constitute the abandonment of our allies on the battlefield and would assign a most inglorious mission to our troops who, for the present, have high morale and complete confidence in their ability to cope with the Viet Cong in the field. The effect of such behavior on our Vietnamese allies could be disastrous. At a minimum, it would destroy all confidence in Vietnam in ultimate success and would encourage the timid and the wavering to turn to the Viet Cong for protection and to the Liberation Front for political accommodation. Another serious result of such passivity would be the impossibility of obtaining honorable terms at any peace table. The Communists are tough enough to deal with when one has the upper hand. They would never give us acceptable terms if the military situation reflected weakness on our part and a readiness to withdraw. Our only alternative would be to accept dishonorable terms or to continue to sit out the war indefinitely on a supine defensive. I can hardly see the American public or this Congress long supporting such a course of action. Thus, I am obliged to conclude that the so-called holding strategy is really not an alternative way of reaching our objective of an independent South Vietnam free from attack. We could never reach it on such a course. Rather than being a true alternative, it amounts to the modification and erosion of our basic objective and hence appears to me to be unacceptable.

Present Strategy Is Best. In conclusion, I feel that our present strategy is the best that has been suggested and that it is important that we adhere to it, always striving to improve our performance within the confines of its general concept. Certainly, it is not without risks, but little of value in this world is accomplished without risk. It seems to me that the risks entailed are warranted by the importance of our stake in Southeast Asia. Congress recognized this importance in the wording of the joint resolution of August 1964: "The United States regards as vital to its national interest and to world peace the maintenance of international peace and security in Southeast Asia."

I subscribe to these words and believe that we should live by them and by the words of President Johnson when he said in regard to our commitment in South Vietnam: "We will not be defeated. We will not grow tired. We will not withdraw either openly or under the cloak of a meaningless agreement."

ABOUT THE AUTHORS

BARNETT, A. DOAK, is a professor of government at Columbia University and acting Director of that institution's East Asian Institute.

Born in Shanghai in 1921; lived in China until 1936. Received B.A. and M.A. from Yale. Served in the Marine Corps, 1942-46. A correspondent on Southeast Asia for the Chicago Daily News Foreign Service, 1952-55. Head of Department of Foreign Area Studies, Foreign Service Institute, Department of State, 1956-57. A research fellow of the Council on Foreign Relations, 1958-59. Associated with the Ford Foundation, 1959-61. Joined Columbia faculty in 1961. Author of "Communist China: The Early Years" (1964), "China on the Eve of Communist Takeover" (1963), "Communist China in Perspective" (1961), "Communist China — Continuing Revolution" (1962), "Communist China and Asia" (1960), "Communist Economic Strategy" (1959). Editor of "Communist Strategies in Asia" (1963).

ECKSTEIN, ALEXANDER, is a professor of economics at the University of Michigan.

Born in 1915. Received B.S., M.S., and Ph.D. degrees from the University of California. Consultant in economic affairs for the United Nations Economic Commission for Europe, 1950-51. Senior Economist, U.S. Department of State, 1951-53. Research associate at Harvard University, 1956-59. Professor of international economics at the University of Rochester, 1959-61. Joined University of Michigan faculty in 1961. A former director of the Association for Asian Studies.

Author of "The National Income of Communist China" (1962) and "Communist China's Economic Development and Foreign Trade" (1966). Contributor to "Prospects for Communist China, Moscow-Peking Axis" and "The Economic Development of China and Japan."

FAIRBANK, John K., is professor of history and director of the East Asian Research Center at Harvard University.

Born in South Dakota, 1907. Received B.A. from Harvard and Ph.D. from Oxford University. Joined Harvard faculty in 1936; advanced to associate professor in 1943 and full professor in 1948. Served as Special Assistant to the American Ambassador to China in Chungking in 1942 and 1943. Attached to the Office of Strategic Services and the Office of War Information, 1942-45.

Author of "Trade and Diplomacy on the China Coast" (1954) and "The United States and China" (1948). Co-author of "China's Response to the West" (1954), "Next Step in Asia" (1949), "A History of East Asian Civilization" (1960), and "A Bibliographical Guide to Chinese Works" (1950).

FULBRIGHT, J. WILLIAM, Democratic Senator from Arkansas, has been chairman of the Senate Foreign Relations Committee since 1959.

Born in Sumner, Missouri, 1905. Graduated from University of Arkansas at 16. Attended Oxford University as a Rhodes Scholar. Graduated from George Washington University Law School in 1934. Special attorney in Anti-Trust Division of Justice Department, 1934-35. President of the University of Arkansas, 1939-41. Member of House of Representatives, 1943-45. Senator since 1945. Author of "Old Myths and New Realities" (1964).

GAVIN, JAMES M., a retired Army officer, is chairman of the board of Arthur D. Little, Inc., a research and engineering consulting company.

Born in New York City, 1907. Graduated from U.S. Military Academy in 1929. Served as advisor to General Eisenhower during World War II. Army's Chief of Research and Development, 1955-58. Retired from Army in 1958 after 33 years of service. Ambassador to France, 1961-62. Author of "Airborne Warfare" (1947), "War and Peace in the Space Age" (1958).

GRIFFITH, SAMUEL B. (II), Brigadier General, is a retired Marine Corps officer. Born in Lewistown, Pennsylvania, 1906. Graduated from Naval Academy, 1929. Received Ph.D. in Chinese military history from Oxford University in 1960 following retirement from the Marine Corps in 1956. Served in Peking as a Marine Corps Language Officer, 1935-38. Participated in the battles for Guadalcanal and New Georgia. Served on staff of the Marine Corps Commander at Tientsin and as Commander of Marine Forces at Tsingtao. Member of the Naval War College staff, 1950-51. Chief of Staff of the Fleet Marine Force, Atlantic, 1951-52. Awarded the Army Distinguished Service Cross, the Navy Cross, and the Purple Heart.

Translator of "Sun-Tzu — The Art of War" (1963) and "On Guerrilla Warfare" by Mao Tse-tung (1961). Author of "The Battle for Guadalcanal" (1963) and a book on Communist China's military potential soon to be published by the Council on Foreign Relations.

HALPERIN, MORTON H., is an assistant professor of government at Harvard University and a research associate at Harvard's Center for International Affairs.

Author of "China and The Bomb" (1965) and "Limited War in The Nuclear Age" (1963); co-author of "Communist China and Arms Control" (1965) and "Strategy and Arms Control" (1961); editor of "Policies Toward China: Views From Six Continents" (1966). Also author of "Is China Turning In?", a recent paper of Harvard's Center for International Affairs.

HINTON, HAROLD, has been an associate professor of international affairs at George Washington University since 1964 and a senior staff member of the Institute for Defense Analysis since 1960.

Born in France in 1924. Educated at Harvard (A.B., M.A., and Ph.D.) Served with the Army, 1943-46. A military historian in Okinawa and Korea, 1945-46. Has taught at Oxford, Columbia, Harvard, and Georgetown, and has served as a consultant to the Rand Corporation, USIA, CIA, and the State Department. Author of "Communist China in World Politics" (1966). Also contributor to "Major Governments of Asia" (1963).

JUDD, WALTER H., is a physician and former member of Congress from Minnesota. Born in Rising City, Nebraska, 1898. Received B.A. (1920) and M.D. (1923) degrees from University of Nebraska. Served in China as a medical missionary of the Congregational Foreign Mission Board, 1925-1938. Served in the House of Representatives, 1943-1962; a member of the Committee on Foreign Affairs for 16 years. Currently president of the American Afro-Asian Educational Exchange.

KENNAN, GEORGE, is a professor at the Institute for Advanced Study and Princeton University.

Born in Milwaukee, 1904. Graduated from Princeton in 1925. Associated with U.S. Foreign Service in various capacities, 1927-1948. Advisor to the Secretary of State, 1949-1950. Ambassador to Soviet Russia, 1952. Ambassador to Yugoslavia, 1961-63.

Author of "American Diplomacy, 1900-1950" (1951), "Realities of American Foreign Policy" (1954), "Russia, The Atom, and The West" (1958), "Russia and the West Under Lenin and Stalin" (1961), and "On Dealing With the Communist World" (1964).

LINDBECK, JOHN M. H., is associate director of the East Asian Research Center at Harvard University.

Born in China, 1915. Received much of his primary and secondary education in China. Received B.A. degree from Gustavus Adolphus College in 1937, a degree in divinity from Yale in 1940, and a Ph.D. from Yale in 1948. Served with the U.S. Navy and the Office of Strategic Services during World War II. A Rockefeller Foundation fellow in oriental languages and history, 1946-1948. An assistant professor of political science at Yale, 1948-52. A Public Affairs Advisor on Chinese and Overseas Chinese Affairs, State Department, 1952-58. Became a research fellow in Chinese studies at Harvard in 1959. Spent 1961-62 doing research in Hong Kong. Currently a consultant to the Rand Corporation, the Institute for Defense Analysis, and the State Department.

MORGENTHAU, HANS JOACHIM, is professor of political science and modern history at the University of Chicago and director of the Center for Study of American Foreign and Military Policy.

Graduated from Munich University, 1927. Came to U.S. in 1937. Holds degrees from Clark University (L.L.D., 1962) and Western Reserve University (Litt.D., 1965). Joined faculty of University of Chicago, 1943. Has been a visiting professor at the University of California, Columbia, and Yale. A consultant to the State Department (1949, 1951, 1963-) and the Defense Department (1963-65). Served as a lecturer at the Armed Forces Staff College, the National War College, and the Defense College of the North Atlantic Treaty Organization.

Author of "Scientific Man vs. Power Politics" (1946), "Politics Among Nations" (1948), "In Defense of the National Interest" (1951), "Dilemmas of Politics" (1958), "The Purpose of American Politics" (1960), "Politics in the Twentieth Century" (1962), and "Vietnam and the United States" (1966). Editor of "Crossroad Papers" (1965).

ROWE, DAVID NELSON, is professor of political science at Yale University.

Born in Nanking, 1905. Received A.B. from Princeton, A.M. from University of Southern California, 1930, and Ph.D. from University of Chicago, 1935. Lecturer on Far Eastern affairs at Princeton, 1938-43. Research analyst Special Defense Unit, Department of Justice, 1941. Special Assistant to the director of the Bureau of Research and Analysis, Office of Strategic Services, 1941-42. Special Assistant to the Ambassador to China, 1941-42. Joined Yale faculty in 1943. Director of Staff Officers

School of Asiatic Studies, 1945-46. Representative of the Asia Foundation in Formosa, 1954-56.

Author of "China Among the Powers" (1945), "Modern China" (1959), and "China: A Handbook For Psywar Operations".

SCALAPINO, ROBERT ANTHONY, is professor of political science at the University of California.

Born in Leavenworth, Kansas, 1919. Received B.A. from Santa Barbara College and Ph.D. from Harvard University. Served in U.S. Navy, 1943-46. Joined faculty of University of California in 1949.

Author of "Democracy and the Party Movement in Prewar Japan" (1953). "Reflections on American Relations With Japan" (1953). Editor of the magazine "Asian Survey" since 1962.

SCHWARTZ, BENJAMIN I., is professor of history and government at Harvard University and a member of the executive committee of Harvard's East Asian Research Institute.

Born in Boston, 1916. Received A.B., M.A., and Ph.D. from Harvard. Travelled in Far East in 1961.

Author of "China and the Soviet Theory of Peoples Democracy" (1954), "Chinese Communism and the Rise of Mao" (1951), and "In Search of Wealth and Power: Yen Fu and the West" (1964). Co-author of "A Documentary History of Chinese Communism" and a contributor to "Moscow-Peking Axis, Confucianism in Action," and "The Russian Intelligentsia and Chinese Thought and Institutions."

TAYLOR, GEORGE E., is Professor of Far Eastern History and Director of the Far Eastern and Russian Institute, University of Washington.

Born in Coventry, England, in 1905. Received B.A., M.A., D.Litt. degrees from University of Birmingham. Lived in China and travelled in Far East, 1930-39. Resided in Peking from 1937-39 under Japanese occupation. Became U.S. citizen, 1943. Joined faculty of University of Washington in 1939.

Deputy Director U.S. Office of War Information in charge of Pacific Operations during World War II. Director of Cultural Relations for the Far East in State Department, 1945-46. Member of American delegation to SEATO conference, 1957. Author of "The Struggle for North China" (1941) and "America in the New Pacific" (1942). Co-author of "The Far East in the Modern World" (1956).

TAYLOR, MAXWELL, a retired General of the U.S. Army, is an advisor to President Johnson on matters relating to Vietnam.

Born in Keytesville, Missouri, 1901. Graduated from U.S. Military Academy, 1922. Assistant Military Attache, Peking, 1939. Served in Italian campaign, 1943-44. Superintendent of the U.S. Military Academy, 1945-49. Chief of Staff of American military forces in Europe, 1949. Commander U.S. Army forces in the Far East, 1954. Commander U.S. Army and United Nations forces in Far East, 1955. Chief of Staff U.S. Army, 1955-59. Chairman of the Board, Mexican Light and Power Company, 1958-59. Military adviser to President Kennedy, 1961-62. Chairman of Joint Chiefs of Staff, 1962-64. Ambassador to South Vietnam, 1964-65. Author of "The Uncertain Trumpet" (1960).

ZAGORIA, DONALD S., is an assistant professor of government and a senior fellow at the Research Institute on Communist Affairs of Columbia University.

Born in Somerville, New Jersey, 1928. Received B.A. from Rutgers and M.A. and Ph.D. from Columbia. Served as an analyst of Communist bloc affairs for the U.S. Government, 1951-1961. He has been a member of the Rand Corporation's social science department since 1961.

Author of "The Sino-Soviet Conflict, 1956-1961" (1962) and has contributed to "The Future of Communist Society" and "Communist Strategies in Asia." Editor of "Communist China and the Soviet Bloc," a 1963 issue of the Annals of the American Academy of Political and Social Science.